The New
Extended Family

THE NEW EXTENDED FAMILY

Day Care That Works

Ellen Galinsky and William H. Hooks

Illustrated with Photographs
by Ellen Galinsky

Houghton Mifflin Company   Boston   1977

To Lara and all the other children who have reached out and found their extended families

Copyright © 1977 by Ellen Galinsky and William H. Hooks. All rights reserved. No part of this work may be reproduced or transmitted in any form by any means, electronic or mechanical, including photocopying and recording, or by any information storage or retrieval system, without permission in writing from the publisher.

Library of Congress Cataloging in Publication Data

Galinsky, Ellen.
 The new extended family.
 Bibliography: p.
 Includes index.
 1. Day care centers — United States. I. Hooks, William H., joint author. II. Title.
HV854.G34   362.7′1   77-21790
ISBN 0-395-25934-7 ISBN 0-395-25949-5 pbk.

Printed in the United States of America

V 10 9 8 7 6 5 4 3 2 1

The authors are grateful for permission to quote from *Family Day Care: A Practical Guide for Parents, Caregivers, and Professionals* by Alice H. Collins and Eunice L. Watson. Copyright © 1976 by Alice H. Collins and Eunice L. Watson. Reprinted by permission of Beacon Press.

Book design by Carol Monacelli

Acknowledgments

We wish to express our gratitude to all of the children, parents, caregivers, teachers, and directors we visited and talked with, and:

to Marjorie Martus, who has a wonderful, wide-ranging understanding of the world relating to children;

to Susan Berresford, who has keen insight and is herself an inspiration;

to Peter Sauer, who is the best judge of child care we know, an innovator in the field, and to the Bank Street Day Care Consultation group;

to Jack Niemeyer, for wise counsel and guidance;

to James Levine, who led us to many places;

to Roger Jellinek, who started this project;

to Dinny Price, a friendly, helpful neighbor who gave us some of our first insights into family day care;

to Ginger Barber, who believed in this book;

to Lorin Driggs, who sharpened our thinking and writing;

to Francis Roberts, for his interest, encouragement, and support throughout the writing;

to Anita McClellan, who made it a book that is a "celebration of child care";

to the Ford Foundation, which so generously aided our study.

And most of all, to Donna Egan, who traveled with us on a Ford Foundation grant, whose joy and judgment we learned from, and who assisted us in innumerable ways.

Contents

1. Myth and Reality — 1
2. Choosing a Child Care Program — 7
3. An Infant-Toddler Preschool Program — 15
4. A Parent-Staff Cooperative — 35
5. A Public School for Teen-Age Mothers and Their Children — 51
6. A Parent Education Program — 61
7. Parent-Controlled Day Care — 75
8. Integrating Children with Special Needs — 91
9. A Parent-Operated, Work-Based Center — 111
10. A For-Profit Center — 127
11. A Comprehensive, Community-Based Program from Infancy through Preschool — 143
12. A Center in Transition — 161
13. An After-School Program — 173
14. Family Day Care — 189
15. An Experiment with Informal Child Care — 211
16. A Local Support System for Child Care — 223
17. Patterns — 239
18. The Political Arena — 255
    Selected Readings — 272
    Index — 273

1
Myth
and Reality

Surrounding every aspect of life, there are myths and misconceptions. They are tied to reality like kites, attached by long strings, soaring above, shifting in currents of the wind.

To begin with: parenthood. Most people today don't think of becoming parents as they did a few years ago. They no longer see images of soft, round babies wrapped in receiving blankets, contented and sleepy. They now know in advance that those babies can turn red with rage, double up with stomach cramps; that sometimes babies cry all day or stay awake all night. The myths and realities of parenthood have recently come closer together.

There is one myth about parenthood, however, that has been relatively untouched. That is the myth of independence. Nurtured in the close circle of the extended family, the myth had some degree of reality. Parents were (with the aid of grandparents, uncles, aunts, and other kith and kin) supposed to do everything for themselves. But today, even without this traditional backup system, parents are still supposed to do everything for themselves. They are the sole guardians, the protectors, the providers for their children. Stepping outside the family for help becomes an admission of failure.

Modern suburban housing is a visual depiction of this value gone askew; separation has been mistaken for independence. Each house stands apart, fortresslike, surrounded by a moat of grass. City apartments are compressed; high-rises with living unit stacked on top of living unit, insulating and isolating the American family.

The reality is a far cry from the myth. Try as they may, parents can never be totally independent. They need others — perhaps someone to talk to, or someone to watch the baby while they run to the store, or someone to care for the child while they work. In countless ways, every day, parents need the help of others.

The statistics indicate that there is an increasing number of working mothers. They show that one out of every two school-age children has a mother who holds a job. The most graphic substantiation of this fact is found in a story told by a psychologist in New York City. He wanted to compare children, between birth and three years of age, who were cared for only by their mothers with those who had been cared for at one time or another by other people. His idea was a failure. He couldn't find enough cared-for-by-mother-only children to warrant even beginning the study.

The gap between the myth and the reality becomes a war zone for many parents. Opposing forces line the two fronts. Parents who have to leave their children usually struggle, within themselves, with highly personal questions: "Is it wrong?" "Is it right?" And yet the reality is that all children have always had more than one or two people to care for them.

The negative societal stance toward out-of-home care casts a shadow on the places that provide such care. When most people are asked to describe a day care center, they picture it as dark, dingy, and overrun with kids. Some describe a place cordoned off by chicken wire, with a cluster of children looking out at the bright sunny world beyond. Family day care doesn't fare any better. Many people imagine family day care as an arrangement that multiplies the problems associated with having a "terrible" two-year-old: messes everywhere, crying children, and the family day care mother at her wits' end.

Most of the recent articles and books have perpetuated the negatives. They have been litanies of complaints. We suspected that some of the criticisms were justified, but that good things were also quietly happening. And we wanted to find out.

A book began to take shape. It would be a book that described different kinds of child care — *good* child care. It would be a book that shared the good things caring people were doing with young children, and one that consequently brought together some of the best thinking about child care in the country — a book about reality and diversity.

It was easy to plan for diversity. We would get in touch with national day care organizations and local information and referral agencies and ask for their recommendations. We would then select programs all over the United States — in rural regions, in the crowded cities, in the North, South, East, and West. We would choose programs that were small, large, formal, informal; that were located in homes, centers, work places, and schools. These programs would represent some of the cultural complexities of America. They would be paid for in different ways: by government, by a patchwork of funding agencies, or by the individual users themselves. And they would have ties to a variety of educational philosophies — from open education to traditional schooling, from behavior modification to Montessori.

It was more difficult to define our criteria for a "good" program. We decided right away that we would not attempt to designate the "top ten or fifteen" child care programs. We were after a sampling of those that were good — solidly good. But what did we mean by "good"? We felt that in making judgments we would have to rely on our insight and experience as educators. In addition, we asked ourselves three subjective questions: Would we want to work there? Would we want to enroll children there? Would we feel comfortable as parents in such a program? If the place under consideration could meet our criteria, we would check our perceptions with several other respected professionals who were familiar with the particular program and with child care in this country in general. Because we wanted this book to be useful to both parents and child care professionals, we decided to look at each of these good programs along many of the same dimensions: their beginnings, their goals, their space and schedule, and parent participation, for example.

Thus we began, in June of 1975, with a visit to a community-controlled day care center in New York City, the Children's Pumphouse. That summer we traveled to Pasadena, California, to see several family day care homes, and in the fall we went to the Children's Center in Biddeford, Maine, a center that includes both children with handicapping conditions and normal children in its program.

We found, interestingly enough, that each form of child care has a group of negative prejudices associated with it. They represent the problems that each form of child care can fall prey to. We came to the conclusion that the places we were calling good had dealt with their typical pitfalls. They had found some way to avoid the dangers that were potentially hazardous in their particular form of child care. Therefore, our studies had even wider-reaching implications than we had originally assumed.

We learned that these good programs were in a continuous state of evolution. Indeed, in the coming year some of the programs we saw may deteriorate, some may close, others may expand to the point where they will be unrecognizable. But at the time we saw them, they were good. We realized that by our writing about a place that was quietly doing a creditable job in Bethesda, Maryland, or Frogmore, South Carolina, or San Fidel, New Mexico, we might elevate this place to the station of a "model." The concept of models has gained a large amount of currency in the educational community over the past few years. Essentially, this concept means that certain programs are refined and then replicated or copied, sometimes detail by detail, sometimes in their overall mode. The disadvantage to the idea of models is that it often calls for change by prescription. The model program may be accepted by the leaders of a community, but in putting it into practice, the practitioners discover that it never quite fits. In the wake of models come pressure and resistance. A program that was developed, in a large city, for the children of middle-class professional people may have less relevance for a poor rural area, and vice versa. We agreed with the statement, made to a visitor, by Betty Van Wyck, director of the Children's Center in Biddeford, Maine: "Our program is just one way to do it. In another building with another staff it would be different. Don't copy us. Look at us and look at other programs and find your own style."

If, indeed, we did find one factor that was common to all the programs, it was that they were not transplants; they were organic outgrowths of a specific community and they stayed responsive to, and completely in tune with, the people they sought to serve.

Another common factor we found was that all adults in the programs were expected to have a personal relationship with the children. Teachers, aides, maintenance staff, administrative people, and volunteers spent a part of their time caring for the children, and they felt comfortable with a new title, "caregiver," that could be applied to a wide range of child care jobs.

The kinds of child care we as a society create ultimately reflect our feelings toward children. Throughout America, from the northwest coast of Oregon to the northeast coast of Maine, from a native American reservation in New Mexico to a rice island in South Carolina, we have discovered many people who care deeply about children and their families. This book is both a sharing and a celebration of that fact.

2
Choosing a Child Care Program

Wherever we traveled, whatever program * we visited, we talked to parents. Often we started our conversations with the question, "What led you to select this program for your child?"

We found their routes to each of the programs to be many and varied. Some had heard of programs through friends and neighbors: "A neighbor said we should check it out." Some came upon them by chance: "I happened to be taking a walk one day and I noticed a day care center." "I saw these kids every day in the park with a nice young man, so I asked him where he was from." Others had seen notices: "There was a brochure tacked up in the supermarket." "I saw a sign at the pediatric clinic." Still others made a purposeful search: "I found this center listed in the Yellow Pages." "We have a day care information and referral service here in town so I asked them about family day care and they gave me a list of places to look at." Several parents in one community had heard about the day care center from the real estate agent who proudly told prospective renters or buyers about the fine day care center in the neighborhood.

---

* Authors' note: We use the word "program" to refer to any child care arrangement, from a day care center to a family day care home to a baby sitter.

Whatever the path that led a parent with a child in hand to the door of a center or family day care home, few traveled this route without strong swings of emotion. At times they felt apprehensive. They felt as if they were about to "dump," "pawn off," even "abandon" their children. They felt guilty. They felt a questioning uneasiness: "How will I know what's available and what's right for my child?" And at other times parents found this search an interesting adventure.

Few, if any, of the parents had any specific guidelines to help them judge what kind of program they should choose for their children. Still, almost without exception, they wished for some magic yardstick against which they could measure a program and feel comfortable with their choice. Our observations of a great variety of child care programs led us to the understanding that there is no such thing as a magic measuring rod, but we can share our observation techniques and the knowledge we gleaned from parents and staff members who have lived through a situation that must seem unique to each parent at the time he or she goes through it.

Betty Van Wyck told us of the two basic guidelines she has offered to parents over the years in helping them to decide whether a program is right for them and their children. She encourages all parents to visit the prospective program for as much time as their schedules will allow. "Trust your own instincts," she says, "and ask yourself if you would like to spend a day there. What about a week? A year?" Then she advises them to note the children's reactions when a visitor enters the room. "Do all or a majority of the children stop what they're doing and focus on the adult visitor? If they do, it usually means there isn't enough going on for the children." There are many other factors that matter in a good program, but we agree with Betty Van Wyck that, given the exigencies of time, these two simple guidelines may serve a parent well in making an initial evaluation.

During our stay at each location we tried to look at the mosaic of the individual qualities that made up each program. We found that the size of the program, the source of funding, and any of the other elements that are commonly used to differentiate child care programs are important but certainly not the most important ones for judging a program. We came to feel that it is the quality of life for children, parents, and staff that distinguishes one program from another. We then developed a basic group of open-ended questions that we found ourselves asking constantly during the course of our observations. In sharing the procedure we followed, we hope to furnish caregivers and parents with some guidelines that may prove helpful in selecting and maintaining a program that provides high-quality care for children.

Here are some of those questions:

"What is the flow of the daily schedule?"

>*Arrival:*
>How do children act when they arrive?
>Do they come in eagerly or hesitantly?
>How do parents and caregivers interact during this time?
>How are children greeted by the caregivers?
>
>*Activities:*
>Are there ample opportunities for the children to work and play?
>How do the caregivers involve the children in the work of the day?
>Is there a choice of activities?
>Are they appropriate for the children's ages and stages of development?
>Do the activities foster the children's physical, social, intellectual, and emotional growth?
>Are the activities primarily adult-directed, child-initiated, or both?
>Do activities include both experiential and symbolic learning?
>Do adults allow children to explore and discover for themselves?
>Do adults use the individual interests and learning styles of the children in developing their curriculum?
>
>*Transitions:*
>How are shifts from one activity to another handled?
>Are transitions smooth?
>Is there a minimum of waiting time between activities?
>Do the children know what to do?
>
>*Lunch and snacks:*
>Are these relaxed, social times when caregivers and children enjoy sharing food and conversation?
>Are children encouraged to eat nutritious and balanced meals?

Nap time:
Is it a restful period?
How do the adults help children who have trouble relaxing?

Departure:
What is the quality of interaction between caregivers, parents, and children at departure time?
Do they talk together in a friendly and helpful way?

"What are the materials and space like?"

Materials:
Does the program provide a good variety of stimulating materials?
Are they attractively displayed and readily accessible to the children?
Are materials flexible enough to allow for imaginative use?

Space:
Is the space aesthetically pleasing and comfortable?
Does it reflect respect for the child; that is, are children's art work and other projects prominently displayed?
Is the space as accident-proof as it can be?
Is it organized so that children can function independently?
Does it allow for freedom of movement?
Does it provide for both group and individual activities?
Does it provide possibilities for privacy?

"What support services does the program offer?"

What health services are provided for children? For families?
What social-support services are offered?
Are there opportunities for staff training?

"What are the human relationships in this program?"

Caregiver-child:
Is there a caring and individual relationship between teacher and child?
Is there genuine respect for each child's racial, socioeconomic, and cultural background?
Are boys and girls treated equally?
Do adults enable children to learn?
Do they act as providers of materials and learning experiences?

Do children feel free to express their questions and feelings to caregivers?
How are behavior problems handled?
Do caregivers help children understand problems and seek solutions?
Do they respect children's needs to let off steam and show emotions?
Are they accepting of all children who are disruptive?
Do they help children develop their own self-control?
Do they console and comfort unhappy children?

Child-child:
Do children respect each other?
Do they have fun together?
Do they learn from each other?
Do they console and comfort each other?
Do they help each other?

Caregiver-caregiver:
How do the caregivers interact with each other?
Do they enjoy being with each other?
Do they seem to be working together and learning from each other?

"What relationship do parents have to the program?"

Do parents have any say in the setting of goals?
How is the parent kept informed of his or her child's experiences in the program?
In what ways are parents linked to the daily life of the program?
Do parents have ready access to teachers?
How do parents and teachers communicate? Is the relationship friendly and accepting?
Do parents feel secure about procedures for emergency notification and medical care?
Do parents feel that their association with the program provides opportunities for their own growth?
In what ways does the program respect and reflect the values and goals of parents?

This last item is the key criterion. Over and over parents told us that this was the decisive factor in their selecting a program. "It felt right," they said. "It clicked." "You know when it's the right place."

The necessity of harmony in values between the child care program and parents is emphasized in the recent

work of the social scientist Ronald Lippitt. In *Socialization and Society,* edited by J. A. Clausen, Lippitt states that the parents and the teachers, the primary shapers of the child's social development, must communicate and collaborate with each other. He claims that if the values of parents and teachers differ markedly, the child will be faced with problems. Parents advised us to tell other parents to look beyond the brochures and spoken words that describe a child care program; to look at people's behavior, and, most of all, to trust their own instincts.

The range of choice in child care possibilities differs from community to community. Parents may have a wide spectrum of tempting programs to choose from or, conversely, a limited, narrow one. Regardless of the realities of each community, we hope that parents and child care professionals will find it useful to journey with us, looking at the following fourteen programs. These programs can serve as a measure for assessing what one likes and doesn't like about child care programs; and they can serve, as well, as a source of ideas for changing and improving the programs that one has at present. Dr. Sue Aronson of The Learning Center in Philadelphia told us a saying that her grandmother used, and it most fittingly conveys the way the people in these programs felt about sharing their ideas: "There is no end to the good you can do if you don't feel obligated to take credit for it . . . If it's a good idea, fine. Take it and use it."

3
An Infant-Toddler Preschool Program

The Learning Center
Philadelphia, Pennsylvania

It was a cold morning in January. Fleets of yellow school buses began arriving at the base of the wide arcade of stairs leading up to the Ben Franklin Institute, a science museum in Philadelphia. School-age children filed off the buses, lined up, and began the walk up the steep steps. Into their midst, a small van pulled up. The doors opened and a woman got out, pulling behind her two infant strollers. Then she and a man reached into the van and unbuckled the seat belt around a toddler and put her into one of the strollers. They helped other children out of the van, one by one, until there was a group of ten very young children around them. Passersby turned to stare, their incredulous looks seeming to ask "A group of infants and toddlers? Who are they? And what are they doing here?"

But anyone who followed the group through the museum would have had a clear answer to those questions. This was, in fact, a field trip for Unit II from The Learning Center in Philadelphia. The children, accompanied by their two teachers, Alice Coles and Gary Kose, went to visit the airplanes first. "Look at that!" exclaimed a toddler, pointing with delight and awe to the big, shining, metal machines. "How do helicopters stay up in the air?" asked a three-year-old. "I went on an airplane to visit my grandmother," said another child. From the airplane exhibit, the children went on to see boats and trains. They climbed into a big locomotive and had a demonstration ride a few feet across the museum room. Their enthusiasm still unabated, they ended up, an hour and a half after they had arrived, at a machine that demonstrated the principles of gravity by dropping a ball onto a roped-off area. Not one child had cried or even fussed. One infant dozed in his stroller as the group got ready to leave.

It was definitely a learning experience for these ten young children from The Learning Center. But would that have changed the minds of those who are opposed to out-of-home care for infants? The opposition to infant group care comes from several sectors. There is the common-sense cultural bias that says that children belong with their mothers during their earliest, most formative years. Psychological theory has been used in support of this tenet; one example is the work of René Spitz, which showed that infants in some institutional settings became dull, apathetic, even withered. More recent studies, however, have pointed out that the children who had become so damaged by institutional care were receiving only physical attention. Provence and Lipton (1961) have attributed apathy in those children to the lack of stimulation and the absence of individual relationships in such institutions.

The Bowlby Report, published in the early 1950s, concluded that children need to be raised by one main person, the mother or a mother substitute. Further work, particularly that of Ainsworth, Yarrow, and Pederson, suggests that there is a psychological phenomenon that has been labeled "attachment." Essentially, this refers to the formation of the relationship between mother and child — a critically important relationship that becomes the archetype of all ensuing relationships for the child, and opens the child's feelings and mind to learning. It is through the mother's interaction with the child that cognitive learning is stimulated. Opponents of group care for infants feel that removing a child from his or her mother for even part of the day will interfere with this attachment process.

Proponents of infant day care argue that studies of attachment merely look at what is, and not at what might be. The father's part in this dynamic relationship, for instance, is ignored in most of the studies. Furthermore, it can be argued that infant day care does not undermine the mother-father-child relationship. A father from The

Learning Center says, "I don't think that [infant day care] makes children less attached to their parents at all. I think the quality of time a parent spends with the child is more important than the quantity." A 1970 study by Caldwell, Wright, Honig, and Tannenbaum supports this father's observation. Infants who had been in day care from six months on showed no difference in attachment patterns at thirty months of age than home-raised children.

The most critical factor is then the quality of the child care. Putting a helpless infant in a barren environment is obviously detrimental. But putting an infant in a warm, loving, interesting, reliable, and stimulating place — such as The Learning Center — where he or she has individualized attention from consistent adults, may enhance the child's development.

Beginnings

Paradoxically, The Learning Center (TLC) was first thought of in institutional terms. It was originally planned to resemble "a newborn nursery, run by nurses, staffed by nurses." In 1971, however, Dr. Sue Aronson, a pediatrician, was appointed by the Medical College of Pennsylvania to design this center. Her ideas differed from the original plans. "My basic philosophical set," she says, "is that heterogeneity of age, sex, race, and socioeconomic status is a very constructive principle, and that it does a great deal to enrich the lives of the people." So she designed a center that derived half of its population from the predominantly white, middle-class Medical College population, including staff and students, and half from the predominantly black, low-income community surrounding the college. "It could be a real bridge between the institution and the community," she says.

Sue Aronson decided that the center should not be located on campus because, as she explains, "Clearly any space on the Medical College campus was going to be very constrained and constantly being competed for by other programs. Day care does not have a high priority in the minds of medical educators." After walking around the neighborhood, she heard that there was a parish house on property belonging to St. James's Church that might be a possible site. "So I trotted down there," Sue recalls. "I met the sixteen-year-old son of the minister and we took a ruler and went into this vacant, dilapidated, almost condemnable building and measured it."

She established a planning group drawn mainly from the community; the medical students, though they expressed interest in day care, were too busy. The planning group negotiated with the church. "We managed to organize a pressure group of high-level society people. These were people who were in touch with the banking community and who could speak to the church vestry members about the wisdom of embarking on an adventure like this. We basically confronted them with a business deal they could not refuse." Knowing that the building might be condemned, the planning group offered to pay rent for the facility and to renovate it at the same time. They went through the zoning and licensing procedures and began to plan the renovation accordingly.

"It was quite clear to me," Sue says, "that a pediatrician shouldn't be the director of a program like this; it needed a person trained in early-childhood education." After six days of intensive interviewing with the newly formed personnel committee, Marlene Weinstein was offered the job of director.

Sue Aronson wrote a proposal and secured federal funds to begin the program. The program was in the unique position of having families whose incomes would eventually be at the middle-class level qualify for state support because, as medical students, they had low incomes. Renovations were completed and the center opened with ten children on July 1, 1972. By the end of the summer, it had expanded to accommodate thirty children in three separate groups.

"From then on," Sue says, "Marlene Weinstein built a staff and a program."

Goals From the outset, one idea has been central to The Learning Center: center life should, to some extent, re-create family life. In each unit there are ten children: two babies in their first year, two toddlers between one and two years old, and six preschoolers between two and four. This age range approximates the spread of ages in a young family. Furthermore, each unit has a male and a female caregiver, paralleling the mother and father in a family. Because of the staff's belief in the importance of the attachment process (whereby one of the natural parents becomes the primary person for the child), The Learning Center tries to reproduce this phenomenon by having each of the caregivers take primary responsibility for one

of the infants, one of the toddlers, and three of the preschoolers. "The infant," Marlene Weinstein states, "has a role like the one he or she has in the family. The infant is special, the most special person in the room."

At The Learning Center, therefore, a foremost goal is the creation of a familylike atmosphere with a secure relationship between each child and the caregivers. In Unit II, for instance, the children were having juice when a baby in a nearby crib awakened. Alice Coles, the primary caregiver for this child, jumped up, but before she had reached the crib, a toddler was there, patting the baby's head. Alice diapered the baby and sat down to give her a bottle. She talked to a visiting mother about how this baby was changing every day. The other children, after finishing their juice, moved to a cutting-tearing-pasting activity. When Alice put the baby in a chair to watch and play, a preschooler picked up the bottle and gave it to the baby, just as he had seen Alice do.

Marlene Weinstein comments on this episode: "When I talk about the goals of the program, I say that the most important component of our curriculum is not the wonderful activities that the children have, but the very warm, really affectionate relationships."

The staff at The Learning Center understands well that it does not replace the family; it draws from the best features of family life. Doug Sauber, the supervisor, and Judy Okin-Wertheimer, the social worker, both feel that their center is a support for families with young children. "It's a stressful time for families," Doug says, "because they are still learning how to deal with children. The center can be a resource for them."

Caregiver Ralph Wynder says: "I don't want a child to look on me as a mother or a father. I want a child to think of me as someone who is there to aid him and give him love. That child has to carry on when he leaves us, and I want him to look forward to going on."

Independence is a frequently mentioned word when the staff is asked about its goals. "I believe," says Marlene, "that children should be given opportunities to discover what they can and can't do." Judy says, "I think about the day care setting being an opportunity for children to have certain kinds of experiences that will contribute to a strong sense of self and an ability to make decisions, to be independent and autonomous." These kinds of feelings grow in the children, she believes, when they are in an environment where they feel safe and respected, and where their physical, social, and psychological needs are satisfied. Gary Kose, a caregiver, also feels that it is important that members of the staff not show children too much or lead them, but, rather, let them explore. He says he wants to provide a situation where a child can interact with a variety of materials, a variety of adults, and a variety of children.

"Building relationships is one of our first priorities," Doug says. The staff encourages the children to form close ties with each other. Older children often help care for the babies, bringing them bottles, pushing them in their strollers, and comforting and consoling them.

With such diversity in the population of the program, one would expect differences in the goals parents have for their children. TLC is admittedly closer to the goals described by the medical school parents, which stress the importance of social interaction and personality development. Judy says that some community parents want more emphasis on educational learning and wonder why their children are playing so much. A parent says that most people at the center are so grateful to have been able to procure good child care that they avoid some of the dissension that might otherwise occur.

Admission

Admission to The Learning Center is based on the policy of accepting 50 percent of the children from the Medical College and 50 percent from the community. Within these divisions, however, there are finer breakdowns. Children of Medical College students are given first priority, faculty members' children next, and college employees' children are accepted if places remain available. The community places are filled on a first-come, first-served basis, provided eligibility requirements are met, with preference given to the younger children of families currently enrolled. Teen-age mothers from the community are encouraged to enroll their children at the center, but with the stipulation that the mothers remain in school.

Since most of the children in the center are subsidized under federal funds, the first step in the admissions process is the determination of eligibility. This is handled by the social worker, who obtains financial information from a family and sends it to the Department of Public Welfare, which decides whether the care will be free or paid for by the parents. If the family income is below 65 percent of the state median-income level, care is free; there is a sliding fee scale for those above this level.

Once eligibility has been determined, the director sends a letter to the family, offering enrollment of the child. The parent or parents and the child visit the center to get acquainted. They tour the building with the social worker, are given an overview of the routines, and learn what is expected of them as parents. Judy Okin-Wertheimer, the social worker, says that the most common con-

cern of the parents on this initial visit is whether their child, who up till now has had individual attention, will fit into a group situation.

Following the get-acquainted visit, a long interview is held with the parents, the social worker, and one of the caregivers in the child's unit. Judy calls it "a way for them to know us and for us to know them." From the interview, the parents and staff work out an initial care plan for the child. The staff asks the parents to be available for the week or for as long as it takes for the child to adjust.

Selecting Caregivers As it does with admissions policies, the structure of the center predetermines some aspects of the selection of caregivers. Each room is staffed with two teachers, one male and one female, one of whom is white and the other nonwhite.

The director explains that what she looks for in caregivers is competence. Her definition of competence includes "the ability to be nurturing, to communicate with other adults, and to see oneself as a model." She adds, "I am not so interested in specific training because I think we can offer that here, but I am interested in a basic view of children." The current caregivers include people with college degrees and people who have received most of their training on the job at the center.

TLC's procedure for selecting caregivers begins with an examination of the applicant's résumé. Each person who is considered for a job is given an interview by a parent-staff committee. The candidates are asked why they want the job, how it fits in with their career plans, and how they see their role with children and with parents. Then they are asked to respond to several hypothetical situations: "What would you do if . . .?" Final candidates are asked to spend a day with the children. The director says, "In this visit we are looking for the person who can touch easily, who bends down to the children's level, who can deal with stress situations, who has the specific skills." There is a sixty-day probationary period, but Marlene Weinstein feels that a year is needed for the staff to get to know a new caregiver. The family atmosphere at The Learning Center, which appears so relaxed and casual, has strong underpinnings; they begin with the thoughtful selection of staff.

Grouping

The family atmosphere is reinforced by the mixture of ages within each group. The management of such a wide age range may seem a formidable task, but the staff of The Learning Center finds the advantages well worthwhile. The director says, "One of the beauties of this kind of arrangement is that you cannot stereotype your activities." Alice Coles provides some examples of inventive activities: "If the older ones are cutting, the younger ones can rip. When you're fingerpainting, you can give the infants and toddlers chocolate pudding to fingerpaint with; they can have a good time playing with it, and it's all right if they eat it."

Doug Sauber points out that there is another side. "You also have to worry about the older child doing something that may harm the infant. It's a challenge to keep the infants satisfied and cared for and still keep the activities going."

Space and Daily Schedule

The building in which The Learning Center is housed is an unusually beautiful old stone structure. The renovation has emphasized the strong structural Gothic details. Walls are painted white in contrast to the dark wooden ceiling beams. The four rooms used by the children are carefully arranged. In each room there are two cribs, not stashed away or hidden in a corner, but out, central to the room. Some part of each room is fenced off, usually carpeted, furnished with mobiles and mirrors, and reserved as a safe playing space for the infants. There are sinks in

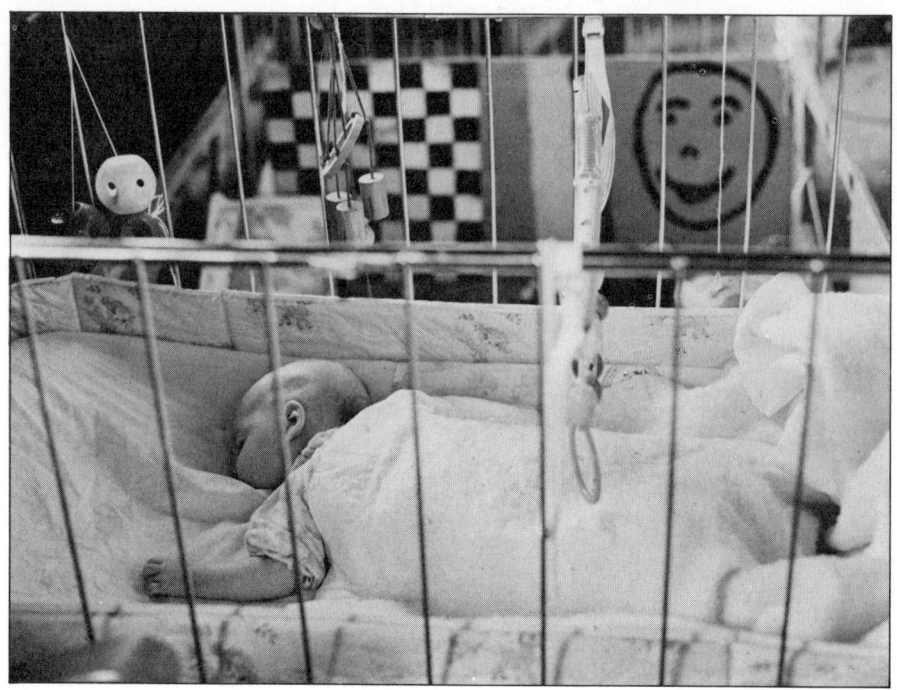

each room and next to them are long, narrow counters for the caregivers to use when changing the babies.

With the exception of the infant equipment, the rooms look like comfortable preschool classrooms divided into activity areas. There are groupings of tables and chairs; shelves with toys, records, puzzles, and games. In addition, adult-size furniture, such as sofas and coffee tables, are provided for parents and staff. Each room has a housekeeping area with child-size refrigerator, stove, bureau, tables, and chairs. The housekeeping area is the children's "sacred territory" — their place to be alone or together, but without the adults. A quiet area, with a rug, sofa, and bookcases filled with picture books, is another feature of each room. The rooms contain many textured surfaces, such as large corrugated letters of the alphabet decorating the walls, that provide the children with a variety of tactile experiences.

The basement of the building has a large all-purpose room, where the children can play group games, run, climb, and dance. Outside playground space was a problem since the neighborhood surrounding the center is constantly subjected to burglary. Marlene consulted a local architectural firm, which, for a very reasonable fee, designed two pieces of equipment — one for climbing

An Infant-Toddler Preschool Program

and one for sand-and-water play — that can be folded and locked at night.

The center is open from 7:30 A.M. until 6:00 P.M. Daily schedules of each room follow more or less the same pattern: arrival, breakfast, circle time with songs or games, free-choice activities, snack and juice, outside time, and lunch constitute the morning; naps, free play, and departure complete the typical day.

Activities are planned by the two caregivers in charge of each room. Once a week they fill out individualized planning sheets, writing down what they feel each child needs; for example, "Josie needs more large motor activity," "Walter needs to learn to hold a scissors," "Nan needs to learn to wait." On this form, they then list the activities they plan for the individual children.

Discipline

"Discipline is your whole relationship with a child," says Marlene. "It should not be just punishing bad behavior." As an example, she talks about two children who couldn't be quiet during nap time. "I think the important thing to think about is why they weren't able to be quiet. Was too much being asked of them?" Marlene may help these children by saying, "I know you don't want to be quiet, so

"PLAYGROUND IN A WHEEL"
© ALLEY FRIENDS ARCHITECTS

I'm moving your cots over here to help you be quiet." She tries to avoid the "no-no, bad behavior" approach, feeling that there's always a reason for misbehavior, even if the reason is only to test the adult. Teaching children not to hit or name-call, Marlene says, takes time. "It takes time the way learning to walk or learning to be toilet-trained takes time."

The staff shares Marlene's view that discipline is "your whole relationship with a child." Steve Walker, a caregiver, says that a lot of behavior problems occur when the room or the day is structured poorly. Doug Sauber looks for alternative outlets for aggressive behavior and bad language. When the children began swearing, he let them know that this language was unacceptable and then suggested that they choose a substitute word. The kids chose "wallpaper." "That word really didn't mean anything and it sounded a little bit silly, but the children needed some way to get rid of a lot of aggression — they needed to be able to say *wallpaper*. And it worked for them. We are trying to get them to verbalize things, but we want them to know that a curse is a verbal hit."

Marlene believes very strongly in her center's way of disciplining, working, and being with children, but at the same time she acknowledges that their way is only one way. "There are marvelous adults produced by people who whipped their children and there are marvelous adults produced by people who never laid a hand on their children, and there are miserable adults produced by both. It would be terrifying to believe that there is only one way, and that you deny the kid anything of value if you do things in only that way."

Parent Participation

We are able to agree on our decisions in our parent group meetings. It's just beautiful!
— Ella Honoré, parent

It is perhaps remarkable that parents from such diverse backgrounds and with different special needs can come together on something so personal as the care of their very young children. The parents in this program come from three groups: medical school parents, community parents, and teen-age parents, also from the community. Dr. Sue Aronson reports, "We have found that there are special needs that the medical school parents have — special guilt problems they have as parents, special discipline problems they have in terms of setting limits for their kids because of their guilt. We have also found that our adolescent parents have special needs as adolescents. We like to individualize our approach. I think it is fair to say that we look at each family and ask ourselves what they need."

Marlene finds that the community parents tend to have more experience in being parents. They may have more than one child and consequently are more relaxed, whereas most of the medical students are parents for the first time, and tend to be very uncertain. One of the ways the center has been most successful in dealing with parent anxiety is to utilize the "big brother" or "big sister" principle. When a parent is troubled about some aspect of care for his or her child or has feelings that need to be worked through, he or she is teamed with a parent who has experienced similar difficulties. John Trimbur, a parent, comments, "The center provides a union of parents who have been through similar experiences, and that helps parents over a lot of anxieties."

Parents play an important role in the Policy Advisory Committee (PAC), which is made up of two parents from each of the child care units and four community members. There are also a half-dozen standing committees, on which parents serve, to deal with such things as personnel and health and safety. The center staff has tried holding full parent meetings, but these are usually poorly attended; however, smaller groupings based on the individual units are popular. Marlene explains, "I find the small unit groups of parents make it much more comfortable and more parents can participate. In the full group there are always parents who like to talk, who talk well, and who predominate."

Most parents cherish the informal daily contact they have with the staff when they bring and pick up their children. This is supplemented by the daily experience sheet: a mimeographed form that provides space for parents and caregivers to write to each other about each child. The caregivers make a few notes about each child every day; parents too jot down important information about the child in a parallel column. Both the parents and the caregivers find that this form provides a very valuable exchange. The parent who is in a rush can glance at the form and get the highlights of the child's day. The caregiver gets valuable information from the parent about the child's health, feelings, interests, and activities. Both groups admit that the forms refresh their memory and help them to see each child in a more complete way.

Each year there are two formal parent-teacher conferences, in which parents and caregivers review together the child's past six-month period at TLC. This is also a time when the parents are encouraged to raise questions and to talk about how they hope their children will develop in the next six months.

Parents work as volunteers at the center and their help is especially welcome when groups go on trips. Many parents have helped with setting up the rooms and with building furnishings for the rooms. They come together for parties, to run a clothing exchange, and to attend discussion sessions on parenting. These sessions often include trained professionals as guests.

Food Food is another subject parents and staff talk through together. When each child is admitted, a food plan is drawn up as part of the initial care plan. Menus are prepared and distributed to parents a week in advance. Throughout the year, parents are invited to offer suggestions and to share information about their children's meals. The center buys the food and prepares the meals. The caregivers speak of meals as "connecting times," because of the many opportunities they offer for the children to make contacts with each other. A family feeling is created by having the children and adults eat together at a large table.

Health As a result of their relationship to a medical college and through the efforts of Dr. Aronson, the center has one of the most comprehensive health plans to be found in any kind of child care. Every child is eligible to be enrolled in the Pediatric Group Services of the Medical College.

The Pediatric Group Services of the Medical College has a part-time satellite office at the center, which is staffed by a pediatric nurse, a pediatrician, and the social worker. This setup provides families with excellent physical and emotional care. John Trimbur says, "The health plan is more than just a convenience. The office staff is very supportive with basic problems, like the child's first cold. It's scary, but they can help you see it's not such a big deal; they can get you over the hump."

Each child, on arrival, is given a daily observational

health check by a staff member. If there are problems or concerns, there is a discussion between the parent and staff member. Any unusual behavior or suspected sign of illness is recorded on the daily experience sheet by both parent and caregiver. In addition, the parents have health-assessment sessions with the staff on a regular schedule: for infants under one year, every two months; for children under two years, every six months; and for children over two years, at least once a year.

The Learning Center's vision of health care, however, extends far beyond excellent professional service for children.

Sue Aronson based this plan on the premise that health care is most effective when it is incorporated into the other disciplines, and when it is integrated into the work of those who relate most frequently with children. "Frankly, most of what healthy children need doesn't depend on the medical professional; it's mainly common sense."

She has thus developed a program that serves TLC and many other centers, the National Health Advocacy Program. In this program, a member of a center's staff is chosen or elects to be the health advocate. It can be a teacher, secretary, director, or social worker. The program requires twelve days of training, spread over several weeks, and concentrates on methods for improving the health care of a center. It becomes the health advocate's job to champion preventive health care in the center.

Training

From the beginning, TLC has been a demonstration center. Student teachers are accepted not only from the Medical College, but from other nearby institutions, such as the University of Pennsylvania, Temple University, and Beaver College. The placements are for students who are majoring in nursing, child care, social work, psychology, and nutrition. The director sees The Learning Center as "a laboratory where students can learn about child growth and development in a very reasonable way." Student training ties in with efforts to encourage the center's staff members to continue their own learning. Each caregiver who supervises a student is given an amount of free tuition credit at one of the participating colleges.

Staff members are also encouraged to take the Day Care Services Workshops offered, free of charge, by the Department of Welfare. The weekly staff meetings are the most consistent staff-training sessions. These are times when the staff talks together about individual children or problems. During one staff meeting, for example, they talked about one of the older children, aged three. He was described as a "loner" who got upset when he couldn't get what he wanted. He talked very little and spent a great deal of time sitting and staring into space. He was a good eater and a sound sleeper. However, the caregiver who had asked for this discussion was concerned. "His staring is becoming more prolonged," she said. She had talked with the mother, who said, "He's just stubborn." The nurse who had observed the child felt that the staring was not a medical problem. After sharing all the information about the child, the staff set some plans for the next few weeks:

- Caregivers should be alert to what was happening before the child went into a "blanking out" or "prolonged staring" period.
- They should keep track of how long he remained in the staring state.
- They should interrupt the state physically (he does not readily react to verbal interruption) if it goes on too long.
- Caregivers should note the child's behavior after he comes out of these periods.

Through this concerted effort the caregivers were able to help the child's mother and themselves become aware of the dynamics that were affecting the child; and in the process they helped themselves to feel more comfortable and confident in working with him.

The concept of modeling underlies The Learning Center's training. Doug Sauber, the supervisor, stresses that " 'model' is one of the major words at TLC — a model for children, for parents, and for other staff, a model for volunteers, and for the students who are looking at you through the observation windows, and, of course, a model for ourselves."

Funding

Most of the families served by TLC qualify for child care services under the main source of federal money for day care, Title XX. For those with low incomes, the center is completely free; for others there is a sliding fee scale. A few parents pay the full fee. TLC is designated as an infant-toddler center, and therefore qualifies for the highest rate of funding, which is $75 per week per child. This may seem high, but Judy Okin-Wertheimer points out that it averages out to less than $2.00 per hour.

The Title XX monies do not cover the total operational costs. The center's staff must raise the mandatory 25 percent of the budget, as specified in Title XX legislation. The center depends on fees, grants, and services provided by the Medical College of Pennsylvania. As the director says, "Without the Medical College as a backup, we would have been down the river a long time ago."

Problems and Changes

The problems that The Learning Center faces are common ones, and confront other publicly funded child care programs: crises in funding, threats and actual withdrawal of money and services, changing of guidelines and requirements. Politics on the city and state level becomes the enemy of the peaceful life of the day care center. It is seen almost as a foe ready to strike at any time. "I'm not a very political person," the director says, "and I think that has been to my disadvantage. Politics comes into play because you have to be able to read between the lines and know what effect something is going to have." A simple attendance report, for instance, turned out to be the basis for future funding. "You have to have the courage to say, 'I'm not going to fill that form out.' You learn not to assume that people are motivated as you are, and you try to protect your own money. This is the problem — people [from child care centers] do very little working together, but do a lot of fighting over the same pot and, in the end, it is very self-destructive."

Another problem that Marlene sees is that city and state employees who are responsible for administering child care aren't well supervised themselves and the quality of the administration can vary widely.

Marlene wishes that there could be a very good course in day care administration that deals with these issues. She wishes there were more opportunities for directors to get together and help each other. "I've learned lots of things just in being the director," Marlene says, "like how to adapt your ideas to reality."

Infant-toddler centers are still an unusual kind of child care. The problems that arise have not been worked out as thoroughly as have those that beset centers for other age ranges. For the staff, there is the stress of the wide age range in each unit. The infants can tie down the caregivers: feedings take longer, infants need more holding, and they always require careful watching. The infants can also disrupt the work of older children: pulling off a three-year-old's fireman's hat or knocking a bead game onto the floor. The staff has recently solved this problem by separating the older and younger children in the afternoons, taking each group off to do something special.

Among the parents, there is still a mixture of feelings about putting their infants into day care. Some parents feel totally positive, because this experience will make "infants more sociable." Having a place that is "just for the child" is important, one parent says. "Giving parents time for their own work" is valued by others. Marlene Weinstein says that she doesn't want to convince parents that infant day care is the only way. But she and the parents believe that The Learning Center is a wonderful experience for children, that it gives them nurture and many new relationships and much to discover about themselves. The Learning Center does, indeed, fit its acronym, TLC, providing as it does so much tender loving care.

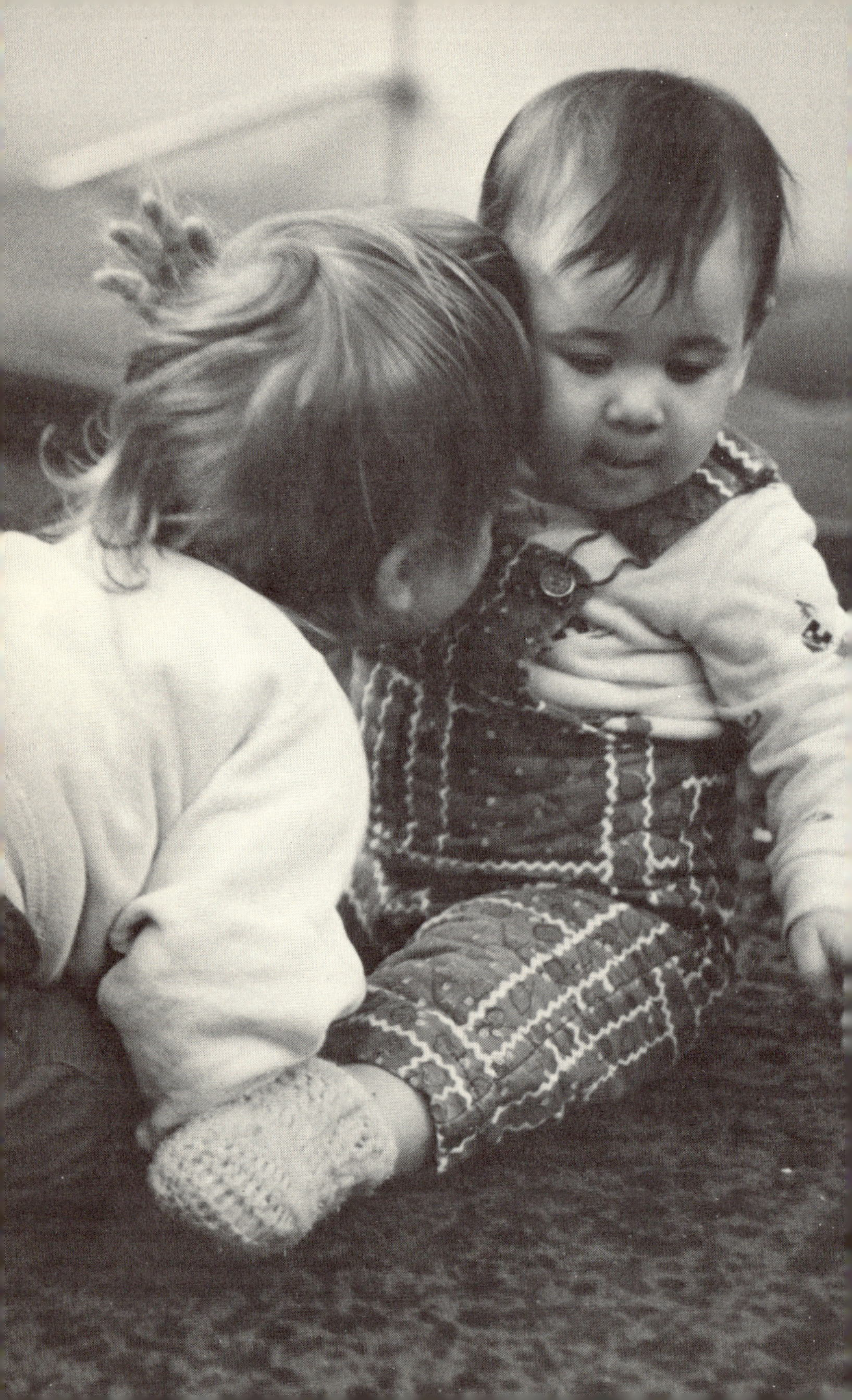

4
A Parent-Staff Cooperative

The Family Center at Bank Street
Bank Street College of Education
New York, New York

It was 9:00 in the morning. Pete Macdonald sat on the yellow-flowered couch in the living room area of the Family Center at Bank Street. He was holding a book on his lap, and two small children snuggled on either side of him, pointing to pictures in the book and naming them.

"Cat . . . oooooh, a cat," said Lara, who is almost two.

"Dat," said Scott, who is a year and a half, trying very hard to say the word the way the older girl had.

Lara took Scott's hand and they crawled into an open wooden box beside the table and hid from Pete, poking their heads out and then disappearing gleefully inside the box.

"Scott needs a diaper change," Pete said. He handed Scott a diaper from a nearby cupboard. "Come on, Lara," he said. "Let's give you a clean diaper, too." The two children, clutching their diapers, headed out of the room, leading the way to the bathroom down the hall.

A visitor in the room turned to the teacher, Phyllis Silverman. "Is that man a teacher or a father?" she asked.

"He's a father," Phyllis answered. "He's the father of the little boy, Scott, and he often spends time here in the morning before going to work at nine-thirty. Visitors do have trouble knowing whether someone is a parent or a teacher. This center belongs to all of us — parents and teachers. We all feel it's our place. What we say is that it is a parent-staff cooperative. That doesn't mean that the parents teach — they don't. What it means to us is that the center is our place and that we all cooperate in making it the best place possible."

Beginnings It was a feeling of dissatisfaction with the manner in which parent-professional relationships are usually handled that led Phyllis to the job of teacher at the Family Center at Bank Street. "In the schools and programs where I worked before," she says, "there were numerous statements about a partnership between home and school, but they were mainly rhetoric." She says that educators often assumed an attitude of superiority, a stance that suggested that this or that parent "has messed up his child's life."

It was, likewise, feelings of dissatisfaction with the status quo that brought the original group of parents of very young children together several years ago. Nancy Portnof had arranged her college class schedule so that she could be home during the day with her infant son, but she found the American ideal — the mother staying home and devoting herself to her child — didn't work for her. Her son, Gabriel, was often bored. He seemed to need and want other children to play with on a regular basis. Paula Weinberger took a year-long maternity leave when her son was born. At the end of that time, she wanted to go back to work, but she had trouble finding a baby sitter. "There weren't that many choices in my neighborhood," she says. Donald St. John-Parsons also had uncomfortable feelings about using baby sitters as a method of child care. He didn't like the idea of one adult and one child alone all day in a New York City apartment, feeling that it would be more healthful to have his child learn the give-and-take of a small group. Ellen Galinsky * didn't want to leave her new baby for very long stretches of time. "I was just seeing her out of her pajamas in the morning and again into her pajamas at the end of a long day." She wondered if it wouldn't be possible to have a program for infants and toddlers in the Bank Street College building where most of these parents worked.

The Bank Street staff was lukewarm to that idea: some staff members worried that separating such young chil-

---

* Author's note: It was my interest in starting this center that led me to team up with a long-time colleague at Bank Street, William Hooks, and to research and write this book. E. G.

dren from their parents would impair the relationship between them, a relationship that is of critical importance in determining the children's growth and development. Other members of the staff had seen substandard infant centers, places where babies were lined up in cribs, unnoticed. Still others thought that it was not the obligation of employers to provide child care service to their employees. Within the college, however, there were as many supporters as critics — staff members who believed that child care is a pressing need of parents and that Bank Street should let this group of parents go ahead.

In September of 1974, the dean of Bank Street, Gordon Klopf, gave the parents a space, rent-free. In the several weeks of discussion that followed, the parents found that they had more in common than a sense of dissatisfaction. Each held ideas and ideals about the way he or she wanted to raise children; but, working alone, it was often difficult to achieve these ideals. Maybe as a group they could.

They felt that they wanted to minimize the conflict between career and family. Having a center in the place where they worked would make it possible for them to see their young children during the day. Consequently, this group of parents decided that one criterion for admission would be that parents live or work close enough to the center to spend time there each day.

"Child care usually means that you give up the child to someone else for eight or more hours a day," one parent says. "But we didn't want to do that. We wanted a situation where we could drop in in the morning before work or at coffee break or lunch time. We were warned that parents wouldn't want to come over during the day, that seeing their children would interfere with their own work. This may be true of some parents; it hasn't been true for us. We are delighted to be able to have time with our babies and still continue our work. We have the best of both worlds and we are as pleased as we can be."

Rena Yannapoulis walks four blocks from her job at a library to have lunch with her son, Ion. Ellen Galinsky takes Lara out to lunch with the people in her office. "It's another kind of familylike group for Lara," she says. "Lara has close friendships with the people I work with. I can't think of a better experience for her than to know and to be comfortable with so many people — older people, younger people, men and women — from her earliest days."

Before the center opened, many of the parents felt trapped by the difficult aspects of parenthood. Some described feelings of resentment about losing their independence; others, the loneliness of New York City apartments. Many discovered competitive tensions among their friends where their children were concerned. Still others felt a loss because their own relatives were hundreds, even thousands, of miles away. Therefore, in designing their center, all of these parents wanted to incorporate the best qualities of family life — namely, the help and support that each member gives the others.

Groupings A large program, they decided, would make an adult group that was diffuse and a children's group that was confusing, perhaps overwhelming, for the babies. A small program could be tightly knit and familylike. The first year that the Family Center was open, 1974–75, it had five children, aged six months through two years, and two teachers. The following year, keeping the same age range and number of teachers, the center increased to eight families, with no more than six children present at a time. In that way, it could offer flexible child care: parents could sign up for two, three, four, or five days a week, depending on their work schedules.

In order to create a familylike feeling, the parents and staff arranged the center to look like an apartment. The larger of the rooms is divided into two areas: one a living room, the other a kitchen. An adjoining room is a bedroom. Down the hall there is a bathroom with a changing table. In each area there is both adult furniture and child-size replicas of the same furniture. For instance, the bedroom has the children's cribs and doll cribs with dolls; the kitchen has a refrigerator and a toy refrigerator. The rooms are painted bright colors, decorated with mirrors and clusters of photographs of each child, but are otherwise kept simple. Most of the equipment is stored in a long wall of cabinets. This equipment is carefully organized so that it can be brought out when needed and put away when not in use. For instance, one day Ion returned from the park, singing. Calley Bittle, a teacher, found a record with the same Pete Seeger song Ion was singing. The children sang along as they took off their gloves, snowpants, and sweaters. Ion got up and started to march in time to the music. Calley then went to the storage cabinet and pulled out a box of instruments — tambourines, triangles, and drums — and the children gathered around the box, each choosing an instrument and then playing it. Calley says that it is very useful to have a repository of equipment "so that if you decide to do music, fingerpainting, or woodwork, it's all there, ready to go."

Space and Daily Schedule

The space that was given to the center had previously been college office space. Bank Street's building is new, and these rooms are well-built and attractive, but they are in the basement and have no windows. In order to make up for what might be a confined, closed-in atmosphere, Calley and Phyllis have kept the space open, and have also planned the schedule so that there are times during the day when the children are using other spaces.

At 8:45, one of the teachers arrives and gets the room ready. There is no fixed time at which the children have to be there — they can come whenever it suits their parents. The children often play in the hall first thing in the morning so that they can greet the other children as they arrive. When Fiona comes off the elevator in her stroller, pushed by her father, Donald, she is welcomed by Ion, who jumps up and down, shouting, "Fiona! Fiona! Look, I'm playing with a bus!" Contrary to many research reports and child-development measures, these infants and toddlers do more than "parallel play." The children at the Family Center form friendships, even in their first year, and can be clearly observed doing such things as waiting for a certain child to arrive in the morning or playing in a genuine give-and-take way. At 10:00, the second teacher arrives. The morning plans usually involve dividing the group in one way or another. On a nice day, the older children may go to a park four blocks away to see the peacocks strut and spread their tails, while the younger children walk up to the corner to Broadway to look in store windows. On a cold day, some children might go into the bathroom to play with soap bubbles and shaving lather while others stay in the rooms and hammer.

At midmorning, one of the eight-year-olds from the Bank Street School for Children comes to work with the babies. Every morning, a different child comes. This experiment grew out of the research of Dr. Beatrice Whiting, of Harvard. In the primitive societies that she studied, she found that preadolescent children regularly had child care responsibilities, and it was a beneficial experience for both the younger and older child, particularly the older one, who developed compassion, responsibility, sensitivity, and ease with children.

The children from the Family Center have lunch together at 11:30. They sit in highchairs or low seats around the wooden table. Each child brings food from home, and often the children share what they have. "The sharing," Phyllis Silverman says, "was at the children's urging. They may not eat a food at home, but when they see another child eat it, it becomes an instant delicacy."

One of the parents' and staff's objectives in the program was to have the children learn to eat healthful food. In a group where this isn't the norm, it is difficult to deny candy or cookies. At the center, however, it's possible to create a group standard of eating. No one brings sweets or dessert. All of the food is fresh and, as far as possible, free of additives. Midmorning and afternoon snacks are supplied by the center — perhaps pretzels from the health food store or fresh fruit bought at the local fruit stands.

After lunch, the teachers take turns putting the children to sleep, one by one. "The children like going to sleep," Phyllis says. Calley attributes this to the nap-time procedures. "We go into the sleeping room with one child at a time and hold him or her on our lap and relax." The routine for each child is different. Cyrus likes listening to songs. Ion likes hearing stories. Pamela wants to be held while she drinks a bottle.

Lara doesn't go to sleep then. Her mother takes her out to lunch at 12:30 and she naps later. Ion's mother comes at 1:30, to have lunch with him after he has napped.

During the time the children are sleeping, the teachers each take a one-hour break. Working with babies can be a demanding job, and the teachers feel that their job is more likely to be rewarding if they are given some time to themselves during the day. Having teachers who are relaxed is important in the dynamics of this particular center. One of the center's main goals is to create a peaceful haven — an antidote to the busy, sometimes frenetic pace of the city.

The parents' accessibility is a distinct advantage to having the center in the building where many of them work. They feel, as does Uri Bronfenbrenner, of Cornell University, that the results of separating children from the adult world can be devastating. In a paper presented at the Symposium on Ecology of Child Development, Dr. Bronfenbrenner spoke about the significant effects of the isolation of children from the adult world of work: "Once children saw what their parents did for a living but also shared substantially in the task; now many children have only a vague notion of their parents' jobs and have had little or no opportunity to observe the parent (or for that matter any other adult) fully engaged in his or her work." Dr. Bronfenbrenner goes on to say that "it appears likely that the absence of such exposure contributes significantly to the growing alienation among children and young people."

At 4:00, the teacher who arrived at 8:45 leaves for the day. At that time, an eleven-year-old girl from the Bank Street School for Children comes to help. In the beginning of the year, she dropped in every day, and was so effective with the children that the people at the center asked her if she would work as a teacher's helper.

Goals

One of the fears of the people who condemn day care, particularly day care for infants and toddlers, is that it will lessen the individualism so prized in American society, producing in its stead human beings who have their allegiances to groups and who follow whatever the groups dictate. The parents and staff at the Family Center feel quite the opposite is possible. And it is perhaps this feeling, beyond all else, that led them to form the center. They say that raising a child alone in an apartment or home until he or she is two or three makes it more difficult for that child to adjust to people later on. They feel that the child has difficulty in socializing, and is more likely to feel ill at ease with other people. Since the beginning of history, infants have been born into groups, whether they were clans or families or communities. The parents at the Family Center feel that group life is not the deviation, but the norm, and that where it doesn't exist, parents and professionals banding together and creating their own groups is a reasonable alternative.

Within group life, just as within family life, there have to be safeguards. In the best kind of family, the center members say, parents don't relate to the children en masse. They treat children as individuals. The Family Center can follow this pattern because it is small enough to permit each child to receive a great deal of individual attention. The schedule is set up in such a way that children can pursue their own interests. The curriculum — if that is the right word to use about babies' activities — is developed from cues the teachers take from the children. Ion's interest in fire engines will be the impetus behind a trip to the fire station. Pamela's interest in exploring her face and her body will lead the teachers to bring in many mirrors. The atmosphere that this kind of program produces is one that is relaxed yet rich, one in which spontaneity and adventuresomeness are valued.

Phyllis Silverman explains her commitment to this value: "I am spontaneous because children are spontaneous. They use everything around them. If you, as an adult, make them do just what you want them to do, you are taking this opportunity away from them." Phyllis's interest in human potential sprang from an observation that she made of her own generation. "My friends are intelligent and talented," she says, "but they've had great difficulty in fulfilling themselves." This is so, she believes, because they held themselves back the way they were held back by those who took care of them. They hadn't learned to trust themselves and be adventurous.

Discipline

While the parents and staff want the children to soar ahead as individuals, they also hope that the children will be caring of, and kind to, each other. It is a commitment to teaching the children how to live well within a group that underlies their approach to discipline. When Lara, for instance, pulled Scott's hair, she was told immediately that "pulling hair hurts Scott." And when Ion pushed Adam over in his rush to get a ride on a bike, the adult said to Ion, "You knocked Adam over and that hurt." The emphasis at the Family Center is helping the children to understand, to sympathize with each other's feelings. The teacher poses, or helps the child pose, a solution to the problem. "Lara, did you pull Scott's hair because you wanted the book he's reading?" she asked. When Lara nodded, the teacher suggested, "Let's ask Scott for a turn with the book," or "Let's find another book about cats." The children have, in fact, become compassionate toward each other.

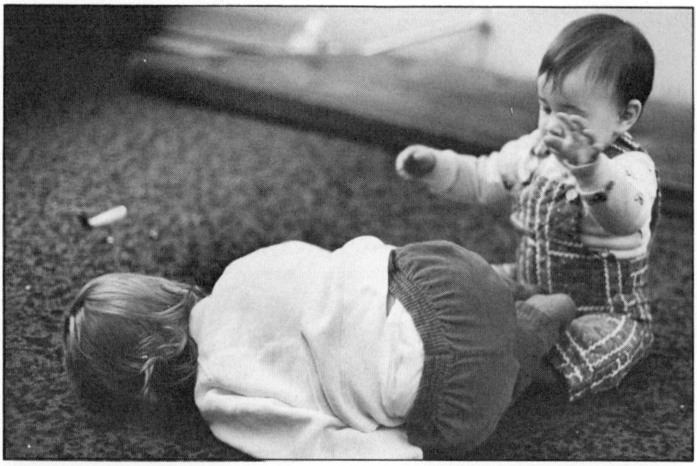

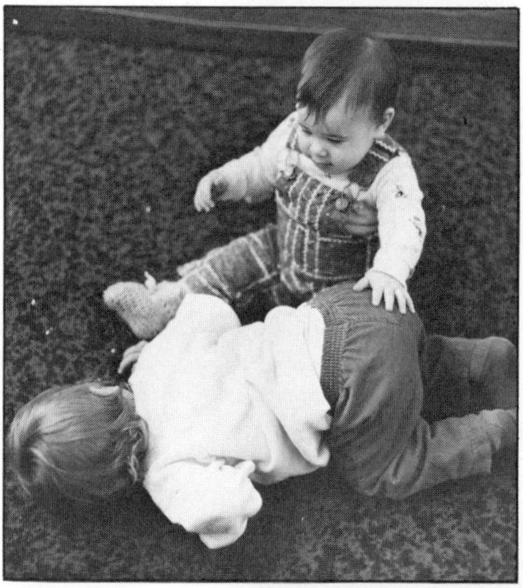

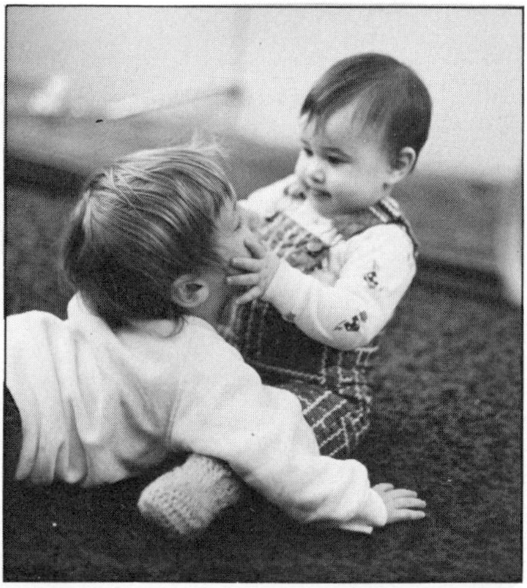

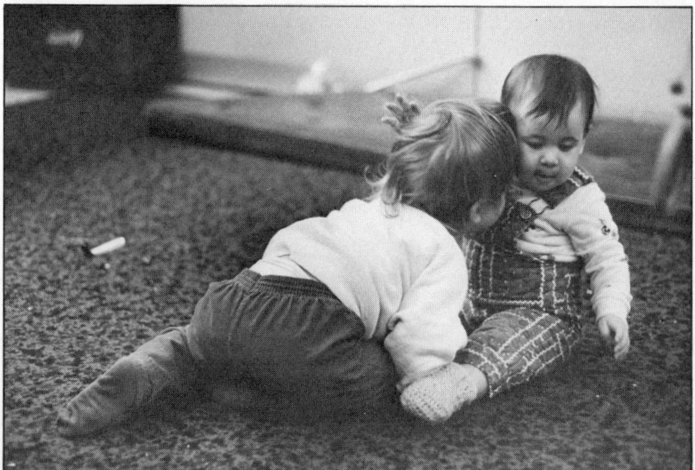

The qualities that the Bank Street families came to cherish most depend on the kind of care given to their children. "We have seen infant care programs," a teacher says, "that were confusing and chaotic, where children received only minimal physical care. The children in such programs, at the age of three, seemed more babyish than most three-year-olds, clinging, very often demanding and unable to share or give at all."

"We founded the Family Center at Bank Street to provide child care for our children," Ellen Galinsky reports. "But it had another, equally important function — it provided an adult group for us as parents. There is no amount of preparation that can convey the changes that occur when one becomes a parent. It is an experience that is earthshaking, and I think all of us wanted other people to talk with about this thing called parenthood."

Parent Participation

For this reason, parents and staff have monthly meetings. "Being a parent is not just the job of a woman," Maritza Macdonald, Scott's mother, states. "We hold our parent group in the evenings so that both parents can attend." At these meetings, the parents talk about what's on their minds. Discussions cover the gamut of parental concerns. Their tone is one of honesty, where, for instance, two children's parents might talk over what they don't like about the relationship their children have formed. Parents also talk about what they don't like in themselves as parents, and try, with group support, to make changes in themselves. The parenting meetings are also beneficial for staff. Phyllis Silverman reports that listening to parents talk makes her feel more "responsive and responsible to the parents and children."

Parents can also share in planning curriculum. At regular lunch-time meetings, once or twice a month, the staff and those parents who are available talk about the children. From their knowledge of the children's development, they plan activities for them. Together, parents and staff keep a journal, writing down anecdotes about the children. The parents then have a unique kind of baby book — a year's worth of stories — to keep.

"We were told that working parents would be too busy to want to take this responsibility," Paula Weinberger, Cyrus's mother, says, "but we find that parents of infants and toddlers want to do it. I think it's because they want to have an active say in the experiences their children are given."

In this program, there is no director. The functions of director have been taken over by a steering committee, which consists of a teacher and two or three parents. In a weekly meeting open to all parents and teachers, the steering committee makes the week-by-week decisions that keep the center going. In the event that major decisions, such as hiring or firing, have to be made, the steering committee brings recommendations back to the whole group for their consideration.

A parent-staff cooperative, in the case of the Family Center, does not mean that parents work regular hours as teachers. Because the parents have jobs or school programs, the members of the Family Center decided that the staff would take complete responsibility for teaching, though the parents can and do fill in during emergencies. The meaning of a parent-staff cooperative here is that both parents and staff take an equal, side-by-side part in administering the center.

Administration is handled by committees, and two people are responsible for each committee. These deal with admissions, hiring, budget, relations with the college, and fund-raising.

Funding Fund-raising is a necessity because the center operates solely on parent fees. The actual fee is determined by the parents and staff. In 1975–76, they decided against a sliding fee scale, putting the daily fee at $11.25 (approximately $1.40 an hour). It is an expensive price for parents to pay, and most don't have high incomes (generally, the families fall in the middle-income range), but as a group they decided that child care was a priority for them, and they wanted to pay their teachers as well as they could. The only expenses out of their $14,650 yearly budget are salaries, snack food, and supplies. When large pieces of equipment or material are needed, the parents and staff have a fund-raising event, such as a white elephant sale or a food sale, to pay for it.

The people at the center try as often as possible to find furniture that has been discarded and stacked up on the streets of New York. With fresh paint and a few repairs, an old rocking chair was made to look like new. Weekly ads in newspapers are another source of supplies. In addition, a letter is sent to the parents of the Bank Street

Children's School, asking for donations of outgrown toys. In general, the effort of the members of the center is to use the free and less costly resources of their community.

Problems and Changes

One benefit of being in the Bank Street College community is that one has many knowledgeable people to call on for help in solving problems. One college staff member, for instance, volunteered her time for a once-a-month lunch-time meeting and was also available to parents. The group found her help invaluable. Phyllis Silverman reports, "She was someone to talk to about the things — which turned out to be everything — for which there are no cut-and-dried answers. She could listen to what we were saying, slow us down, and help us put things back together again." One of the major areas the teachers worked on as a staff was their relationship to parents. Calley Bittle says, "I had to learn to become less judgmental of differences in peoples' lifestyles." Both teachers say that the fact that their adviser is not their director or boss, and can stay strictly in the role of helper, is an advantage. "When I was teaching in other programs, I used to resent people coming in and *telling* me what I *had* to do," says Phyllis.

One of the traditional problems of cooperatives is that as the founding parents leave, the group tends to lose its momentum. Recognizing this as a potential pitfall, the group that formed the center made two provisions. The first was that most children admitted to the center be in the six-months to one-year age range so that parents would usually have three years at the center; the other was that one of the parents of the youngest children be admitted to the steering committee. As a result, the transition from year to year is smooth, and the leadership has continuity.

The fact the parents and staff try to work in a cooperative way, has been a source of strength and weakness for the center. It has sometimes meant that things don't get done. This was particularly true in the interval when the center expanded from five families to eight. With five families, the decision-making could be casual, but the addition of just three more families turned informality into confusion, and the parents and staff had to create decision-making procedures and structures. It also took some time for the group to realize that there had to be leaders taking overall responsibility, even within the steering committee.

Another problem that the center has faced is its relationship to the college. The center is not a regular college program, but a guest program. Perhaps the place where this tenuous relationship is felt the strongest is in the assignment of space for the center. Is it all right to have a center in a basement? The parents and staff at the center agree that it would be nicer to have a program in a room that was designed and built for infants and toddlers, with indoor-outdoor space. Furthermore, operating in a basement is a violation of the New York City licensing code. The center's consultant from the New York City Department of Health has been helping the members gain a temporary license, with the agreement that the center will move into a more appropriate space within the college. Plans are now underway to incorporate the center into the college program.

Despite the problems, the parents and staff feel their center is an overwhelming success. News of the center has spread, and numerous people call the parent who handles admissions to ask if there is space for another child. "When we talk to these parents, we help them find other child care or we help them start their own child care program in the places where they work or in their apartment buildings," a parent states. "Originally, I felt very worried about the trend toward infant and toddler care," she continues. "It could be a devastating or destructive experience. But parents and staff working together in cooperative ways can provide a system of checks and balances for each other."

"A cooperative works best if it is small," Maritza Macdonald says.

"The key to maintaining a cooperative is selecting staff," Paula Weinberger insists. "It took a long time to decide what kind of people we wanted to hire. Then it took us a long time to find just the right people. But the result was worth every bit of the time, for we have helped to ensure the quality of our center."

The continual process of creating their center has been an exhilarating experience for these parents and staff. At the end of its first year of operation, Ellen Galinsky wrote in her journal: "We lumped our dissatisfactions and dreams together and have tried to create a form of child care. Sometimes it becomes misshapen, veers too far in one direction or another, and we have to keep reshaping it. If any of our hands let go, what we are making begins to weaken. But with all of us together, we are forming something, something beautiful, unique in its emerging, replete with our hopes for our children."

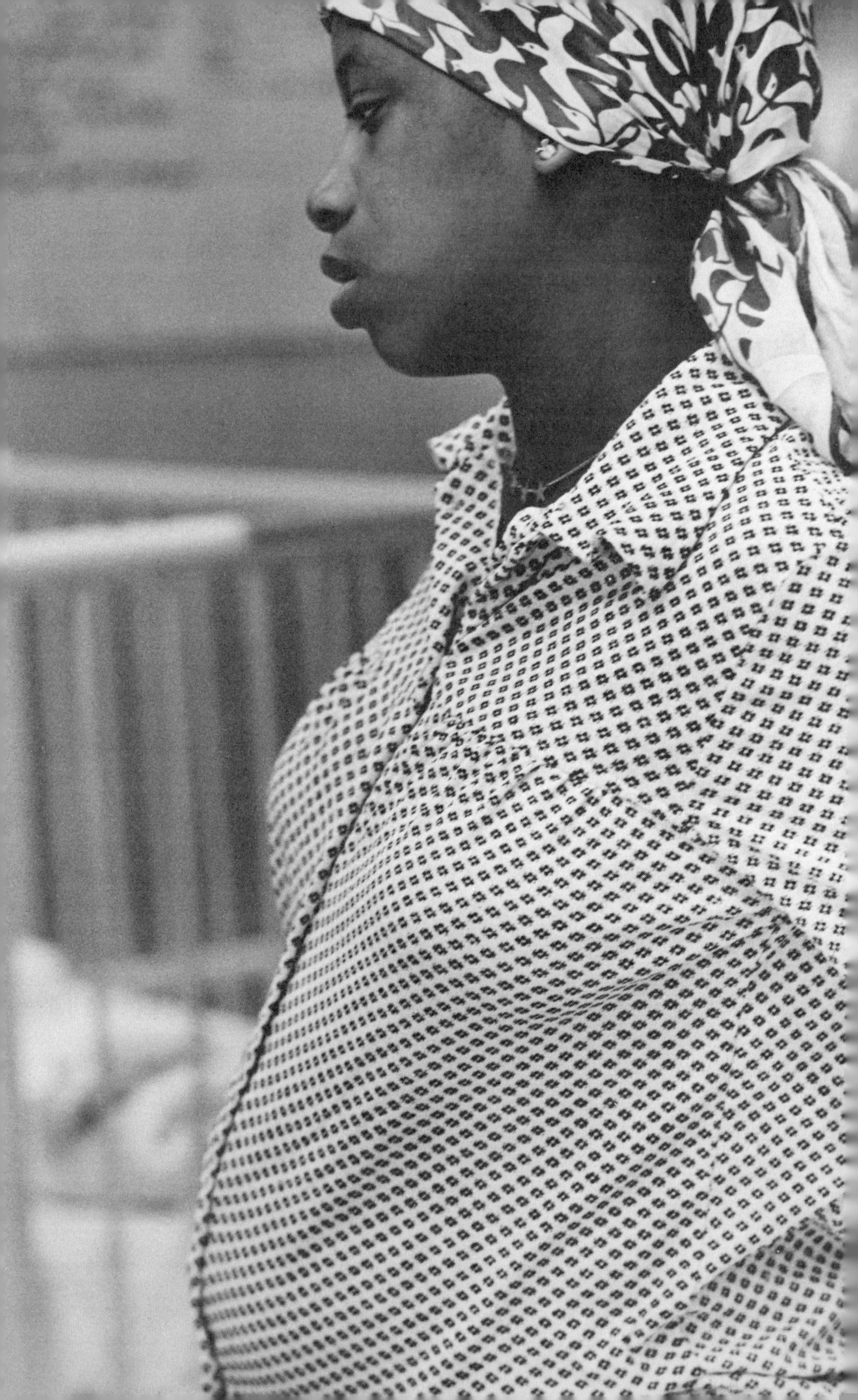

5
A Public School for Teen-Age Mothers and Their Children

The Durham School
Philadelphia, Pennsylvania

Signs tacked to the hallways and doors announced that there would be an African dance and drum concert at the Durham School. When the day finally arrived, children and their teachers came eagerly into the auditorium. After most of the people were seated, another group came in and sat toward the front — teen-age girls, some pregnant, others carrying infants. They sat down just as the concert began with a resounding drumbeat. As the dancers moved, the girls clapped in time to the music, rocking and swaying with their babies. The older school children nudged each other, whispering, "Look, the baby's dancing too." Even when one baby started to wail, no one looked disapproving or asked that the baby be taken out. Babies and their teen-age mothers are an integral part of the Durham Elementary School.

At present the Teen-Age Mother Program serves an average of ten girls per year. They all voluntarily elect to drop out of their regular public school and continue their education at the Durham School. Here they have the chance to incorporate parenting into their required public school curriculum and to have their newborn babies in the same building.

52 The New Extended Family

Beginnings Durham is not an ordinary public school. In addition to the Teen-Age Mother Program and a nursery for infants and toddlers that serves the teenagers and working parents, it has a Head Start program for three- and four-year-olds, a school serving kindergarten through fifth grade, and a Learning Resource Center for teachers, pupils, and community people. These programs are housed in a single, old-fashioned school building in South Philadelphia. It exists because Lore Rasmussen had an idea that a true community school should encompass all of these components, and that it could exist within the framework of the present school system.

Lore Rasmussen is an educator with creative ideas, and she has the ability to communicate them with enthusiasm. Lore describes the process of establishing this unique combination of services at the Durham School: "It was difficult to convince the Welfare Department. At that time, legislation only allowed for four infants in a group." She discussed this dilemma with a woman in the state Welfare Department, who was so taken with the idea that she suggested examining the legislation carefully for an "experimental" loophole. The loophole was found and Lore gave her presentation to the Philadelphia Board of Education. In making this presentation, she stressed the importance of the mixture of infants, preschoolers, elementary school children, school-age mothers, and community people. One of her fears was that some components would be approved and funded and others eliminated. But in the spring of 1970, the funding agencies concerned — federal government, school district, and Welfare Department — miraculously came together and approved the launching of all the programs in the fall of the same year.

Lore's first concern was to find the someone who could head a program that had no precedents, and who could chart new courses while at the same time dealing with agencies that were not likely to nurture this kind of experimentation. Lore turned to Dr. Peter Buttenwieser, who already had gained a reputation for his innovative and alternative approaches to education. Lore says, "My first real job was to convince Peter, and the more excited I got about the project, the easier it was for me to convince him."

Peter Buttenwieser accepted the job, and the work of setting up the five components was accomplished during the summer of 1970. "We decided to start everything all at once," Peter explains, "on the theory that unless you start everything at once, you will get only what you start with. So we decided, no matter how crude, we would go with the whole plan. It wasn't that hard at the time to bring new ideas together. There were no precedents. I think that right now it would be unbelievably hard to pull off the same thing."

Schooling for pregnant teen-agers is not a new idea in education. In many parts of the country there are special schools for pregnant school-age girls, and there are infant care programs for the babies once they are born. But the Durham School is a departure from the usual pattern. To begin with, in most programs, the infant care lasts for only one year. At the end of that time, the new mother has to find her own child care if she wishes to continue her education. If her own mother is not available or is not willing to baby-sit, the teen-ager is often forced to quit school. At the Durham School, the babies may stay the next year and the next — they can stay until they finish fifth grade.

Durham differs from other programs in another respect. The atmosphere in programs for pregnant teen-agers is often condemnatory and condescending. The teacher and administrators, sometimes unconsciously, take the attitude that these girls have done something dirty, something dreadfully wrong, and that they should be reminded of this every day. And so they are looked upon and spoken to in a way that makes them withdraw or fight back. At Durham, in the words of the social worker, "There is no attack or judgment made." One of the teachers says, "We are friends as well as educators of the girls."

Goals

Many teen-age parent programs concentrate on education alone, which they define as "keeping the kids from falling behind or failing." At Durham, education is defined more broadly. It encompasses teaching parenting as well as the required school subjects. If one had to delineate the major goal of the program, it could be said in two words: teaching responsibility. These teen-agers are really children themselves, and for most of their lives people have made decisions for them. In becoming parents, however, they are taking on an immense responsibility, and they don't know how to handle it.

Deidre Grose, teacher of the teen-age girls, makes a

"responsibility contract" with each girl, setting out in detail how the schoolwork will be accomplished. The girls know what they are expected to cover in algebra, English, world history, and other subjects. But how and when they do their work is their own choice. Deidre cites the example of a girl who hated Spanish but loved algebra. "She finished algebra in two months, and next she did Spanish. She decided that she would rather do it that way, instead of doing a little bit of this and a little of that each day. It is up to the girls to work out how they get their work done." Deidre uses regular school textbooks as well as worksheets she has devised herself. In essence, she individualizes the program for each girl. As Deidre puts it, "It means I do a lot of work."

Space and Daily Schedule The parenting part of the program is a combination of classes and on-the-spot observation and work. The girls' classroom connects to the Infant Center, and part of each day is spent in the center itself. Before her own baby is born, each girl takes care of a baby in the center, with a caregiver who can help her learn about child care. She learns not only from watching caregivers, but by taking actual responsibility for all the baby's needs at certain times during the day. She is involved in changing diapers, feeding, cuddling, and infant stimulation. Deidre comments, "We aren't too concerned about the educational thing — we can handle that. If we can get the girls into that nursery and make them feel comfortable about being parents, then the rest will fall into place." All of this is viewed as preparation for the arrival and care of the pregnant girl's own baby.

In the Infant Center, the staff caregivers take care of the babies from 9:30 to 11:00 A.M. while the girls are doing their required school studies. At 11:00 the girls are responsible for going in and feeding and caring for the babies. They are also free to come into the center if their babies are upset or crying. The caregivers are very conscientious about demonstrating both care and stimulation of the infants, but they do so with a high degree of sensitivity toward the young mothers and mothers-to-be. One caregiver, Corinne Patterson, explains: "It is modeling, but it is never being condescending. They are so young, but you must never talk to them as if they were children, or in a punitive way. You must do it in a way that is never threatening." Another caregiver, Joanna Waldman, adds, "To many of the girls, when you have a baby that means you are a woman, and we must really approach them with care. We can't jump on them or they'll just turn us off."

The staff of the Infant Center assumes that opportunities for learning will affect the infants' physical, social, and mental growth. One day each week staff members discuss child care and child development with the young mothers and mothers-to-be. Their developmental approach to infants is an eclectic one. Joanna Waldman describes it: "We use a bit from this person and a bit from that person — Kuno Beller and Piaget, for instance. But we don't just use Piaget; we combine his theories with the knowledge of the mother and what we see on a day-to-day basis and what we find that fits. We have behavioral inventories and we work with what the expectations might be according to the scales and our observations. But it is not rigid; the kids are never judged on a rigid basis. It is very, very open." Using this flexible approach, the caregivers help the mothers to engage in interactions with their babies, which include talking, singing, exposing the babies to sights and sounds and to tactile and other sensory experiences.

Babies participate in a wide range of activities. They are taken on trips outside the school buildings, sometimes with their mothers, at other times with the professional caregivers. They are included in almost all of the school's social activities.

Health and nutrition are considered vital elements in both the mother and infant programs. Most medical services are provided by the nearby Penn Urban Medical Center. When the mother takes her baby to the Medical Center she is encouraged to ask questions so that she will understand the health procedures. Special instruction is given to the mothers at the school by a nurse to prepare them for labor and delivery. They visit a hospital delivery room and view many films about pregnancy and childbirth. Girls who have already had their babies discuss their experiences with the pregnant teen-agers. Nutrition is also a part of their regular curriculum, and they are provided a balanced lunch each day.

Health and Food

The teen-agers are taught to be responsible for their own actions. An example is the annual year-end trip, which they take with their teachers and without their babies. They are expected to plan the trip, to set up the budget for it, and to arrange for baby-sitting for their own children. In Deidre's words, "I didn't want the girls to assume automatically that their own parents would baby-sit. We had a really big problem with one of the girls, and it was a good learning experience for her. She went home and said she was going away and *told* her mother to take care of the baby. Her mother said, 'Oh no, I won't.' Her mother held her off for about three days until she went back and *asked*."

The teen-agers are also given responsibility in a summer work program. They can work at different jobs throughout the school, from helping the cooks to being caregivers themselves. They fill out applications and get Social Security numbers. Deidre says, "They learn that if they come in late, they will be docked pay, and if they don't show up they will lose a day's pay. Then comes the day when they get paid. We go to the bank with them to get their checks cashed, and it really is a big moment when they get that first check."

Becoming responsible entails learning many other skills. One of the primary ones the teen-agers must learn is to be straight with themselves, to say what they think and feel. Every day they watch a soap opera on television with their teacher and use that as a forum for talking about why people act the way they do. They are also encouraged to express their own emotions. Deidre tells of one of the girls who was causing a commotion in the classroom. When pressed, she finally admitted that she had only $3 to spend on a new Easter outfit for herself. Deidre agreed to help her shop for material and a pattern and to teach her to sew. Then she said to her, "The next time something like this bothers you, you should be able to tell me instead of going through all sorts of other ways."

Problems and Changes The major problem the staff encounters is one of attitude on the part of the new mother when she returns to school after the birth of her baby. Deidre Grose describes the situation: "After she has the baby, there is some form of rebellion and rejection. I've never seen it fail. It takes a lot of different forms, and sometimes it can take the form of acting out. She is no longer the center of attention — the baby is. And she is interested in boys again. She wants to be a girl again, and it's a real problem: suddenly having to play so many roles — mother, daughter, student. There is no amount of warning you can give her. Every one of them goes through it in different ways. And we have to work on an individual basis with each girl." The most effective method the staff has developed for working through this difficult time is to help them express these feelings, to show them what resources they have, to allow them to make choices, and to support them in their decisions.

The question often arises in infant centers as to whether the relationship between the caregiver and the infant dilutes the mother-child relationship. The Durham staff finds no such problem; on the contrary, they feel the caregiver strengthens this alliance, and it becomes a caregiver-child-mother relationship. As Deidre puts it, "The child gets the sense that everyone cares about him or her."

Another aspect of the program for young mothers is the support provided by a part-time social worker, Edith Cunningham. She is an on-site confidante, counselor, and provider of social services. As Edith says, "I'm there if the girl just needs to take a walk."

There is a strong camaraderie among the girls and the

staff, and most of them express regret that they can remain in the program for only one year. However, many of the mothers maintain close contact with the school, since their children can stay on through grade school. "I wish I would *never* have to leave!" exclaims one girl. "Teachers here have patience, they listen to your problems, they help you with what you need help with, and there aren't too many kids in one classroom," remarks another. An expectant mother says, "I haven't had my baby yet, but I will feel okay about bringing it here. I will trust it here." Still another young mother simply but beautifully expresses the continuity of the kind of learning she has experienced at the Durham School: "They treat babies nice here; they treat us nice. You see mothers treating babies nice, and you learn that you can do this at home. Treat your baby nice so when she has children, she will treat them nice, the same way you treated her."

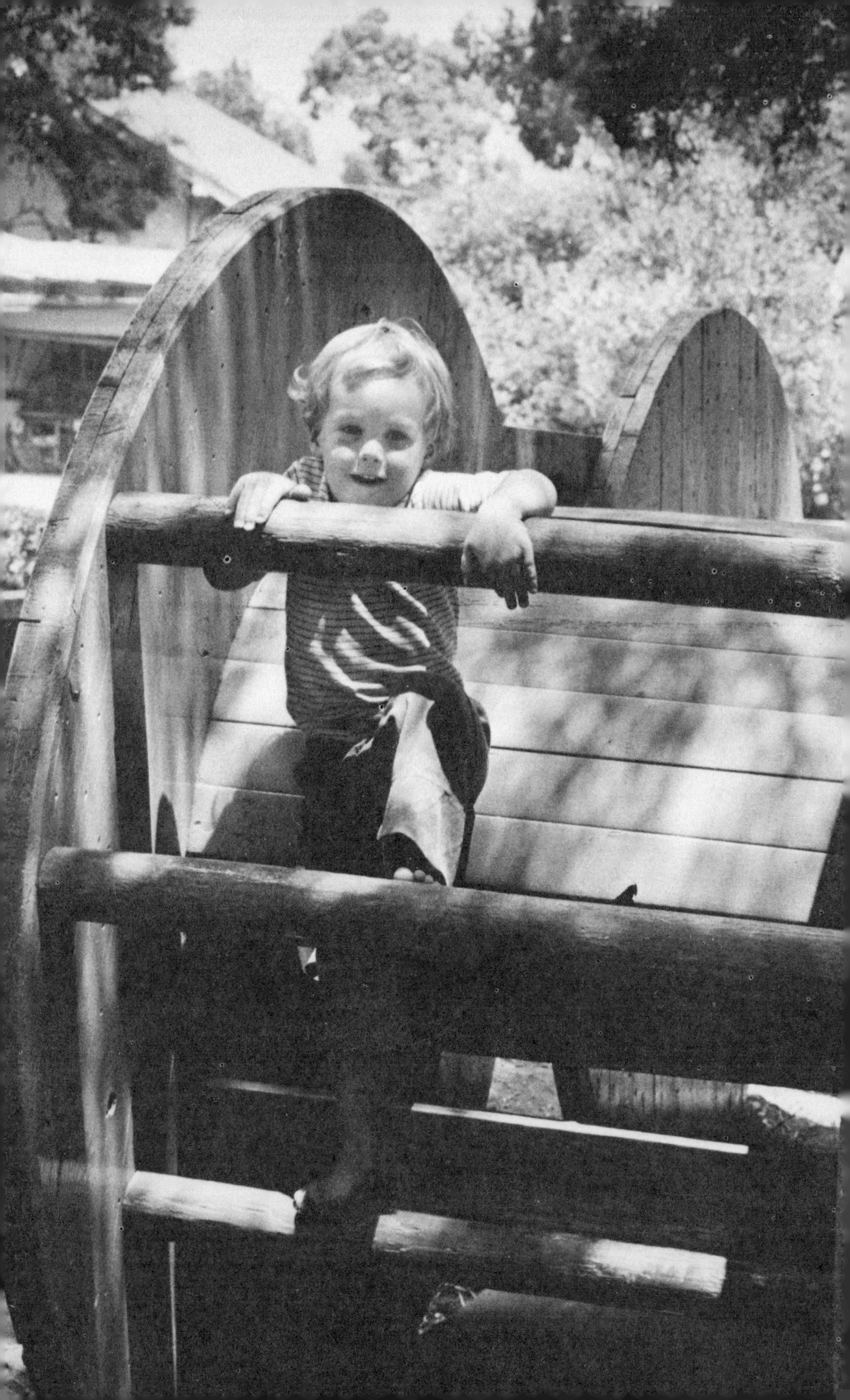

6
A Parent Education Program

The Infant-Toddler-Parent Center
Pacific Oaks College
Pasadena, California

"I have a question," a young mother named Heather says. She is nursing her three-week-old baby and addressing a group of about fifteen mothers, who have children as young as hers or as old as two and a half years. All of the participants are in the Infant-Toddler-Parent Center at Pacific Oaks, a small college of education in Pasadena, California.

Heather continues, "Kevin, my son who's almost three, wakes up every night. My two-year-old daughter, Brooke, wakes me up in the night, too, and now the baby wakes me up every other hour to eat." The rest of the mothers and the program's founder, Jerry Ferguson, nod sympathetically.

Heather says that she isn't getting any sleep at all. If the children happen to be quiet, she lies in bed, tense, wondering who is going to cry next. She has tried a variety of approaches. Thinking that perhaps the two older children felt lonely and scared at night, she moved them into a room together, but that didn't work. "They woke each other up and got each other going and were screaming all night long. It's ridiculous, but I don't know what to do."

Her problem may indeed seem ridiculous to some people, but certainly not to those who have lived through sleepless nights of children's crying. And for these mothers, the chance to talk about things related to being a parent and a woman with others in the same situation is, as one of them put it, "lifesaving."

"I had a real hard time fitting into the role of mother," explains Poppy Dully, another mother in this group. "It was so new to me. I went to childbirth classes and everything, but I found that when the baby came, I was bogged down."

"New mothers stay at home and go crazy," says Linda Getze, also a parent. "They have no place to go and no one to talk to."

Jerry Ferguson believes that parenthood today boxes people into their homes and apartments, trapping them, in a sense. The Infant-Toddler-Parent program, she thinks, can help nonworking mothers break out of confinement and isolation by providing, twice weekly, a time for them to be away from their young children and be with each other. The Infant-Toddler-Parent Center has two groups: one that meets on Monday and Wednesday mornings, the other on Tuesday and Thursday mornings, each serving about fifteen families. The children, with the exception of nursing babies, play in a beautifully designed play yard adjacent to the building where the mothers talk. The groups meet once a week with the program's director, Molly Noxon (who succeeded Jerry Ferguson, the founder of the program), and once a week by themselves. The mothers help each other, as the program's brochure states, "share problems, solutions, information, and techniques."

The word "comfortable" is an important one in the Infant-Toddler-Parent program. When one mother reaches an impasse, the other members of the group help her dig into her own feelings and attitudes to find what's comfortable for her and to fashion solutions accordingly.

A century ago, families were larger than they are today, and they generally stayed together. A new mother then had the advice, knowledge, and actual helping hands of her own parents and older relatives. Furthermore, she probably had had a large share of the responsibility in the raising of her younger brothers and sisters. In today's mobile society, a new mother is likely to be far away from her own parents. If distance doesn't separate them, the changing patterns of family structure contribute to the isolation of family units. And, because family size is smaller, it is possible, even probable, that one can become a parent without ever having touched a small baby. People become parents with less preparation than for any other job in today's society.

There have been attempts within society to remedy this situation. One suggestion is that parenting be taught in high schools, colleges, and special courses. Another trend has been the creation of parent-child development programs. These programs reach out to both the mother and the baby, teaching them together. In general, parent-child programs are so-called intervention programs; that is, they teach a certain number of defined skills to parents who might not otherwise learn them, and at the same time they provide stimulation for the child who would otherwise be deprived.

Goals

The Infant-Toddler-Parent Center at Pacific Oaks is of this genre, but it differs greatly from the majority of parent-child development programs. In the Pacific Oaks program, people don't speak in terms of "intervention," but rather in terms of "support." They try to provide a friendly, supportive atmosphere. Though they emphasize skills for the mothers and stimulation for the children, their method of reaching their goals is different from that of other programs. In most other parent-child programs, the skills that are taught are predefined, often by researchers, and are then taught to mothers either by experts or mothers who have been trained as "model mothers."

"It is easy to tell other people how to run their lives," Poppy Lully says, "but what's fantastic here is that they want you to do what's comfortable for you. I wouldn't want to go to a place that was going to tell me how to do this and how to do that."

Jerry Ferguson says, "I couldn't begin to tell or even guess what would be good for another person to know. I just don't think I am qualified to do that."

By that statement, she is not referring to her educational qualifications, which are, in fact, impressive. She has a doctorate in education, a degree in architecture, and is the mother of two young children. What she means is that she believes that people do not learn parenting by following a recipe method, but by being allowed to open up, express themselves, and find their own solutions.

Most of the parent-child programs that follow a structured, authoritarian approach have been designed for poor people. Pacific Oaks, on the other hand, tends to serve a more middle-class constituency. Does this mean that the Pacific Oaks program is more applicable to the middle class? Jerry Ferguson thinks not. She thinks that people, regardless of their background, should have a say about what skills they are taught. They should be given responsibility. In Jerry's opinion, there are no sure-fire answers to parenting. At Pacific Oaks, the parents have the opportunity to hear many solutions to a situation. If Jerry or Molly feel that a proposed method would harm a child, they will say so. But within the range of normal solutions, they believe parents do have many options.

Beginnings The Infant-Toddler-Parent program did not have its origins in the needs of parents at all. That it has come to be one of the few programs that are truly responsive to parents' own needs is indeed interesting, considering its beginnings.

In the early 1970s, some members of the Pacific Oaks College staff discovered that, for the most part, their students had read about infancy but lacked actual experience. "I said to my graduate students," Jerry reports, " 'How can you get a degree in human development if you've never picked up a baby?' " The students, it turned out, had no access to babies. "The next semester," Jerry says, "I taught a class on infants and we imported babies [from well-baby clinics]. But I thought that that was a real crummy thing to do to the babies — to have students pick them up and poke at them. I thought we should offer something in return to the children we observed."

In the summer of 1971, Jerry announced the opening of

the Infant-Toddler-Parent Center through notices tacked up in doctors' offices and local markets. Fifteen mothers responded; all but one of them had boys between the ages of fourteen and eighteen months. "I was about seven months pregnant at the time," Jerry says. "It was the blind leading the blind, and we just all had a pretty fine time."

Jerry discovered that the mothers wanted to leave their children for a short while and talk to other mothers. The graduate students welcomed the opportunity to take care of the children during this time. A schedule and an environment were then created to serve the needs of the mothers, the graduate students, and the young children.

Space

Because the program is in Southern California, it can be centered on the outside space, with the inside considered a refuge for cold or rainy days. One of Jerry's main interests is the creation of learning environments, and the play yard may be one of the most beautiful spaces ever designed for young children. Built of natural materials, mainly wood and brick, it is divided into three spaces. A ramp with high brick walls leads from the parking lot into a semicircular central space, the area intended especially for babies. It is the highest space, surrounded by a brick wall, with built-in planters. Though this yard is enclosed, steps do lead out to the yard on the right, and an underground tunnel goes into the left yard. An overhanging tree has a swinging cradle for babies to sleep in. Colorful cushions can be folded and stacked to create all kinds of cozy places for other babies to lie down, crawl, or sit in. "In this place," says Jerry Ferguson, "there is a lot of room for adults to sit down. I wanted the adults in the central yard to be immediately available to the children." From their high vantage point in this yard, the adults can see into both of the other yards.

The yard to the left is for the toddlers. It consists of a variety of spaces, with steps or tree stumps for the children to use in climbing from one level to another. Most of the material here is malleable: a bowl of cornmeal for feeling, soap suds for water play, sand, and water. Next to the building there are long cabinets for storing a variety of equipment — wheel toys, and buckets and funnels for mixing and measuring. In this yard the adults sit on the walls but can easily get up and move around. Children at

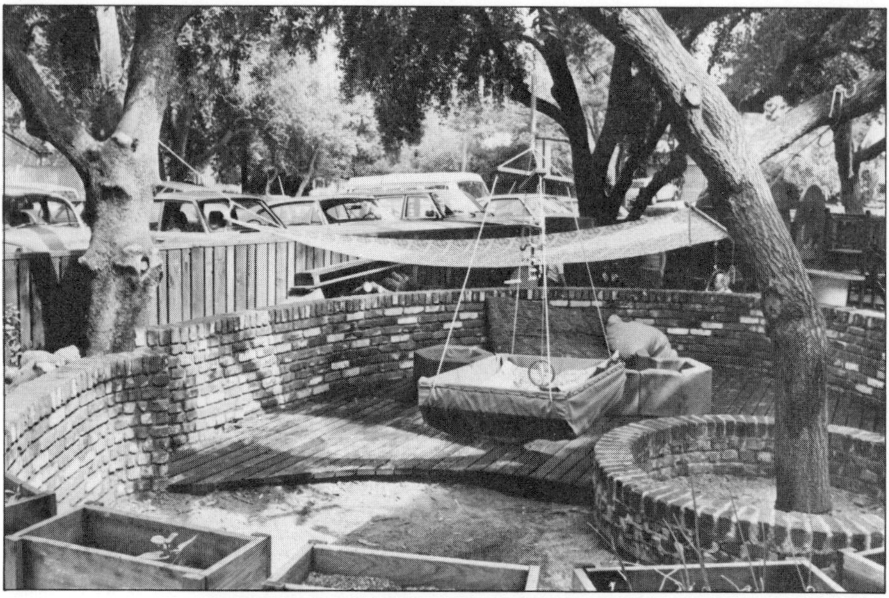

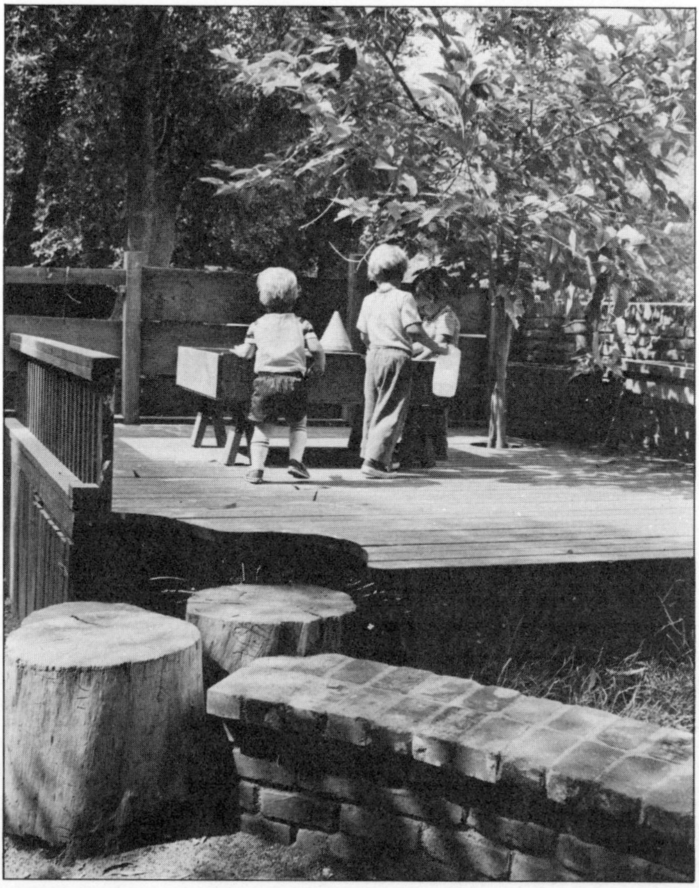

this age are inquisitive and independent, so the seating is designed to make the adults immediately accessible but not directly involved in the activities taking place in the yard.

The yard to the right is the space for the oldest children, the two-year-olds. More challenging climbing equipment is here: industrial spools, slides, and ladders. A rope-and-tire swing hangs from a tree. A playhouse with cut-out windows stands next to the brick wall. The design of this section emphasizes children's growing autonomy. Originally, there was no seating for adults in this yard, and they had to stand, but because they tended to leave and go to the other yards where they could sit down, seating has now been added.

Jerry says, "I'd hate to see every bit of equipment

embedded in concrete, so the environment you come with is the environment you leave with. Every semester there are changes in the yard that are made by whoever wants to make them — parents or students. It is a neat thing to have the environment responsive to the people and the people to it."

The environment provided for the children is also a very responsive one. There are materials to investigate, materials to be changed: water, dough, shaving cream, and sand — things children can make an impact on. Children who are in a sensory-motor stage of development need materials to walk over, climb onto, throw, push, poke, and shape. Jerry says, "In developing the Infant-Toddler-Parent program, we responded to the developmental needs of the children rather than watering down a kindergarten program."

Admissions Those who participate in the program are mostly nonworking mothers, though some work part time. At one time a father joined. In the beginning, admissions were on a first-come, first-served basis, but now the center has developed a list of criteria emphasizing diversity of race, lifestyle, sex, and age.

Since this program is primarily a parent-education one, children aren't admitted unless their parents participate in the parent groups. The admission decisions are made, by both staff and participating parents, whenever an opening occurs in either the Monday-Wednesday or Tuesday-Thursday group. It is the belief of staff and parents that the two groups should have continuity, growing and changing slowly, the way a family does. Originally, one of the groups was for younger children and the other for older ones, but now there are children of mixed ages in both groups; the staff finds this a more successful method for parents and children. More experienced parents and children can thus serve as models for the newer ones.

Daily Schedule On a typical day, the program director and the several graduate students who make up the staff of the center arrive at 9:00 A.M. and begin to get the play yard and indoor space ready. At 9:30, the parents and children begin to arrive. They often stand outside and talk for a while. On the first day that a parent brings a new baby to the group, she is surrounded by other people, who admire the baby and ask about the birth. Usually some of the parents go directly inside, perhaps to fix a bottle or change a diaper.

One or two children may stay inside, but most go into the yard to play, hiding away in the playhouse, scaling the large climbing structure, pushing or being pushed in the rope-and-tire swing. The arrival time has purposely been made long — an unusual procedure in comparison with most programs. This arrival time provides parents, staff, and children with an easy, relaxed beginning to the morning.

At 10:00, Jerry or Molly announces that she's going over to the meeting room. The mothers, judging for themselves the proper moment, begin saying good-bye to their children and joining the parents' group. They always explain to their children where they are going and when they will be back. If a child needs special care at this time, one of the student teachers helps the child with the transition. The parent's actual departure, the staff feels, should be made quickly, for prolonged good-byes are difficult for a child to take.

Parent Participation

The mothers, the director, and some of the graduate students then sit down together to talk about what's happening. The attitude in these groups is nonjudgmental. People feel free to discuss their feelings about very personal matters. In one meeting, a young mother talked openly about her lack of sexual desire following childbirth.

The tone of the meetings, originally set by Jerry Ferguson, was maintained by Molly Noxon when she took over the job of program director. Poppy Dully says, "Molly is really open about herself and has gone through lots of changes, and she has been very willing to talk about them." The part the leader plays in the discussion is interesting. At times she talks about her own life, her children and concerns, as an equal member of the group. Linda Getze says, "I really don't look at Jerry and Molly as professional people. If I have to stop and think about it, I do, but I don't think of either of them as my teacher or my shrink or anything like that." But the leader does take overall responsibility for keeping the group functioning well.

In the meantime, the children are playing in the yard. Some work at tables in groups or play in the sand; others climb or ride or toddle around, exploring. A group stays close to a student teacher, perhaps listening to a story, perhaps just talking. What is most striking is the ease with which the children follow the hints of their own curiosity, and the daring and sense of adventure with which they explore. The play yard is a place to make messes in — to get into water, to paint in a way that might make some mothers uncomfortable at home. But in the play yard, messing is acceptable and is considered by the staff an important way to allow children to make a personal impact on and with materials.

Another interesting aspect of the program is the relationships that form among children. Jerry Ferguson says that it has become apparent to her that the development of a child's ability to socialize is a function of his or her being around other people. The caregivers in this program are student teachers. The children are cared for, by several students, in a large group of about fifteen to twenty. "A primary caregiver makes sense in a day care situation," Jerry says, "but this program only lasts an hour and a half. The premise that we are working with is that we are an extended family for each other. You don't just leave the baby with Granny; you expose him to a whole family."

Selecting Caregivers and Training

The graduate students in the program are enrolled in a course in Infancy, taught by Jerry and Molly as their core program. That means that Infancy is the central portion of the students' teaching-learning program for that semester. They have other experiences that branch out from, but still relate to, the core. Working in the Infant-Toddler-Parent program is one such experience.

Students in the Infancy program are expected to assume a great deal of responsibility for the center as a part of their study. Sometimes this responsibility takes the form of building equipment. Last semester, for instance, one student made the children's playhouse; another built a large machinelike gadget for the children to play with. Olive Odione studied children's food preferences, and planned and carried out the snack program. She found, to everyone's amazement, that, when given choices, the children choose high nutrient foods. She also discovered that they prefer meat and cheese to many other foods and that they like cold foods when they are teething. Her snack program emphasized preparing the food with the children. She served an assortment of finger foods in large bowls — a simple procedure that calls for the children to use the skills of discrimination and selection.

At about 11:15, one of the students joins the parents' group. She has written a short description of what each child did during the morning. There is much laughter and kidding as the mothers hear about the exploits and antics of their children.

The parents return to the yard at 11:30. Jerry Ferguson and Molly Noxon want the parents to talk with each other, play with their children. So they built into the program an opportunity for such exchange by providing a time for it to happen, between 11:30 and 12:00. One parent might push her child on the swing, another look at a book, others help pick up the toys and clean up. The parents' departure is as casual and relaxed as their arrival, and they often leave in groups, to have lunch together. "I have made my most important friends here," Linda Getze comments.

Just as students are welcome at the parents' meeting, parents are welcome to stay for the staff meeting, which begins at 12:00 and runs until 12:30. It is a time for everyone to get caught up on both the children's and the parents' part of the program. The staff meeting is a combination of the academic and the personal. Staff members sometimes delve into their own feelings about parenting. "The best thing we have to offer mothers and babies is 'together' people," Jerry says. "The staff meetings are the way we keep ourselves together."

Funding

This program is operated on parent fees. Children aren't enrolled — families are. A family pays $165 for a semester of approximately seventeen weeks. A tuition-exchange policy makes it possible for families to attend, without paying the fee, in return for their working in the program. Scholarships are also available.

The fees cover part of the director's salary; the remainder is donated by Pacific Oaks College. The tuition also pays for snacks and materials. The space is rent-free, another donation by the college, but all materials have come out of the program budget.

Because the play yard is so beautifully designed and built, one might think at first that it was very expensive. A second look reveals that most of the things in the yard are inexpensive natural materials — stumps of logs, sand, and so on. It is the way these materials are put together that gives the yard its handsome look.

The staff has devised a number of ways to keep working

on and improving both the indoor and outdoor space. One is the abovementioned tuition-exchange plan; parents build equipment — the barbecue pit, for example — in return for free tuition. Student projects help enhance the play space also, and the program holds regular workdays when parents participate in repairing, maintaining, or doing other jobs for which no money is available.

Workdays are one of the main ways by which fathers become part of this program. Men do get feedback from their wives' participation, and there have been "fathers' days" on Saturdays. One mother reports, "My husband came and he was so excited to find other fathers to talk to. Fathers say they can't stand by the water coolers and talk about their two-year-olds or their problems; this is not part of the culture of middle-class men." The fact that the Infant-Toddler-Parent program reaches mainly only one of the parents may or may not be seen as one of the program's deficiencies. Some mothers feel it is a lack, and that more should be done to include fathers. But there are also mothers who appreciate the opportunity to be with other mothers and to talk about their own concerns as women.

Problems and Changes

The biggest problem the Infant-Toddler-Parent Center has faced is, in Jerry Ferguson's words, "the lack of understanding and support from the major institution involved, Pacific Oaks." The program is what it is today, she feels, because of the people in the program. They have made happen what has happened, and to some extent they have had to push hard for what they have. Staff members at Pacific Oaks support the program verbally, but when it comes to having to share their space and resources, they have created some problems. One year, for instance, the program had no indoor space. A parent says, "All that you hear about southern California isn't true in the spring — it rains and it is cold, and having twenty babies and no indoor space was really a hassle." With the great help of the graduate students particularly, the program was able to obtain a small space, which, however, the members considered inadequate. Then there were no bathroom facilities. "We kept saying we needed a bathroom," Jerry recalls, "and they [Pacific Oaks staff members] kept saying that we didn't have any kids in our program who were toilet-trained. We didn't really come to a meeting of minds, so one Saturday we just came here and cut a hole into the adjoining bathroom and had access to the toilet. You know, you just have to do things like that sometimes." On the other hand, Jerry admits that being separate from the college has given the parents and staff the distinctly good feeling that it is very much their own program.

Because the parents in the program are on the premises, a license to operate is not necessary; however, they would like to comply with the licensing standards. Their small indoor space and lack of an adequate bathroom make this impossible for the present, but there are plans to move the whole program into a new space in another building that Pacific Oaks has purchased.

In the meantime, the Infant-Toddler-Parent Center continues to prosper. This program helps people learn the skills of parenting, but, beyond that, it helps them become strong, more capable adults. It is a program in which children grow, student teachers grow, and parents grow.

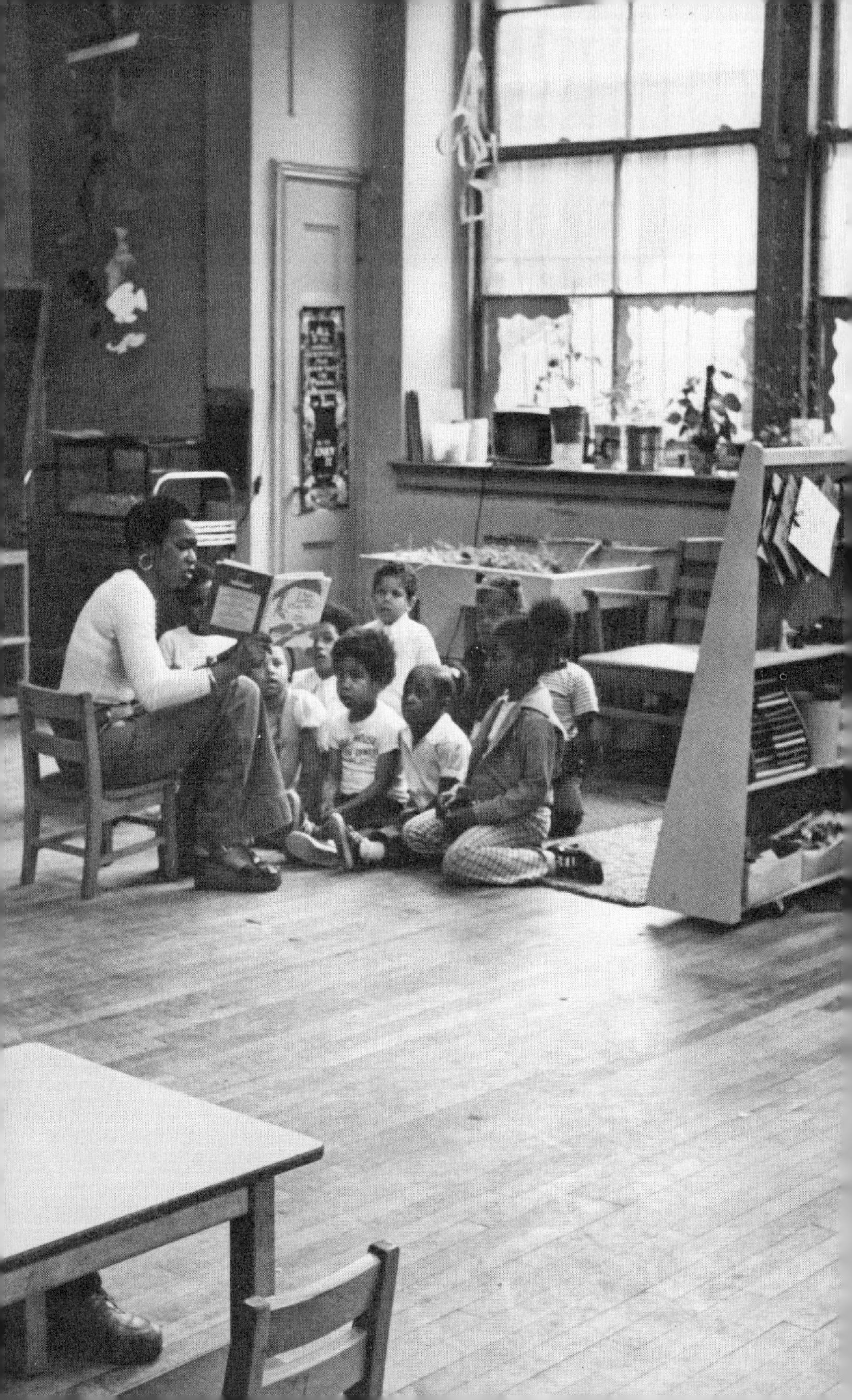

7
Parent-Controlled Day Care

The Children's Pumphouse
New York, New York

The Children's Pumphouse is a parent-controlled day care center. If one idea could be singled out as the most controversial among educators, it might well be parent control. To many, it connotes anarchy, a lack of structure, confusion, even abuse. They often feel that parents are trespassing in the territory of professionals, treading into areas that they neither understand nor are equipped to handle. On the other hand, many parents feel frustrated and helpless when they have no say in what happens to their young children for the long hours the children spend away from home. These parents and some professionals are becoming increasingly aware that it is the parents who have the primary responsibility for the care of their young children, and that child care must reinforce this responsibility. To the group of Harlem families who established the Children's Pumphouse, parent-controlled day care seems the best way to realize their goals.

When one walks into the Children's Pumphouse, any notion one may have had about anarchy caused by parent control is immediately dispelled. One enters a large open space in an old church building in New York's Harlem — a space that has been carefully transformed into a learning environment for young children. It is an area that is busy; both children and adults are involved with finger-puppets, story-telling, game-playing. "Inventive" is the word that comes to mind. The children create fanciful buildings, ramps, and fortresses with small and large blocks. The room is ingeniously arranged to accommodate thirty-three children and six teachers.

The atmosphere has an ebb and flow — sometimes highly active, almost bubbling over, but still orderly — as the children work with one thing and move on to another. At other times there is a hush surrounding a group caught up in the lure of a story, or deeply involved with an abacus. Moving, laughing, tussling, experimenting, imagining, thinking, and learning — this is the Children's Pumphouse.

Beginnings Not long ago, the Children's Pumphouse existed only in the thoughts of Irma Garay. Every day, when Irma was working as the director of Community Services in a large public building on 126th Street in Harlem, she saw women come in and out of the building, bringing their children with them. She listened to the women complain that although they would like to work they didn't know what to do with their children. "I thought of the idea of starting a community parent-controlled day care center where the parents are the board. They're the ones who make policy, goals, and objectives."

It took a long time for that idea to be realized. A group of parents and community people formed around Irma Garay and began to work. The first thing they did was to look for space. There were few spaces big enough for a center and within financial reach. The group started to meet in Saint Mary's Episcopal Church. During one meeting, someone asked, "Why don't we start the day care center right here?" They wrote a proposal and asked the church to donate the space. The church agreed to give them one large room downstairs and one room upstairs, providing that the center would pay rent when it was able to.

Almost two years after Irma Garay had the idea of starting a day care center, the Children's Pumphouse opened, with fifteen children ranging from babies to five-year-olds. "I didn't have any age limit," Irma explains, "and we were constantly changing diapers."

A love for children and the willingness to work without pay were the principal attributes required of caregivers. Initially, the parents were volunteer teachers in a room with homemade and donated furniture. Irma Garay and the parents called on everyone they knew to help. Irma, herself a grandmother, enlisted her sister, brothers, and children to work in the center.

The parents decided on a fee of $10 a week. They raised money in many ingenious ways; for example, they prepared and sold food to the people in the rest of the building.

Irma was the director, janitor, cook, and, sometimes, teacher. "I used to come in about six o'clock in the morning. Mop. Clean up the cages of the animals. Sweep so that everything would be nice and dry and clean when the children arrived. When they came at eight o'clock, usually a volunteer parent would come in. If she couldn't get here, I would have to give them their snack, and then start cooking. Sometimes I was here till past twelve at night. I don't know how I did it."

But Irma and the parents and staff did do it. Irma explains, "By trial and error, we have been able to build up good children, a good staff, and a good program."

Basic to the program is a dissatisfaction with the usual lot of black and Hispanic children. "All people are supposed to be equal. Then why is it," Irma asks, "that black and Hispanic children get the lowest grades in college? Is it the people themselves, or is there something else?" The conviction at the Children's Pumphouse is that something is lacking in the education of these children. "If someone could come up with something when the children are young, when they're exploring, when they're interested and curious . . ." That, the parents and staff believe, would make the difference.

That is what the Pumphouse program tries to do: give children a solid foundation for entering public school. The parents and staff feel that this foundation depends on the children's feeling good about themselves. They want children to go into public schools believing "they can accomplish anything; that they can do great things. We teach the children that they have to respect each other. We find that the most important thing is how they relate to each other and how they feel about themselves. If one child hits another, the child is asked, 'Why do you feel this way? Everyone has bad days; maybe today is yours.'" **Goals**

The staff and parents believe that one of the most important ways that children learn to feel good about themselves is by having opportunities for self-expression. Teachers are often heard asking children what they think about the many experiences the Pumphouse offers. To reinforce experiences, a variety of materials — clay, wood, blocks, paint, to name a few — is available, and children are constantly encouraged to use the materials in whatever ways appeal to them. Each child's individuality is openly acknowledged and appreciated.

The staff at the Children's Pumphouse believes that children have greater self-respect when they have solid underpinnings of knowledge and skills. The goal of the Pumphouse is to serve the community by preparing its children for school. And so it has become a school in itself. And, as such, it has midyear evaluations and graduation exercises.

Admissions Admissions are on a first-come, first-served basis. The Pumphouse now has thirty-three children, ranging from

2.75 to 5 years of age. Those families who qualify for funding through the New York City Agency for Child Development (ACD) must be processed and certified for eligibility by a social worker.

Selecting Caregivers

In selecting caregivers, the Pumphouse organizers turned to their community parents and friends who were interested in children — interested enough to devote many hours to volunteer work. Even today, after the center has become more formalized, a prime criterion for selecting caregivers is their love and understanding of young children, and their intimate knowledge of the community in which the children live. The Pumphouse staff is convinced that it can supply the necessary teaching skills through in-service training, but that caregivers must bring with them warm, loving feelings about children.

Space and Daily Schedule

Through a long period of experimenting with different types of room arrangement, the staff found a way to provide thirty-three children and six caregivers with a diverse and supportive environment for learning. The space is set up as one large open classroom with well-defined activity areas. The noisy activities, such as block-building and dramatic play, are carried out on one side of the room; reading, math study, and other quiet activities take place at the opposite end. Many low bookshelves, filled with games, puzzles, toys, books, and materials, are arranged to form private islands for table work and small-group activities.

The room has a festive air. Children's paintings line the walls; the windowsills are filled with plants the children are growing in recycled plastic containers and tin cans; a pet rabbit, a cage of gerbils, and an aquarium provide care-taking opportunities for these children, who see very little animal life in their city surroundings.

The children and parents begin arriving at Pumphouse at 8:00 A.M. A few of the children go upstairs to the kitchen to have breakfast before joining in the free-play time, during which they are allowed to follow their own interests. Clay, coloring, cutting and pasting materials are set up by the teachers on tables near the door. The room is a beehive of activity, but it is orderly and well-orchestrated.

At 10:00, the children are signaled by a blinking of the

classroom lights. They sing-song, "Clean-up time! Clean-up time!" as they put away their materials and prepare for a snack.

After their snacks, the children are divided into three age groups for teacher-directed activities. The youngest group goes outside to a nearby public playground. The two older groups work on activities centered on math, reading readiness, or special projects. After about forty-five minutes, the groups rotate, exchanging activities.

Lunch is set up and served by the teachers, and all of the children eat together. Each child has a certain place to sit and has his or her own personally decorated placemat, which makes it easy to find one's place. Sandra Grant, one of the teachers, says, "We found that children this age need to know 'This is mine. This is my placemat and this is my chair and I can go and sit there and feel good because this is my place.' "

A two-hour nap follows lunch. When the rest time ends, the children have what the staff describes as "body movement exercise." This may mean taking a walk, using the playground, or playing indoor games.

At 4:30, parents begin picking up their children, but some children remain engaged in free-play activities until 6:00.

Discipline Throughout the day one can see the staff's approach to discipline. The children are encouraged not only to feel good about themselves, but to respect each other. At the Pumphouse, they are exposed to a climate in which adults show respect for children and in turn expect the children to respect each other and adults.

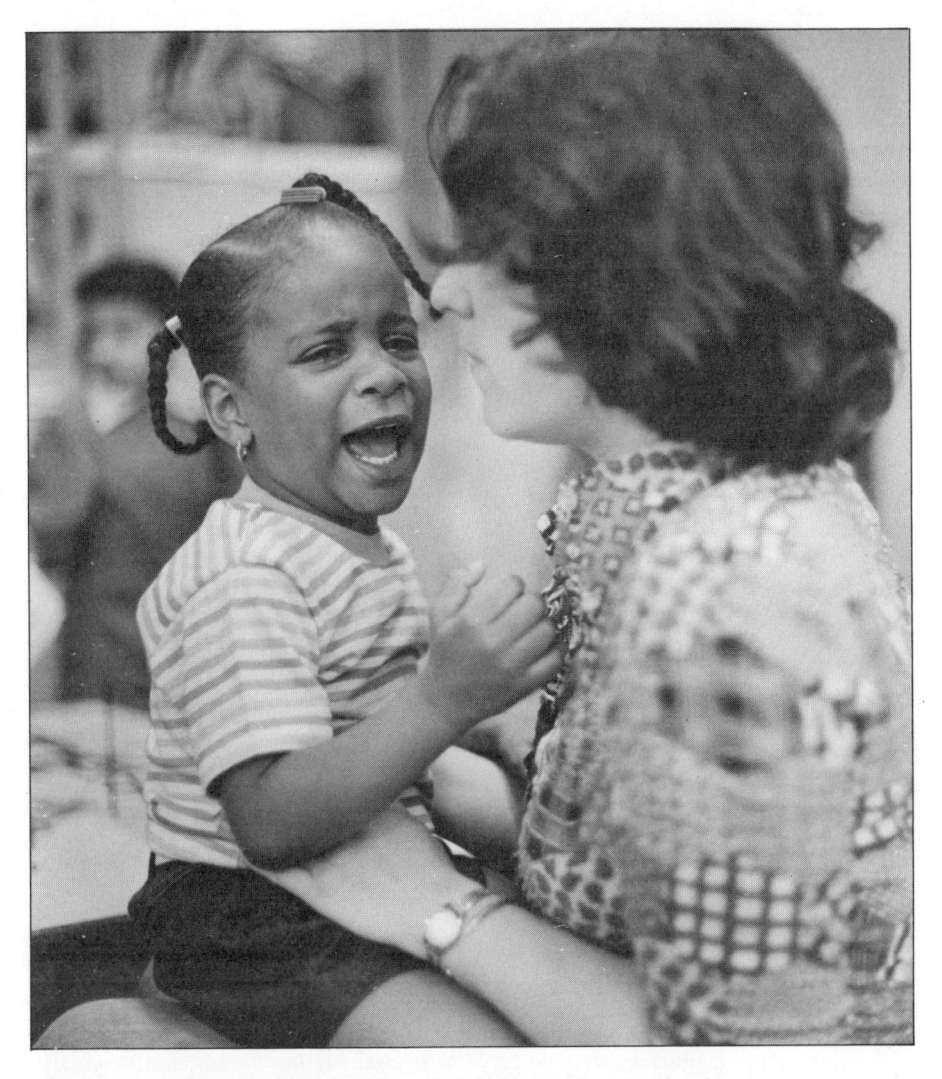

An attempt is made to help children understand why they feel and act in antisocial ways, and how to resolve such problems. "Nothing gets really forced on them. We usually try to have children talk things out with each other. If a problem persists, we have them sit down and cool off for a moment. Then after a while they are able to go back into the group." A teacher gives another example, which puts the matter of respect squarely up to the child: "When one child is finished talking during discussion time and says, 'I don't want to listen anymore,' we say, 'Well, we sat down here and listened to you; now it's your turn to listen to us, and have the same respect for us, whether you want to or not.' And it's working pretty well."

Occasionally there is conflict between parental disciplinary methods and the center's approach. Parent control does not mean that parents should ignore the expertise of educators. Irma Garay gives an example of a parent who "used to come in here — I guess she was tired from work. She would snatch her child and bang her, and I said, 'Listen. Wait a minute. Here we have a certain way of disciplining the child and that's just not the way, because if you hit the child today, tomorrow you will see the child hit someone else.' " After talking it over with Irma, the parent agreed that the center's approach to discipline was more productive.

The subject of discipline has come up in the parent meetings, and concern has been expressed that the children call the teachers by their first names. When the teachers explained to the parents that they wanted to have the children talk openly and freely so that they could establish a warm, friendly relationship and better understand and help the children, the parents began to appreciate the approach.

Encouraging open and free talking, however, does not mean that rudeness and swearing are condoned. There are times when direct, decisive action seems best, and discussion must come later. The director cites such a case: "These children live on the streets. We have a child who comes in here using street talk and cursing. We just pull her aside and tell her, 'Look, we just don't do that here.' "

The Pumphouse approach to discipline is one of the ways of combatting the effects of an often hostile and negative urban environment. Irma Garay sums it up: "This is what we have to live with — the garbage cans, the street talk. What we are trying to do is bring the children up so they don't go that way."

Parent Participation The commonly felt need for a child care center in which the parents of the children are deeply involved in the decision-making process is the cement that holds the Pumphouse together. Initially, parent involvement covered almost every aspect of the center's operation, from answering telephones to raising money. The realization that the parents would have to do things for themselves rather than depend on others has served as a sustaining strength for the center through its many changes.

The parents feel that being a part of Pumphouse is a two-way venture. It provides a learning center for the children and it teaches the parents new ways of child-rearing. This has resulted in training sessions for parents in child development, in personal development, in black history, in Spanish language, and in community-organizing skills. The director dramatically describes how many parents have moved from an almost complete concern with mere survival to an awareness of themselves and their power: "That was all they had — surviving. Now, it may not seem like much to everybody, but they have learned what a by-law is, what it is to write a proposal, what it is to be an effective board member, what an objective is, what rights they have as far as their children are concerned, and what health facilities are available."

Every parent is a member of the Pumphouse board. Meetings are held each month and attendance is mandatory. If parents miss two consecutive meetings, they are fined; continued absence means they, along with their children, are dropped. Irma Garay admits that this seems harsh, but the Pumphouse does not see child care working without parent involvement — without the extension of those things learned at the center to the home, where they can be reinforced.

In addition to the full membership board, which includes some teachers and community persons who are not parents, there is a small executive board, which proposes policy; but all decisions come back to the full membership for approval.

The Pumphouse has its difficulties with such broad-based parent involvement. Some parents attend every other meeting of the board to avoid missing two consecutive meetings. This is frowned upon by the group in general. One parent expressed the frustration of learning the intricate procedure of working as a board member. "I think that as the year is just over, at the last meeting, we found out what we were trying to do the whole while. Next year it may be the same thing all over again." But everyone seems to regard the process as an essential one.

Another difficulty mentioned was the tendency of some parents to get too personally involved. A consultant to the Pumphouse, points out that "sometimes the center becomes the total family. This can lead to hassles; it isn't only an asset." However, on the positive side of this close connection, a parent says of the director, "Irma's the mother of the center; everybody loves her. Regardless of what your problem may be, either she can help you or she can refer you to some place else for help."

Parents have taken on the role of political involvement necessary to keep the center running and have relieved the teachers of bearing that burden alone. Sandra Grant, a teacher, says, "At first the teachers were always running to meetings and demonstrations and having volunteers come in for the kids, and it was bad for the kids. So now it's the parents who are going to a lot of the meetings and working in the politics of day care."

The words of one of the parents sums up the parent relationship at the Pumphouse: "If we really want a day care center, right now, the way things stand with funding, we have to get to the meetings to understand and to fight for our center."

Food Two full meals, breakfast and lunch, and snacks are provided for the children. Aside from salaries, food is the largest item in the Pumphouse budget.

The center has the benefit of the advice of a nutritionist from the funding agency who serves as a consultant, but the menu is often modified to take into account ethnic preferences. "Who says ethnic food does not have nutritional value? We think there's a lot of value, and other people are now finding that out," states Irma. "One of the things I stopped was the kids coming here with their pockets filled with junk. One child sees another with a lollipop and naturally they all want it. I said no, stop it."

The center operates a food cooperative for parents and staff, as well as for some community people. By purchasing large quantities and reselling at no profit, the participants can buy a greater variety of food without spending more money than they usually do. The cooperative provides more than food — it serves as another link between the center and the family.

Health All of the children have regular medical and dental checkups at the local health center. Emergency care arrangements are made with a neighborhood hospital.

Both the food cooperative and the health care plan are examples of the broader view of child care, which is concerned with the needs of the children and their families outside the center.

The original Pumphouse group quickly came to the realization that, despite all of their volunteer efforts, substantial funding would be necessary to achieve the goals they had set for themselves. They applied to the ACD, and after the Pumphouse met some minimal building requirements, it was approved for funding. The director says, "I think they liked us because people down there [at ACD] were so sick of seeing the stereotype of the day care center. The ACD loved the fact that everything we had was homemade."

Funding

ACD provided $117,000 for the fiscal year 1974–75. Good day care is expensive; this amount does not cover all of the operational costs. The center charges fees ranging from $.50 to $10.25 a week, based on a scale developed by the governmental funding agencies. Parents who are on welfare make no payment, but they must be in a training program or looking for a job. The rest of the monetary gap is closed by parent-staff efforts. Emma Moses, a parent, says, "Money happens to be a big factor in the day care center, because we don't ever get enough money to really run this program the way it should be run."

Budgetary problems are part of the daily life at the Pumphouse, and the center frequently exceeds the budget. "I'm always being called down [to ACD] and asked, 'Why don't you keep within the budget?' And I tell them, 'Why don't you bring the budget up to par? The budget is from nineteen sixty-six. Why don't you bring it up to date?' And they know what I'm telling them is reasonable and true. After the hassle — because that's their job and they have to do it — they usually give us modifications on budgets." When they overspend, the parents try to raise the difference, or Irma Garay juggles the budget: "I rob Peter to pay Paul."

The Pumphouse has a unique way of handling salaries. Although the center is funded for salaries of different dollar amounts, the entire salary portion of the budget is pooled and divided equally among the staff. "It is rare to find something like that that really works," a consultant observes. At Pumphouse, it does. It does primarily because all the parents share the conviction — which supersedes petty differences and personalities — that each staff member makes an equal contribution to high-quality education and care for their children.

Training "Pumphouse is not a baby-sitting facility. It is a child development facility, and it's for your benefit and your child's benefit." This is the essential message of the director of the Pumphouse, and the training for teachers and parents working at the center reflects this.

Even before the Pumphouse was funded, the volunteer staff managed to hire a part-time teacher who was working on a master's degree in early-childhood education. She came in for three hours a day and worked with both teachers and children.

In making the transition from a voluntary operation to a funded one, Pumphouse was faced with meeting the training requirements of their funding agency, ACD. The center asked to keep its volunteer workers, but on a paid basis. ACD agreed, with the proviso that the staff begin in-service training. Staff members set aside the two-hour children's nap time for their own education. The entire staff is required to participate in an ongoing child care–training program sponsored jointly by the center and the Bank Street College of Education. Many are working on B.A. degrees. The in-service–training program has included supervised teaching and courses in health education, curriculum planning, open-classroom education, human relations, early-childhood growth and development, and the psychology of women.

Perhaps equally important as the more formal in-service training is the training aspect of the weekly staff meetings. These meetings, which also take place during the children's rest time, give the participants an opportunity "to air things out and get things done." Here, attitudes and interpersonal relationships are examined and discussed. This straightforward self-examination often leads to further training sessions. The need for a better working relationship with parents was an issue that came out of the weekly staff meetings. The staff established parent-involvement classes for themselves. As one teacher puts it, "Parent-involvement classes helped us to relate to parents, to learn how not to turn them off, and how to *listen*. The basic thing is that we listen, and we're not afraid to say that we don't know. And that we'll find out about it."

The open attitude exemplified by "we'll find out about it" makes training at Pumphouse not only a continuous process but an all-inclusive one, encompassing staff, consultants, parents, and children.

Problems and Changes

The Children's Pumphouse today is in some ways a very different center from what it was three years ago, and growth has produced some problems. The advent of funding has plunged the members of the staff of the center, whether they wanted it or not, into politics. To protect and enhance what they have attained, they have had to join picket lines, attend and speak at endless meetings, and band together with other groups into numerous committees.

Because they are still using some parent teachers without B.A. degrees, the Pumphouse staff does not meet the legal requirements for licensing. It is what is called an "interim" center. "I hate that word 'interim.' What does it mean?" says Irma Garay. "It means 'in the meantime,' but you see, we've been going for three years." What it has meant, though, is that the state, when it made budget cuts, stopped paying for interim centers, and the city was forced to pick up all of the cost. Although most of the staff members and the director are attending college, there has been pressure on them to leave the center so that it could become licensed and therefore state-funded. Even Irma Garay, for a while, thought she might have to step down. "They were coming down on me not to be the director because I don't have a B.A. I felt it was my duty to step out; I would hate the center to close because of me." However, she was granted a limited waiver to continue working while finishing her degree.

College training, some feel, has caused problems in the center. The director says, "I think that once people get into college, then everything becomes a problem for them. They can't deal with things the way we used to. If we didn't have one thing, we'd improvise with something else. Now they feel it has to be strictly one way." There are some undercurrents of resentment between those who go to college and those who don't. It is said that "the people who go to college are not coming back to share their knowledge with the rest of the staff."

Learning to work with ACD has, at times, been another problem. Teachers at the Pumphouse will say in the same sentence that the people they work with are "beautiful," that they will "listen to reason"; and then complain about something someone at the agency said or did.

A further problem has been the accumulation of many rules and regulations added by the center. As with any rules, there are those who feel that they make life easier, others who regret the loss of spontaneity. For example, the rule that children must come on time in the morning has supporters, who argue that if you are going to have an educational program, children must be there to be part of it; and protesters, who submit that if a parent doesn't have to be at work until later in the morning, his or her time at home with the child can be very important.

Community control and a parent board, the principles on which the Pumphouse has been based, haven't been easy to maintain. One parent jokes, "If you're having a community day care center, I would suggest you don't put a whole bunch of parents on the board." Then she adds, in a serious tone, "You run into problems with people." Petty squabbles, personality conflicts, difficulties in making group decisions always crop up. "We have thirty-three children," a parent says, "and about fifty committees."

The Pumphouse solves its problems by trying to face them squarely and by talking about them. "We've found that the only way we can work together is by being honest," a teacher says. That honesty doesn't have to be in the form of confrontation or accusation. Rather, it is talking over problems in general. If a teacher is constantly late, for instance, it would not be brought up in the classroom. At the staff meeting, lateness would be discussed in a general way, but a particular teacher would not be singled out for criticism.

The Children's Pumphouse has changed. It has doubled in size; it has gone from a volunteer center to a funded one; from a spontaneous to a systematized educational facility. But even so, the Pumphouse remains a place where people respect each other, and a place where staff, parents, and children enjoy being. The changes, especially the training, have given people a new view of child development. "The training we had in early-childhood education helped us not only as teachers, but as parents as well." Everyone concedes that the children are granted more respect and understanding. Before, if a child was crying, people might have said, "Be quiet."

Now they try to find out what is wrong and help the child. As Irma Garay says, "By trial and error, we have been able to build up good children, a good program, and a good staff."

Almost everyone who comes to the Children's Pumphouse asks, "How did you get your name?" Irma explains that when she was first looking for a place to set up a day care center, she noticed that a gas station nearby had closed down. She wrote to the Humble Oil Company to ask if it would like to do something for the community. The company donated the land, but the parents were never able to raise the money to build there, so under the terms of the agreement the land reverted to Humble. When the center was established in the church building, it was named the Children's Pumphouse — a reminder of the founders' early efforts.

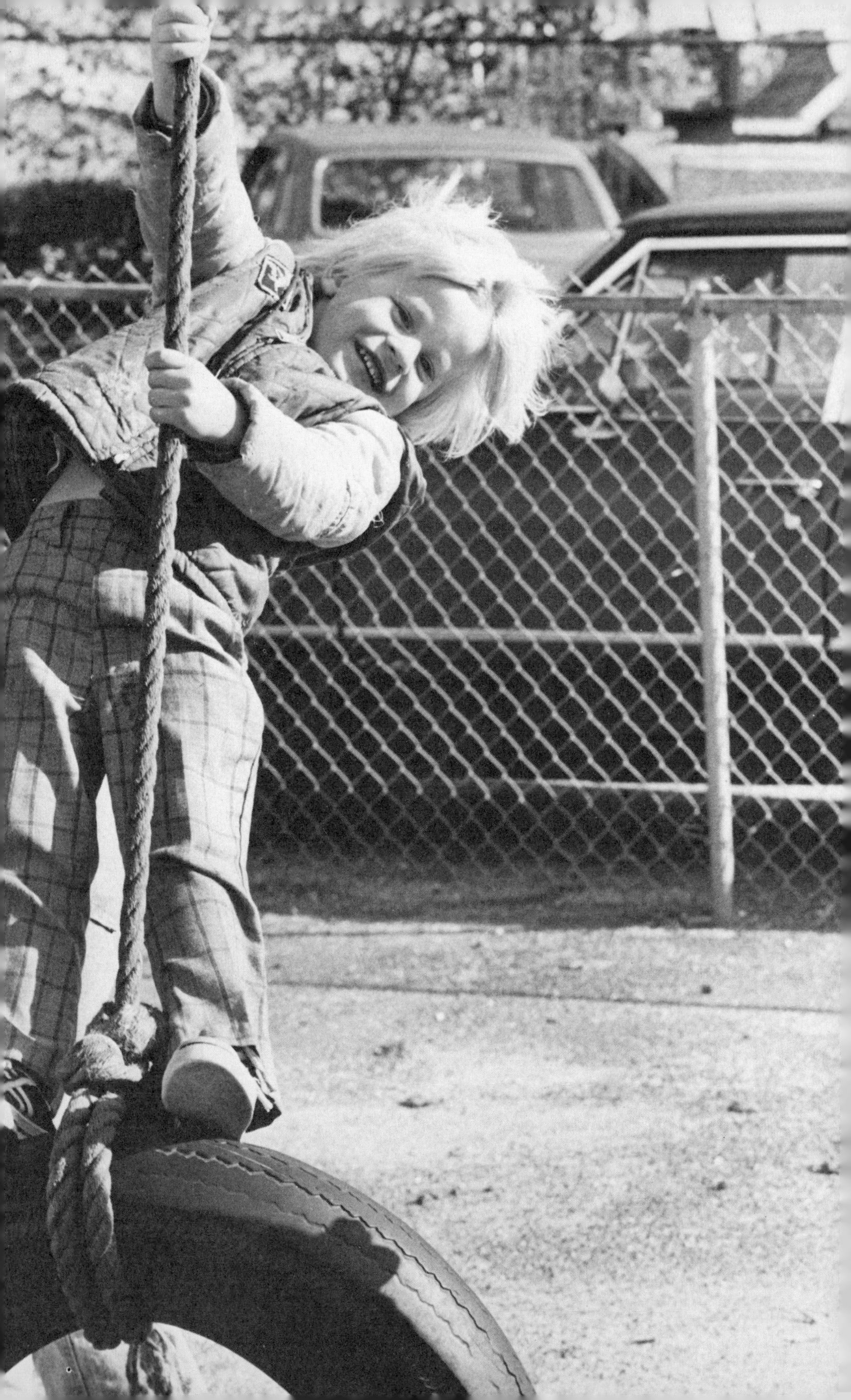

8
Integrating Children with Special Needs

The Children's Center
Biddeford, Maine

> My feeling is that if you put a child with a handicapping condition in a class where children are all blind or in a class where all are cerebral palsied, what they learn is not very useful patterns and they are not encouraged to behave the way other children behave. They cannot be encouraged because the usual things are not going on in the room.
>
> — Betty Van Wyck, director

> The initial message I would give is that we are a program for children — preschool day care. We do integrate children with special needs, but the foremost message is that we are a day care center that thinks about children and staff as individuals, and we allow them the freedom to be.
>
> — Pauline Ruel, secretary-receptionist
> Handicapping condition: cerebral palsy

The history of care for children with handicapping conditions has, for the most part, been one of neglect or of specialized care, and both attitudes have resulted in isolating the children from the mainstream of childhood. Recently there has been a move toward integrating them into existing child care centers, and federal funding has been designated for this purpose. However, neither funding nor shifts in attitude toward the care of handicapped children necessarily prepares centers to do a good job with a mixture of children with and without such conditions. The Children's Center in Biddeford, Maine, has found a way, and quietly goes about treating all children as "individuals."

How this center developed such a program has its origins in the experience of the director, Betty Van Wyck. "I guess it goes all the way back to the fact that I have four children myself," Betty says. "We lived in a very small town while the children were growing up, so I was very aware of a community that raises its own children. It was a town of seven hundred people in Arizona . . . The quality of that kind of life for young children was really great."

In the early 1970s, there was very little organized child care in the state of Maine. The Bureau of Human Relations of the Catholic Diocese (the Catholic Charities Appeal organization for Maine) sensed a need, and offered Betty Van Wyck of the Portland Model Cities program the job of setting up a day care center in Biddeford — a seaside industrial town ten miles south of Portland, with several paper mills and a large French-Canadian population. They also offered her a site: a deserted Catholic school. Betty's job was to make this into a center for young children.

Betty brought to this task her sense of what a community can be. She also clearly understood a critically important fact — that day care and regular schooling are quite different from one another. "One of the things I had seen was that the typical preschool day didn't stretch very well over the ten- or eleven-hour day care day; the process of grouping children by age and keeping them in one room, lunching and napping in the same room, letting them out only for recess, didn't feel very comfortable for either adults or children. Adults would find lots of excuses to go out and get coffee, or get paper and a pen, or make telephone calls; manipulative kids would walk out with the adults, but the other kids would get trapped in that box for the day. So when I looked at this building, I realized that it had within it the possibility of a different kind of system."

The Program Now From the outside, no one would ever know that the Children's Center is a "different kind of system." The building is old and austere. It has the appearance of a fortress, protected by a wire fence, surrounded by a sea of blacktop. Inside, its wide, high-ceilinged halls have the look and smell of an old-fashioned school. But once inside the rooms, one is immediately aware that the Children's Center is, indeed, a different system. Four activity rooms open on to each other. Two staff members stay in each room, and the children, sixty in number, approximately ten of whom have handicapping conditions, are free to go in and out of any of the rooms to choose their own activities. The rooms open and close "like an accordion," as Betty Van Wyck often says, according to the number of children and staff at different hours of the day.

The children seem to move in the large space with self-assurance and ease. They read; they build with blocks; they play the piano; they type. Children from just under three to over five years old all work independently.

Goals

It becomes apparent that every detail of this center, all the way from the overall room arrangement down to the smallest item, is designed to help children become independent. That is a particularly necessary goal for children with handicaps, because the usual tendency of adults is to do things for them, creating in the children, as the director and parents concede, feelings of self-doubt. Betty Van Wyck states that the child who is blind or deaf or has cerebral palsy needs to "find out what's going on and how to get there himself and not always to be led around." These same goals apply to all the children. "Here we just simply assume that all the children will do a little more tomorrow than they did today."

The system at the Children's Center is also designed to encourage children to help each other. That aspect of the program is always visible. A girl claps her hands in front of a blind child, leading him, by the sound, to the bathroom. Nearby, a boy helps a girl pick up the pieces of a puzzle she has spilled. "Our center helps children become caring people, people who grow up having empathy with other people. My own kids are old enough," Betty says, "so that I know that the kids you work with in day care are one day going to be the people who are going to be your bosses or your subordinates. I think that a lot of people, when they start out, aren't quite aware of that. I think you could say that one of our purposes is to help children grow into good caring people . . . good people to share the world with."

This purpose is accomplished by what Betty describes as a series of support systems. The word "support" is critical here. In line with her desire to have a child care center draw from the best in "a community that raises its own children," Betty Van Wyck is against the idea of one person telling another what to do; rather, she believes in people supporting, helping, and caring for each other. She sees this idea falling into a pattern: the staff is the support system for the children; she is the support system for the staff; and the board is the support system for her. Together, they all form a system that supports families. Betty says, "Our style with parents is exactly like our style with everybody else — we *share* with them; we don't *teach* them anything."

Admissions   When a family inquires about the center, the applicant fills out a form, and the name is put on file until a place opens. Priority is given to younger siblings of children already enrolled in the center. "We do that because we feel we are making an investment with the family," says Betty Van Wyck. She feels real concern for the handling of the transition between home and the center, and arranges for a staff member to make a home visit before the child comes to the center. "The home visit is made so that the staff member becomes a friend of the child; it's not for any social work kind of purpose." She reports that members of the staff often become friends of the whole family and that the child feels more secure about coming into a center where he or she knows someone.

"We insist that the child come to the center with a caring person for the first few days — an older brother, a father, a grandmother, or the mother herself, depending on the family situation." Often the child stays only for the morning during the first week. Sometimes the separation procedure takes even longer, especially with children who have handicapping conditions. The center tries to admit not more than one or two new families a week, even in September. In addition, every child starts on a trial basis, and if that works, the arrangement is made final.

One of the reasons the staff takes such care in introducing children to day care is to ensure that "as the children get older, new experiences are not going to be frightening . . . the children are used to different people and different styles."

"Variety" is the key word in the admissions procedure. The center tries to have families from different backgrounds, a balance between boys and girls, a workable ratio of handicapped children (up to 25 percent), and a balance between funded and fee-paying families.

Selecting Caregivers

The desire for differences is also behind the selection of staff. "We're looking for good people to be with children," the director says, "but I believe there isn't just one model for children — there are hundreds of them. We look very hard for variety. We look for males and females, we look for quiet people, and we look for noisy people. We look for people of different ages — older and younger — and we look for some people with different points of view."

In selecting professional caregivers Betty seeks people with both training and experience. The present staff includes caregivers with day care experience, training in teaching young children, social work background, and Montessori training. It includes people with experience in the public schools. "That is an important balance for us," the director says, "because we find that if we don't have people like that on our staff, we don't make good contact with the public schools."

The paraprofessional staff is, in general, hired locally so that the overall staff reflects the different groups within the community: the French-Canadians, the young people who live along the beach, the people who work in the paper mills, the older wealthier families. "We try to offer with our variety of staff a variety of points of view so that children learn to get along in a variety of situations."

Grouping The pattern of interage grouping also helps the children learn how "to get along in different situations." Interage grouping is particularly helpful for the children with handicapping conditions. Betty explains, "A three-year-old isn't much different than a six-year-old who is functioning several years behind her chronological age." The staff also believes that children will naturally form their own groupings and that those formations usually cluster around interests rather than age.

Space and Daily Schedule Parents begin arriving at the center with their children between 6:30 and 7:00 A.M. These are people who work the early shift at one of the Biddeford mills. In the spacious entry hall, each parent pauses to sign in his or her child. On a low-placed attendance board the children turn over their own name tags, to indicate they have arrived. Then both parents and children move into the Welcome Room.

The Welcome Room is the space in which the daily program begins and ends, and it is also the transition room for lunch, playground, or other large-group activities, such as trips. Wooden cubbies line two sides of this carpeted room, and low shelves filled with blocks, toys, puzzles, and books line the other walls. A large geodesic climbing frame and two low tables with chairs complete the furnishings of the room.

The children who arrive early are given free-choice time until breakfast is ready. Some look at books or build with small blocks or gather around one of the caregivers for a story. Irene Belanger, a caregiver, says, "At first I thought that I should have a project ready and going. But I was wrong. This is really a waking-up time for most children."

From twelve to sixteen children usually have breakfast at the center. They go down the hall to the dining room, which is set up to help them manage for themselves. There is a low pass-through from the kitchen to the dining room, so the children can reach their own dishes. Several

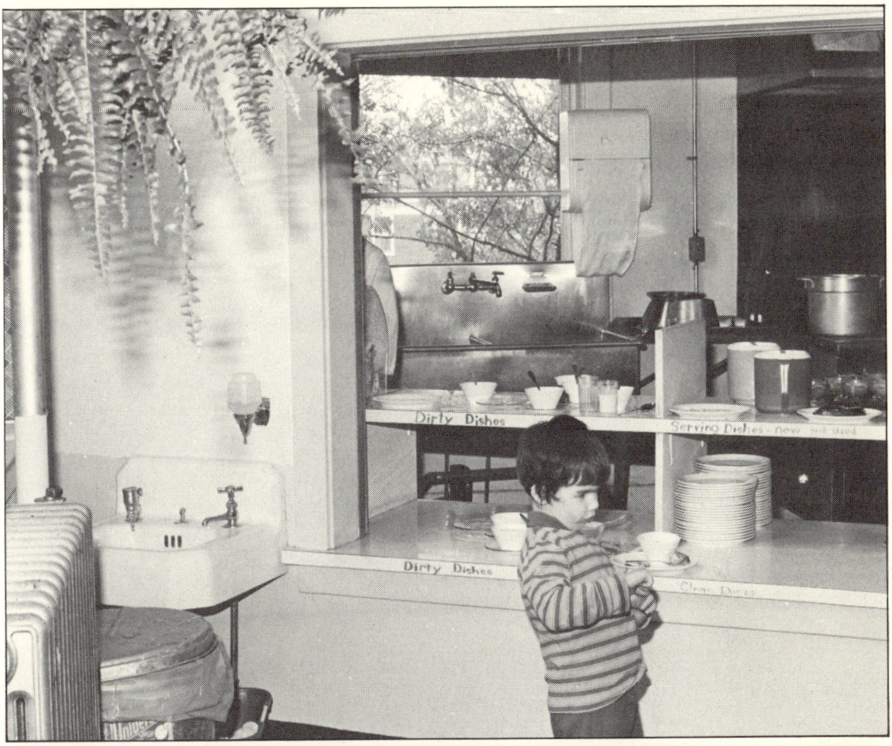
Dirty Dishes
Serving Dishes - new
Dirty Dishes

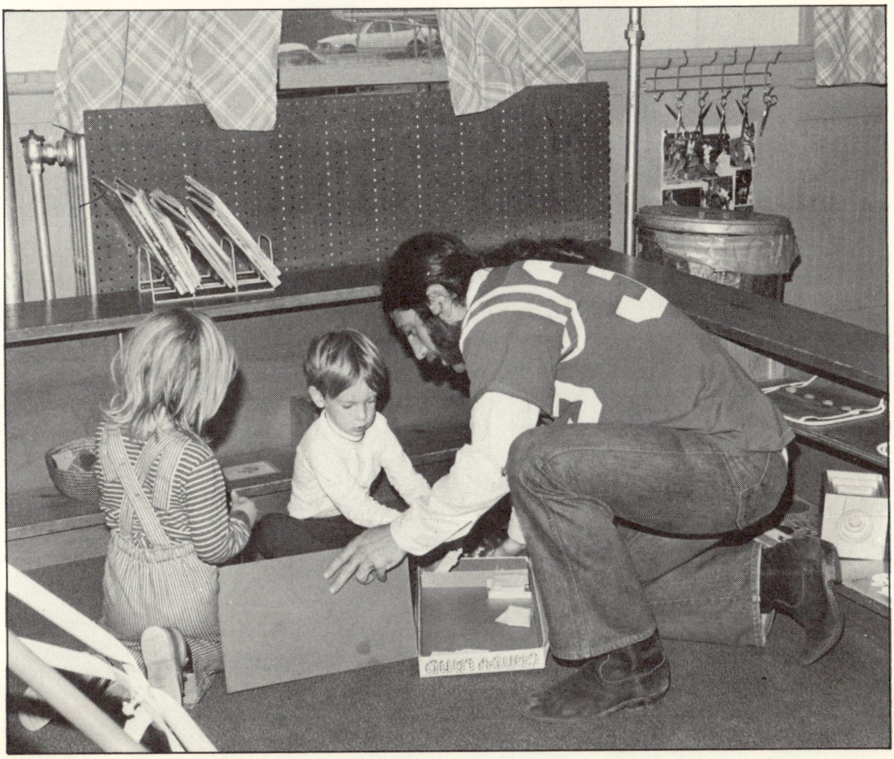

areas in the room are color-cued to help the children: red indicates where clean dishes are kept, blue indicates where dirty dishes should be placed. The children get their own milk from a milk machine scaled down to child size.

After breakfast, the caregivers begin to open the connecting rooms. The names of the rooms indicate the kind of activities they feature. To the left of the Welcome Room is the Game Room, which has a large wooden loft, a housekeeping corner, a book corner, and space for individual and group play. Here there are also Montessori sensorial number and language materials. Two caregivers are assigned to each room; together they plan activities for that space. Beyond the Game Room is the Art Room. Here carpentry, painting, water play, and a variety of arts and crafts activities are offered. To the right of the Welcome Room there is a Block Room. It is largely free of equipment, except for the big block collection stacked along one wall. Here the children engage in dramatic play, enjoy music and movement, view movies, and do their block-building.

There is no set schedule of activities for the morning. The children are free to move from room to room and join whatever activities they like. Jeff Pastor, coordinator of the program, explains, "Instead of having an activity-centered room, we have an activity-centered building." Before children move from one area to another, they are encouraged and helped to clean up and put away the materials they have used.

At 10:00 the pace changes: the playground opens and most children go down the steps from the Welcome Room and outside. The large tarmac-surfaced area, surrounded by a fence, has sandboxes, a free-standing gate for opening and closing, several large tires for rolling, lots of room for running, jumping rope, and playing ball. The children's favorite piece of play equipment was built by a caregiver, Duke Dudevoir. It is a unique multipurpose structure with rope-and-tire swings connected to a large wooden industrial spool. The spool has a crawl-through and hiding space in its base and a rocking horse and steering wheel attached to the top surface. There are groupings of tree stumps for sitting and climbing on.

Snacks are served in the Welcome Room to the few children who choose to work inside on a project, and trays of snacks are taken outside for those in the playground. Between 10:00 and 11:00, the children may work on projects indoors or out. If the weather is good, the caregivers encourage outdoor projects. "It's really easier to clean up outside," one caregiver comments.

Lunch is served in three shifts, at 11:00, 12:00, and 1:00. This is one of the few instances where the children are separated by ages. The youngest are on first lunch (although older children who arrive at 6:30 and are very hungry by first lunch may also eat then), children in the middle range of ages eat second lunch, and the older children third. Duke Dudevoir explains that little is expected of the young children at first lunch, but that, by the time the children move to third lunch, they can just about do everything by themselves, including sweeping up and washing the tables.

Each lunch group goes from the dining room into the Art and Game rooms to use the toilets. The toilets have walls about 4½ feet high but are roofless. This gives the children their needed privacy, yet allows the caregivers to become aware quickly of a child who needs help; this works especially well for the children with handicapping conditions.

A "quieting down" period precedes nap time. The children either listen to stories, sing songs, or participate in finger-plays. When the activities end, the children remove their shoes and go quietly to their cots for a two-hour nap or rest.

At 2:00 P.M. the early nappers are up and participating in activities in the Game Room and the Welcome Room. By 3:00 everyone is awake, the playground is reopened, and snacks are served again. Parents soon begin arriving to pick up their children. As the children leave, the Art Room and Block Room are closed down. The end of the day's activities take place in the Welcome Room. Many of the children become involved in the process of closing down and cleaning up. Children take turns operating the vacuum cleaner; others help the caregivers store away game materials.

All of this interaction between children and adults fits easily into Betty Van Wyck's idea of a program for young children. She feels that children used to learn what they needed to know simply because they were constantly around children and adults, and were close to the natural environment. She stresses to her staff the pitfalls of depending on "activities" alone to carry a program. "What is really important," she says, "is the quality of the relationships among people. You've got to have something going on and that something should be fairly orderly, and you need objects so that children can learn to take care of objects, but they don't necessarily have to be puzzles. There's no reason why Duke couldn't teach the children all the names of the cars that go by instead." Throughout the day this concept is kept in mind, and the staff says it makes a difference in their approach and use of materials and activities.

Discipline In line with their goal of promoting independence in the children, the staff members see discipline as helping the children build self-control; and in keeping with their desire that the children learn a variety of viewpoints, they fully recognize that there is no one way of building self-control. "What works for me today," Betty says, "won't work tomorrow. What works for Irene won't work for Duke, and vice versa. I think we must find out how it feels to the adult and child, and whether it helps the child build the controls he needs."

There are, however, three general guidelines that all staff members follow: to help children not to hurt each other (either physically or emotionally); to help children not to hurt themselves; and, finally, to help children learn reasonable respect for the cultural ways of their community.

Jeff Pastor says, "My philosophy is consistency," and as an afterthought he adds, "most of the time." Betty Van Wyck agrees, and goes on to explain that consistency is not rigidity. As Jeff sees it, the adult must set an example and take the responsibility for making the children aware of the consequences of their behavior.

Quite a different style is used by Duke Dudevoir. "You get down to their level, eye to eye, and you go through a whole trip of explaining why you can't let them hurt somebody. You talk it out with them and it usually works. But if it gets worse and the kid keeps hitting and being a real punk, you bring him over and say, 'Look, you're not stupid; you know what I'm talking about. I can't let you do that. Now sit in this chair for five minutes.' That seems to work pretty well, but not all the time. You have to keep with it."

Irene Belanger first tries talking to a child as a way of

disciplining. If this doesn't work, she has the child sit in a chair until he or she can calm down. If the problem continues, she will take the child to a private spot, where she does not have to raise her voice or embarrass the child before his or her friends.

Conflict or personality problems between staff and children and between some children and others are often resolved by the very nature of the program at the Children's Center. If two children are fighting, they don't have to spend the entire day in the same room, where the situation may well become the biggest thing of the day and ruin the atmosphere for everyone. They are free to move away into any of the four rooms. This option is also given to staff members when they have gone through a trying situation with a child.

In dealing with the use of bad language, the director points out that ignoring bad language doesn't make it go away and that what the children need is very real limits. "The day care child who is using a lot of bad language often comes from an environment where he hasn't had to learn to limit himself or control himself, and therefore what he needs is control, not freedom. The more freedom he gets, the more confused he gets." The director also states that problems emerge more frequently for the staff member who acts in an indecisive way with children and thereby communicates to them uncertainty about the use of undesirable language.

Both nap time and lunch time are good examples of the way the staff handles discipline through self-control. "You can't make a child eat, and you can't make a child sleep, but you can create an atmosphere in which they will probably eat and be able to sleep. We find that the very child who is least able to lie still is the one who is out of control in the room. So that child would need the most practice and the most help learning how to hold himself in a small space on a cot while taking a nap. It is a very helpful thing for children to learn to control themselves reasonably over a period of time." This example, given by the director, is typical of how thoroughly the process of developing self-control is built into all of the children's activities. Children know what their boundaries are; they know where the caring adults are; and they usually feel secure in this knowledge.

Underlying all of the discipline at the Children's Center

is an understanding of what is acceptable and what is not acceptable behavior in the community of Biddeford, and a respect for the families' values and cultural ways.

Parent Participation

It is important to Betty Van Wyck that the staff at the Children's Center have respect for and be responsive to parents. As she puts it, "We become friends. It isn't a duty-type of thing. It's just what happens, and the more it happens, the more I think we have done a better job."

Parents have little to do with the actual administrative or operational aspects of the center, but they are represented on the advisory board to the director. They are always welcome at the center, and often help out in the classrooms.

Potluck dinners, picnics, trips, open houses, the annual Halloween party, the Wednesday morning coffee hour, are a few of the numerous informal parent activities that revolve around the center. Sheila Cook, the social worker responsible for the Wednesday coffee hour, characterizes it as "a time when parents can make connections with each other. A lot of these mothers really haven't had much of a chance to socialize — they are home with young kids, with not very much money." Conversations at the coffee hours cover many topics. One morning, a mother started to talk about a legal dispute she was involved in. It was striking to watch the way the group worked. Everyone offered suggestions. There was no sense of the staff member's being apart from the parents — except that after the meeting he took responsibility for offering to call the Legal Aid Society.

Irene Belanger says of parents, "My house is open to them any time if they want to come and talk." Annie Lambert, a parent, says, "The center's staff really seems to care about the whole family. I know if I ever had a problem, I could come here and talk to somebody who would help me work it out." Sheila Cook says that when she first undertook the job of working with parents, she got bogged down trying to be everything to everyone and, as she says, she was only scratching the surface of what needed to be done. Since then she has found out that "you have to think through goals and decide what you want to accomplish."

Many parents are overwhelmed by the sheer size of the center — sixty children intermingling in four rooms. "The whole thing was very scary to me," Deborah

L'Heureux says. But now she finds that the staff has become "pretty special" to her and that her children "love" several of the teachers "as if they were part of the family."

Most parents mention how much they like the independence that the children acquire at the center. They see it carried over at home. One parent reports that things she tried to do with her child at home became more meaningful because of the reinforcement from the center. Some parents recall that they did question the mixture of handicapped and normal children at first. One parent says, "I was worried about how my children would treat the handicapped children." Another comments, "There are a few kids who are hyper — I was afraid that was going to rub off on my kids, but I've had no problem." But once their children have been in the program for a while, the parents are enthusiastic. The mother of a blind child says, "The interage groupings help my son; he can use younger children as models for things he needs to learn. I think children are the best teachers."

Perhaps the highest compliment paid to the center came from the mother who said, "I never thought I would want to work with young children, but now if you offered me a job in day care, I think I would want it."

Food

One parent who did decide to work for the center is the cook, a Vietnamese who began by filling in when the former cook left. She is now a full-time staff member.

The staff eats with the children and is requested to eat some of everything. "It's part of modeling," says the director. "If an adult says, 'Ugh, rice again!' you have set up a whole table of children who will be saying the same thing." The objectives for the children are to help them enjoy a variety of good foods and to limit the amount of sweets. Children are discouraged from bringing junk foods or candy to the center. And here the rule that they must share with everyone works to advantage — sixty kids are simply too many.

Health

The staff members care a great deal about the general health of the children, but it is an area they don't want to take over. They feel they should help the parents carry that responsibility themselves.

The entrance hall to the center contains a rack with forms for parents to fill out with pertinent medical information. Directly over the rack, out of children's reach, is a medicine cabinet where special or temporary medications, authorized by the parents, are kept. The center has a pediatrician on call, and parents are asked to sign forms granting permission for emergency care.

There is a dental clinic on the floor above the center where all the children have checkups. Staff members also assist some parents in getting immunizations for their children and with the special health problems of the children with handicapping conditions.

Funding The Children's Center has carefully avoided the hazard of single source funding, of being dependent on one agency for survival. Its funding is a patchwork of federal, state, local, and special funds. Federal money, granted under Title XX of the Social Security Act, provides the largest portion of the funding. The Catholic Diocese provides part of the match for the federal money on a one-to-three basis. The state of Maine and the town of Biddeford provide very modest amounts. "This is an old community and a conservative community. Its point of view is that people should be able to take care of themselves — that social services are not really needed," comments the director.

Additional monies come from special agencies, private fees, and donations. There is also money to cover the cost of the food program from the state's Special Food Services Act. All of these sources provide the center with an annual budget of $136,000 (1975) for sixty children. While this pro-rates to well over $2000 per child per year, it is reasonably low when compared with the national cost of center day care, but high when compared with family day care.

Obtaining and maintaining enough funding is practically a full-time job for the director. It involves a complete knowledge of business and of politics — for example, being able to recognize that one funding agency is employing a divide-and-conquer tactic by offering money to be shared among several child care centers — or knowing to whom to turn when cutbacks are made. Betty Van Wyck cites a recent study on why so many child care programs fold. One of the main reasons, she says, is that "they simply didn't know how to run." Watching Betty at a board meeting, one can't help being impressed by her grasp of the intricacies of funding and of the explicit and implicit meanings of regulations and procedures. It seems a herculean task, but she knows how to do it. "Running a day care center is running a business first," she says.

There are private-fee families who pay on a sliding scale. The range is from $10 to $50 per week, but no one pays the top amount. The unit cost for the center is $48 per week per child, and $65 per week for the special-needs children. There are now some half-day, private-fee "nursery school" children at the center.

Everyone pays something for child care at the center. All families are invited to make a donation, regardless of their individual funding, and most families do so on a regular basis. Betty observes, "This puts us in a buyer-seller relationship with the families, and they feel much more comfortable about criticizing us."

Training

"I guess it's basic to our philosophy about working together. We are training together. Any staff member who has been here very long is a model for the staff. A paraprofessional staff member in reality may be helping a professional staff member understand our system." This kind of working-training has produced a close-knit, effective staff for the Children's Center, but it has never been formalized into a training component to produce what the director refers to as "paper qualifications." However, Betty does have ample paper qualifications, with degrees in both early-childhood education and special education.

The center has been criticized because it does not have specially trained staff to care for the handicapped children. According to the director, the paraprofessional staff members are the most comfortable with the mixture of normal and handicapped children since they do not bring with them any great fears about caring for children who are different. "It is the professional staff that is trained by special educators, like myself, to feel that there is a special magic — especially magic equipment — that you use when dealing with a special child. The things that work with an ordinary child work with a special child. You only have to think about them a little more — it really tests your program."

Betty says, "I feel we are training all the time. The center has taken on part-time helpers and has given them on-the-job training. Many of these people have gone on to teach in other day care programs in Maine. Concurrently, the center is also taking student placements from local colleges and nursery schools.

The weekly staff meetings are all considered training sessions. The entire staff — the maintenance man, the housekeeper, the cook, the social worker, and the caregivers — meets together. Everyone knows the children, too, because part of most staff members' time is spent in the classroom. For instance, Sheila Cook, the social worker, spends half to three fifths of her time in the classroom and has regular room responsibilities for planning and curriculum development. She feels this time is invaluable for giving her knowledge about "where the kids are at." At the staff meeting, everyone pools his or her knowledge about the children. At one meeting, the members took five minutes per child, first discussing their observations, then deciding on "next steps." There is a piece of paper taped to the wall in Betty Van Wyck's office on which she and other staff members jot down what they want to talk about at the next staff meeting. These topics range from small problems to matters of procedure.

Problems and Changes

"I guess that problems are always part of the process," Betty Van Wyck says. "In other words, if we stopped having problems, we would have stopped changing and we would have stopped developing and we would have stopped doing a good job for kids. When I was asked to do this job, I said, 'Sure, I'd love to.' But it took me two years to realize that the only way to keep a center open is to run a good business. And you have to be in it at least two years. Most day care directors don't last two years. Most day care directors, like most social-service people, don't realize that the business community can be a tremendous help to you. You should be seeking help from personnel people, from business-management people, from bank people — from all those kinds of experts; that's what you need."

Betty feels that once the program is underway, it is no longer the concern of the director. "Your concern is staff relationships, job descriptions, hiring, firing." Among the changes brought about by this attitude were the development of job descriptions for every position and the development of a policy and procedures manual, "which is always in draft form and always will be."

Betty has become very clear about her own job in the center. "I try to be a democratic person and we run a pretty democratic ship around here, I think. But there are certain things that no amount of voting is going to change. As the director, I run this place. I am responsible for hiring and firing; I am responsible for my staff. The board does not hire or fire staff. I report to the board whom I've hired and fired, and if the board is unhappy with it, they can fire me."

Learning to fire staff members didn't come easily. Betty comments that "social-service people don't like to fire people . . . because we are in a position of helping people. So, if we have a staff member who isn't functioning well, we say, 'Oh, that's because we are not helping him or her enough.' If you do that — if you help people on staff who do not improve when you try to help them — what you do is lose your good staff. And you keep only mediocre staff who can work with poor staff. I've seen it over and over again. It is very hard to fire, but you can fire, and you can usually fire in a positive way, because a person is not happy in a job he or she is not right for."

Betty Van Wyck says that the director of a day care center needs a supervisor to provide support through the many difficult times that arise. "That was one of my problems. When I started, I had no supervisor." Eventually she found someone who knew about administration and could help her.

Betty believes that directors have to protect themselves or they'll burn out. "Day care directors usually work a sixty- to eighty-hour week. How long can you work like that? You simply have to say 'I'm sorry' to some of the demands made on you, or take a day off." She does have a "different kind of system," and as a result she is often subjected to criticism. "A program that is different threatens other people. And we frightened people. It never occurred to me that we would. I just assumed that everybody would think we were just lovely."

She and the staff of the center have been able to move ahead, developing their system in their own way, possibly because of a tactic they use: they make their long-range plans without reference to financing, and they look for the opportunity to "pick up a little piece of it." And they do mean *little*, because another tactic they use is: "Don't do anything in a big way to start out with."

Betty has always had a commitment to combining family day care with center care because she believes some children need to be in small groups. Recently an opportunity arose for achieving this long-range plan. A parent whose older children were in the center said that she needed to work, but what she really liked to do was to stay at home with her young children. The center hired this parent, Priscilla Boissonneault, trained her at the center, and helped her open a family day care program in her home as a satellite of the Children's Center. Eventually Betty hopes to have many such satellite homes providing infant and toddler care, early-morning and late-afternoon care, and an opportunity for small-group placements.

Betty says, "I think that you must question everything

you do. That produces change because it produces problems, and problems always produce change."

By this method, she and her staff have been able to create a center that has its roots in an awareness of how a community raises its children; that is, children of different sizes and shapes and ages, each pursuing his or her own interests, while adults do the same. In essence, it is transposing that kind of life into a center and the forging of that center into a community of friends, where people help each other and children learn to become independent and caring people.

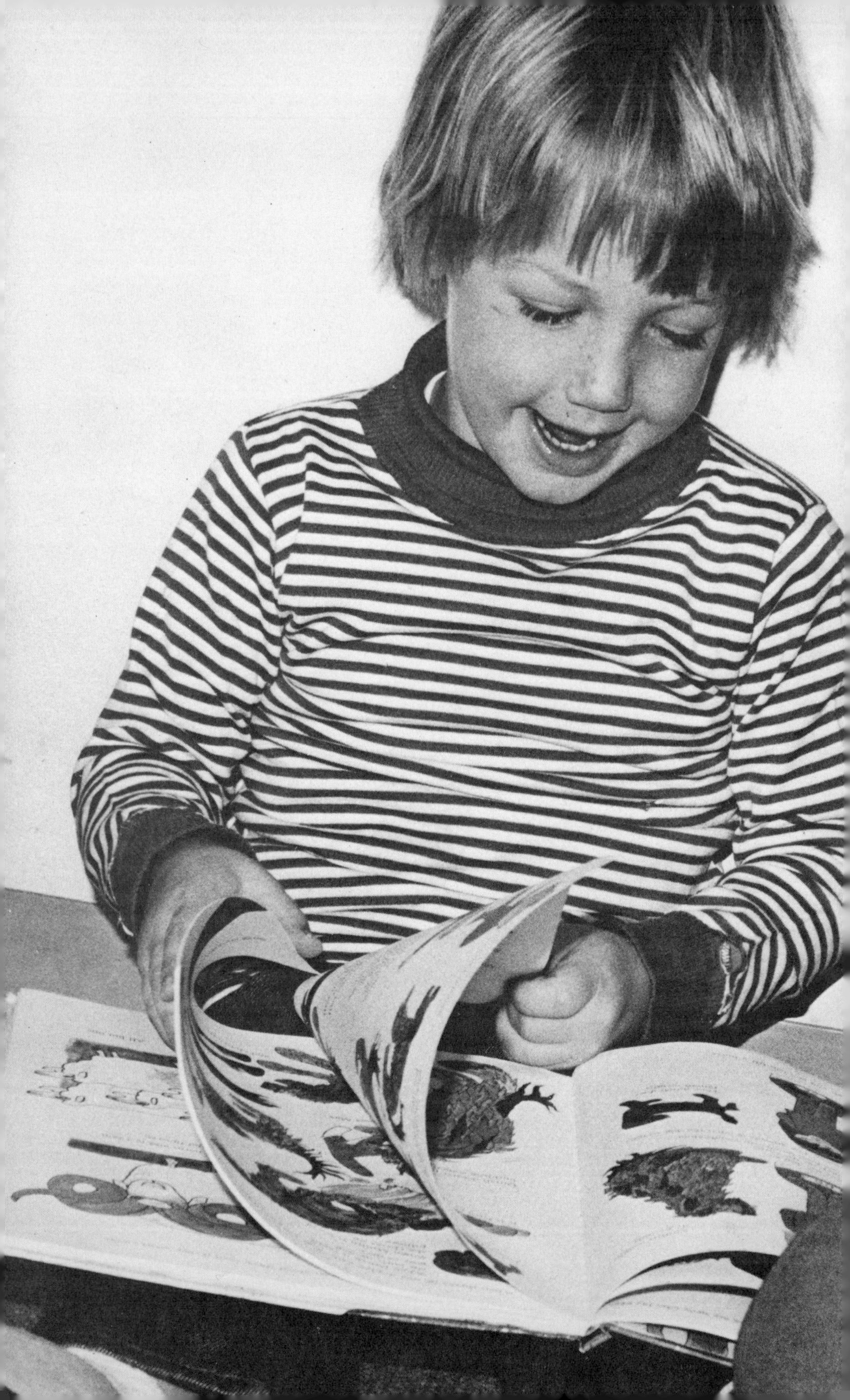

9
A Parent-Operated, Work-Based Center

**National Institutes of Health
Bethesda, Maryland**

Having a center for children at the place where parents work seems an ideal solution to child care problems. The list of the pluses for this kind of child care is long. Parents say: "My child and I wouldn't be going in separate directions." "I could know what is going on in my child's day." "I wouldn't feel so out of touch." Yet there are few centers of this kind. Many employers don't want children "running around, messing everything up" or "disrupting our work." Jean Curtis writes in *Working Mothers* that some employers even oppose having children visit their parents at work. When work-based centers have been established, they have been plagued with problems. Surveying this kind of child care center, Susan Stein, in *Child Care — Who Cares?* edited by Pamela Roby, attributes some of the difficulty to the fact that the centers have been set up without sufficient contact with parents, without the knowledge of what they need and want in child care. These centers have sometimes been exploitative, according to Stein — a means devised by management to tie women to low-paying jobs.

The Preschool Development Program at the National Institutes of Health stands in sharp contrast to the general picture. Occupying half of the ground floor in a low, modern building on the spacious NIH property, it serves close to sixty children of NIH employees. The program has recently been expanded into the Ayrlawn Elementary School, a local public school, with an all-day kindergarten program for five-year-olds and a before- and after-school program for other age groups. At the NIH center and Ayrlawn, the children have a well-run, enriching curriculum.

Beginnings This center had its origins in the parents' need for child care; through a woman's group they began petitioning and pushing for a center. Their efforts, however, were met with resistance and hesitancy on the part of many people at NIH, and they were confronted with the hard fact that there was no money. Coralyn Jones, one of those parents, looks back at that period as "terrible." The parents considered all kinds of moves, from striking to bringing their children to work with them despite the regulations. The basic obstacle was money. NIH is funded by federal tax revenues, and by law this money cannot be spent on such benefits as child care for its employees' children. As a result of these early efforts, an ad hoc committee (which, incidentally, included none of the parents who were petitioning for child care) was set up by NIH for the express purpose of looking at the possibility of day care for NIH employees. "Everyone on the committee was interested," one member reports, "but with no money and no resources, it was difficult to do anything." The one thing the committee did accomplish was to get a commitment from the administration to hire a child care coordinator — Virginia "Jinny" Burke.

"I was hired at NIH in nineteen seventy-one," Jinny Burke says. "NIH had been trying to do something in the field of day care for their employees for about ten years."

Jinny Burke's first move was to check to see if any other monies were, in fact, available. Twice she thought she was about to get funding; twice it was withdrawn because of budget cuts. She then realized that she wasn't going to be able to rely on outside funding. Figuring out the average costs, she developed a sliding fee scale based on income level by which some parents would pay more than others. The overpayment was called a contribution and was tax deductible. In that way, the money to operate the center would come directly from the parents. In the meantime, Jinny found out who at NIH wanted child care, and she and a group of those parents began to meet every few weeks at night or during lunch hours.

Before Jinny was hired, no parents were represented on the ad hoc committee; after she was hired, two parents were added. But that didn't improve the prevailing feeling toward parents, as expressed by the committee. Coralyn Jones was one of the parent representatives. She recalls, "Whatever we were professionally made absolutely no difference [on the committee] — there, we were parents, merely parents."

Unlike the administration, with its distrust of parents, Jinny Burke had a different vision; to her, parents were the key people in designing child care. Those parents who expected her, as an educator, to "write the curriculum and do all the work" were told by Jinny, "It is your child who is going into the center, and I refuse to do this. Now, I will spend all kinds of hours with you in working it out, but I will not do something and hand it to you." This approach was very successful, Jinny states. "After a while we developed good rapport, and the parents didn't feel intimidated because I was the 'expert.' " However, at first the parents weren't willing or ready to assume full responsibility for the center, opting instead to hire Education Systems Corporation, an educational contracting firm.

Finding space for the center was difficult. "We looked on campus and off campus," Jinny says, "and of course it was the same song in all the agencies: 'We don't have space for the child care center.' " The parents heard that Building Thirty-five on the periphery of the NIH grounds wasn't filled to capacity. The parents found out that one program temporarily housed in this building would prefer to be closer to the center of NIH. "So somehow or other that program was reshuffled, and we were able to take over the classrooms in Building Thirty-five." NIH charges the center $3600 a year in rent — a low price for industrial space.

Finally, two years after Jinny was hired, the planning group was ready to enroll children. Jinny says, "When I passed out applications in the dining halls, one guy looked at me and said, 'Lady, you have got to be kidding. I've been here for eight years, and people at NIH have been talking about this ever since I've been here. Is this another survey blank?' And I said, 'No sir, it is an honest-to-goodness application.''

Several donations and a two-week prepayment from each parent enabled the center to open its doors with eighteen children on June 18, 1973. Jinny planned to phase in children every two weeks until the center's licensed capacity of sixty children was reached. "Unfortunately," Jinny recalls, "the company we hired to run the center decided to hire all its staff at once instead of phasing in as we did. So by the end of July, we ran into a problem because the contractor wasn't getting enough money to meet the payroll. We finally got on a better footing by October first, when more children were enrolled." But that "better footing" didn't last very long. The following year the company gave notice that it was going to raise its fees. Jinny Burke told the parents that they should take over running the center. "Otherwise," she said, "the doors will be closed because we can't afford to pay these increases." On Jinny's advice, the parents became incorporated as Parents of Preschoolers (POP) in January of 1975 and took over the operation of the center in March.

"It was hard to get day care here in the first place," one parent says in summary, "but by having the other company run it, we saw that there were a lot of things that we didn't want and that really firmed up our goals. This added a great deal of cohesiveness to the parent group. We now have very firm goals."

Goals The Preschool Development Program, including Ayrlawn Kindergarten Program, presently serves approximately 60 children of all races, ethnic backgrounds, and economic classes . . . Some are children of visiting foreign scientists from Japan, Taiwan, Israel, Belgium, and South America.

Visitors to the Program are struck by the mixture of children chattering in many different languages, learning to play and work together.

The Parents of Preschoolers believe that they are contributing to a most important aspect of their children's social and intellectual development by placing them in a mixed cultural environment that is committed to the belief that young children can most easily learn respect and appreciation for people of all backgrounds.

— *Parent Handbook*

Carol Rudolph, the director, says that her main concern is that children develop the "ability to cope with the world around them." Jinny Burke uses a similar phrase, "learning to cope." Perhaps the reason that both the director and the coordinator use the term "cope" is that it isn't always easy to combine such diversity of cultural and socioeconomic background. These differences in values clearly emerge when one speaks with the parents. One parent says, "I wanted my children to get a lot of love and affection and a lot of personal attention from the adults. I haven't any real great academic goals for them. They are very bright, very verbal, and I'm not worried about their learning in the long run." But another parent says, "I really want to see learning going on. I'm not as educated as some here, but I still want more for my son than I had. I can't for the life of me see paying thirty dollars a week for a baby sitter where they watch television all day."

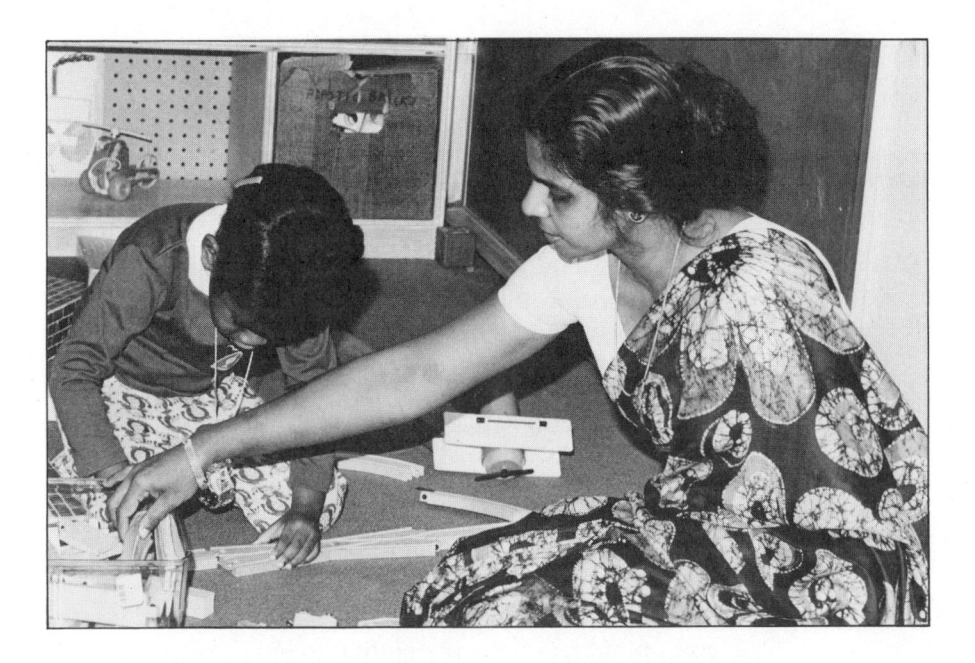

In many programs with a large diversity among the population, the goals have mainly reflected the values of the dominant group. This program, however, has achieved a unique balance by being responsive to all of the parents. The teachers state that they want the children "to be able to live together socially" and "to get ready for school."

Admissions

Admissions are made on a first-come, first-served basis. This applies as long as there are scholarships for the children whose parents cannot afford to pay full or partial costs. Fifty percent of the children receive some kind of scholarship aid.

All applications for admission are made to the coordinator, Jinny Burke, who places the children in the NIH center or helps the parents find other day care. Priority is given to siblings of those already enrolled.

Because the center has shifted from heterogeneous to

homogeneous age groupings, some problems have occurred when the child at the top of the waiting list does not correspond to the age group where a vacancy occurs. Other problems evolve because of the center's desire to maintain a "beautiful mixture of children." According to Jinny Burke, it has gotten to the point where "one gentleman said to me that I was discriminating against Israelis because I wasn't replacing an Israeli child with another Israeli child." The parents have formed a Selection and Criteria Committee to work with Jinny and to seek solutions to such situations by formulating guidelines for admission.

Selecting Caregivers The same desire for maintaining a proper mixture of children underlies the selection of staff. Jinny Burke thinks in terms of racial and national groups and percentages. "It is my feeling that since twenty-eight percent of NIH is made up of blacks, twenty-eight percent of the children in the center should be black, and the same thing with the staff. You have to have a balance and you have got to remember the balance." This is in line with the center's affirmative action plan, which calls for racial and sex balance in hiring practices.

The parents have a Personnel Committee, with staff representation, which interviews all candidates and works with the director in hiring new staff members. Teacher substitutes and volunteers are given high priority for staff positions. Carol Rudolph says, "Since we don't have too much time to spend on staff training, we hire people who are skilled and who come to us with a lot of experience and who impress us with their knowledge of what child care is about." Two of the teachers have degrees in early-childhood education, two have degrees in sociology, one is a pediatric nurse, and the others have had previous experience in child care programs. In addition to these skills, POP chairperson Dr. Edith Miles says, "We look for very loving and affectionate types of teachers."

The center hires two qualified teachers and perhaps a teacher aide for each of the four classes at NIH and for the kindergarten class at Ayrlawn Elementary School.

Groupings When the center was initially set up under the educational contracting firm, the children were in mixed age groups all day, with an age range of 2.6 to 5 years. Some parents felt uneasy about that arrangement. The parents wanted to have a center with a learning environment that allowed specific time for units of study. They felt that the mixed age groupings did not allow for such a schedule, so rearranging the age groups was one of the first changes made when the parents took control of the center.

The classes are now grouped in narrow age units. The youngest group is composed of the 2.6- to 3-year olds; there is a group of young threes and a group of older threes. A fourth group is made up of fours and of fives who have missed out on kindergarten. While the children are age-grouped for all classroom activities, they do mix at free-play time in the mornings and during many outside activities.

Space and Daily Schedule

"My son Albert says that he works at the National Institutes of Health," reports Leepo Yu.

Children and parents begin arriving at 7:30 A.M. Two caregivers are on hand and two of the four connecting classrooms are open. Inside the bright, sunny rooms the children can choose from a variety of free-play activities. By 9:00, the children separate into their age-grouped classrooms, where they have a morning snack of cereal and milk with raisins or bananas. This is followed by circle time, which involves attendance-taking, discussions about the calendar and weather, and singing songs. The center places strong emphasis on units of study, and a good amount of midmorning time is usually devoted to them. These units cover such things as transportation, children of different countries, holidays, art and colors, premath and prescience projects.

A teacher comments: "I have the children do some unit-related activity every day. They do have some choice about when they want to do it, and there is flexibility within the unit itself. But I feel that since they are getting ready for public school, a lot is going to be demanded of them and they can't say, 'No, I don't want to do that.'"

Outdoor activities usually follow. A huge patio stretches along two sides of the building where there are storage chests for play equipment. Beyond, in the large, fenced, sandy playground, there is a variety of equipment: a large climbing dome, tree stumps, tires, huge wooden spools, a slide, four swings, and a tether ball. On rainy days, the children stay inside and have creative dance or indoor games.

Lunch time is organized by the children in their class-

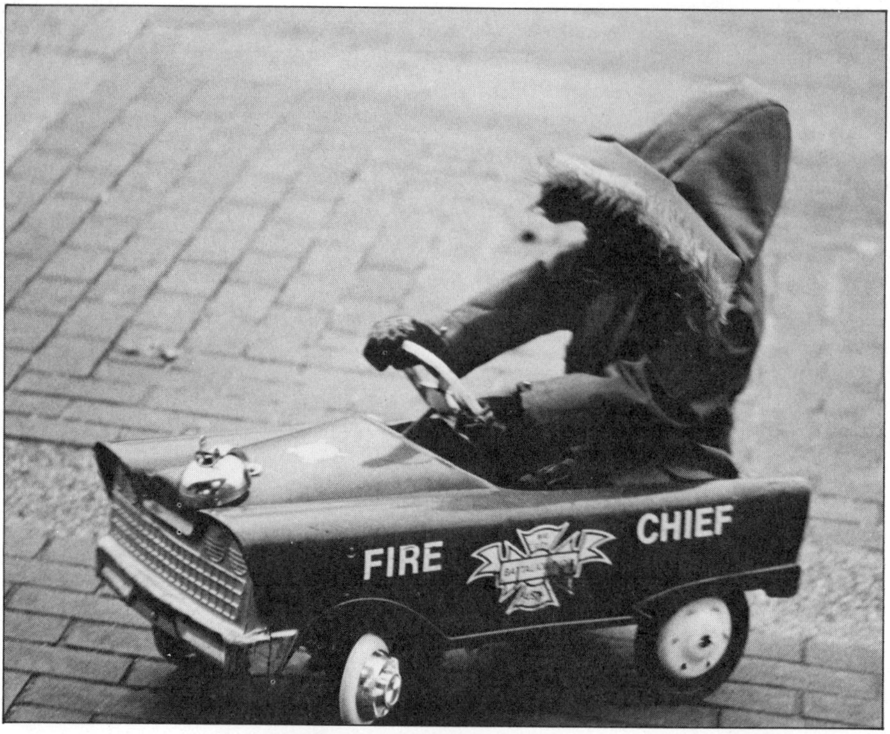
FIRE
CHIEF

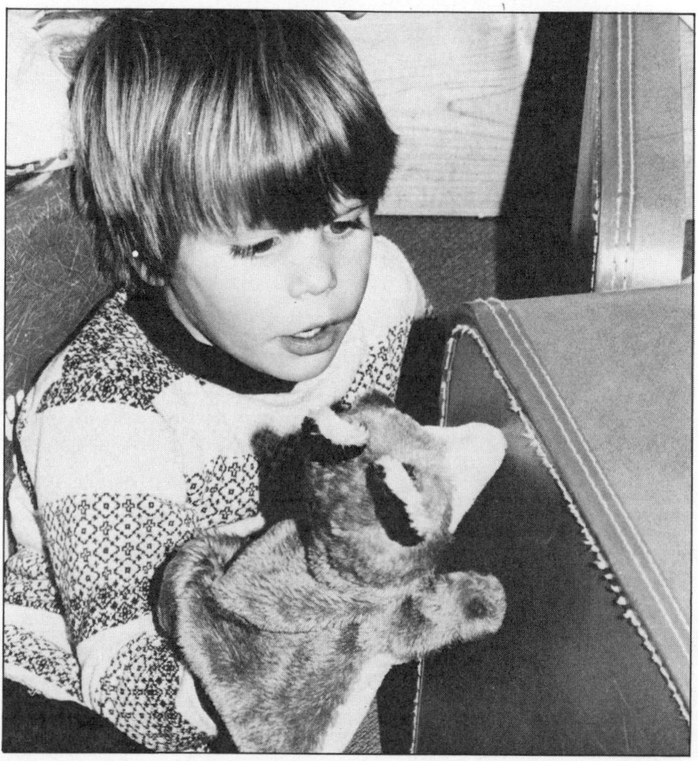

rooms. They set the tables while a caregiver warms the meal. Taking responsibility for clean-up after lunch is stressed in each classroom.

At 1:00 P.M., cots are moved into the classrooms for the children's two-hour rest period. Each child has his or her own spot for nap time, and keeps that place every day. Some of the teachers play classical music softly during nap time. In other classrooms there are rest toys: coffee cans containing miniature toys and puzzles that the children can play with quietly. The teachers use nap time for writing reports, having staff meetings, and making plans.

The afternoon program varies from group to group, but it usually includes a snack, outside activity, and some skills work in the classroom.

Parents begin arriving for their children at 3:30, but staggered work schedules mean that some pick up their children as late as 6:00. Spending time in the classrooms at the end of the day is difficult for parents because of a parking problem. But as one parent comments, "Sometimes a ticket is worth it. It's nice to give your child time to finish whatever he is doing or for you to see what he has done."

The daily schedule is often varied with field trips. The children go to off-campus places of interest and often visit their parents at work. Dr. Miles says, "I think there are many ways that children benefit from being where their parents are working. They also get some idea of the work their parents are doing."

Discipline

The center staff uses what it describes as a "low key" approach to discipline. As the staff members get to know the children, they try to anticipate problems. The director explains: "We use a lot of positive reinforcement. If we see a child whose self-image is really poor, we use as much praise as possible, maybe before the trouble begins — for example, just before one child pounds another on the head with a block."

The teachers and the director agree that matters of discipline really depend on the age and personality of the child, and the style of the teacher. They are also aware that children may have a better relationship with one adult than with another, and they have learned to allow such a relationship to form; this often means permitting children to visit other classrooms during times of stress.

The staff uses a "time out" technique for dealing with

fighting. Children are separated from the group until they have calmed down. Swearing is handled in several ways. Some of the teachers find that ignoring it works best. Others make clear to the children that certain kinds of language are not to be used in the classroom. One teacher found a cure by giving the child a taste of his own abusive language. "I had a child who used to call me a motherfucker and he used to throw chairs at me. One day I got so angry, I bent down and whispered in his ear, 'You're a motherfucker,' and he never said it again."

While each teacher in the center has an individual style of handling specific discipline problems as they arise, the director believes that the most desirable approach is a preventive one. Prevention, she feels, can best be effected by "letting the children get into self-responsibility and group responsibility, by doing a lot for themselves and a lot for each other."

Parent Participation Responsibility is the major factor in parent relationships. It is the parents' center; they are the ones who manage it. The center is run by Parents of Preschoolers, Inc., a non-profit, tax-exempt corporation. Each parent joins the corporation and signs a contract for a minimum of twenty hours annually of voluntary service to the center. This can take the form of acting as a room parent, helping with trips, participating in fund-raising, and service on committees. It is the committees that handle the actual management of the center, dealing with such things as admissions criteria, fiscal management, personnel policies, health, safety, nutrition, curriculum, and fund-raising. As with every group, there is a core of very active parents, many of whom give far more than the required twenty hours per year of service. Barbara Iba, former chairperson of Parents of Preschoolers, calculates that sometimes she spends sixteen hours a week working at or for the center.

Carol Rudolph, the director of the center, was apprehensive at first about working with the parents, but now she finds that the parents have made perceptive suggestions about how things can be done. "I'm finding that I have less to do than when I ran the ship by myself. There are more people to count on."

The parents' influence extends beyond the management of the center. One parent says, "I also think it is important that the teachers know what parents want. We fill out quite an extensive form of what we want for our own child, and that goes to the director and it goes out to all of the teachers." The teachers report back to the parents about how their goals are being met and how the child is doing. The reporting is done informally when the parents bring their children or pick them up, and in parent conferences twice a year. Describing a conference, one parent says, "The teachers fill out a four-page form. They give us a copy and they keep a copy, and they go over it with us and ask if we have any questions. We spend about an hour or so discussing the form. They also tell us about things that we can work on with our child at home." Furthermore, there are regular center meetings, which help keep the parents in touch with what is going on.

The parents publish a monthly newsletter to keep members of the corporation informed of important events involving the center. It includes a calendar of special events and parent meetings, and notes the days the center will be closed. It also provides an open forum for staff and parents to exchange ideas.

Carol Rudolph regards the parents as a rich resource for the center. Not only are the children taken on trips to see their parents at work, but parents are invited into the classrooms. Some scientists have devised simple experiments for the children. Parent volunteers from diverse cultural backgrounds are asked to come to the classrooms.

Peace of mind and convenience are the two things most parents point to as the marked advantages of a work-based center. In their own words: "The convenience is wonderful. You can go over at lunch any time. If your child is sick, you can be right there." "I think the parents feel a little more secure having their children nearby." "Does it pay off in better work attendance? Oh, yes! I think morale is better, attendance is better, and you get a feeling that the company cares about you, which makes your feeling toward the company better." "I think it makes for a much better atmosphere within the industry. It's not distracting, but quite the reverse. It's easier to schedule meetings or meet with committees when you're located in the same spot with similar schedules."

When the center was managed by the educational contractor, a packaged-food service was used. A parent re- **Food** calls: "We looked at the food they were getting — things like Scooter Pies for snacks — and we knew we didn't want it. It takes a lot more work to get fresh fruits and vegetables, but it firmed up our idea of what we wanted." Under Parents of Preschoolers, a real effort has been made to improve the quality of the food.

The children are involved in cooking in their classrooms. Carol Rudolph says, "First of all, cooking is nonsexist. It is also a science project. The kids love to mix and grind, cook and serve. One day a week in each room is usually a cooking day." Often the children make their own lunches — perhaps grilled cheese sandwiches or vegetable soup.

Health The center requires that each child have a physical examination before entering the program, and yearly physicals thereafter are encouraged.

The center takes care of some special health needs:

through NIH the children are given vision tests; the University of Maryland provides hearing screenings; emergency arrangements are made with Suburban Hospital. The center also carries accident insurance on the children.

Once each year a Department of Health employee comes to the center, checks the health records of the children to make sure they are up to date, and, when he or she finds records that aren't complete, so informs the center.

Funding

The principal funding for the center comes from fees paid by parents. There is a sliding fee scale, which ranges from $8.00 to $47.50 per week, depending on the parents' income. The actual weekly cost per child is $38.50, which means those who pay above that amount are contributing to scholarship assistance.

The Montgomery County Department of Social Services provides a considerable amount of income for the center through tuition assistance for eligible children. A percentage of this money also goes into scholarships. The Department of Agriculture provides some food free of charge. Since half of the children require tuition assistance, the parents find it necessary to do fund-raising for the center. They sponsor children's movies, lotteries, and raffles.

Despite the center's being work-related and located on the NIH campus, it receives no money from the federally funded NIH. Jinny Burke feels this is reasonable. "It would be unfair," she says, "for my tax dollars and yours to be spent on child care for federal employees."

Training

Because most of the income comes directly from the parents, there is little money for anything beyond salaries, materials, and rent. The center has only a small budget for staff training — less than $200 per year. Yet the staff manages through the use of local resources to keep training part of its program.

Montgomery County provides a free sixty-four-hour course in child development, which all center staff members are encouraged to take. New employees are given a salary increase after completing the full sixty-four hours. Parents contribute a great deal to staff training. Using the twenty hours they agree to give the center annually, some parents contribute their own professional skills. For instance, a parent who is a speech therapist works with the teachers in screening children and setting up language development programs; a scientist provides science workshops for the staff; a psychologist works with the children. The small training budget is used to bring in visiting specialists in areas of need defined by the staff. Workshops in running parent-teacher conferences are an example of this kind of training

Carol Rudolph sees regular weekly staff meetings as a training time to explore and solve problems and share teaching ideas.

The center also serves as a training ground for others. It trains student teachers from the University of Maryland and Montgomery County Community College as well as high school students and senior citizens who volunteer in the program. One of the focuses of this training is on adults' becoming more aware of themselves. Carol says, "I feel that I need as much staff training as the rest of the people. I called in a consultant and had her monitor me in a staff meeting. She listened to me and heard how I project myself to the group as an authority figure. For instance, how much do I allow for input? How much do I allow people to make their own decisions rather than my dictating to them? That was an important part of my growth, and as a result of her observations I put myself into a sensitivity-training course."

To further self-awareness, the Personnel Committee tried a written evaluation in 1975. Each member of the staff, including the director, was evaluated by the director, staff members, and parents. In addition, each person wrote a self-evaluation. Two parents tabulated the results and showed each person the results of his or her evaluation.

Problems and Changes The greatest change in the life of the center took place when the parents assumed responsibility for its management. Their experience with the educational contracting agency, while largely negative, did help them consolidate their ideas about the kind of child care they wanted, and it gave them the time they needed to reorganize and take complete control of their program. Many of their current problems spring from the fact that it is a work-based center. The relationship between NIH and the center is still tenuous and ill-defined, and one of Jinny Burke's major responsibilities is to act as a liaison. She sees this function as "taking the pressure from both sides and pushing it back so that the program continues to operate." In effect, she relieves the center's personnel from dealing with political situations and frees them for teaching the children. Some parents agree that the center's relationship with NIH is less than firm. They would like more assurance that the center can stay where it is at a low rent beyond the period covered in the present leasing agreement. In addition, they wish that employers would provide child care as a staff benefit.

There are also difficulties associated with the center's being a parent-run organization. Because the parents' stay at the center is, at most, three years, there is always a turnover; often a small group of parents seems to run things. Most working parents are hard put to find the time to participate on committees. But the parents are the main source of financial support, and any change in the organization would result in an increase in costs, which would be an enormous burden on the center.

Finally there has been some conflict over the recent push to make the staff more heterogeneous. This and all of the center's other problems — being work-based, serving a heterogeneous population, and being run by parents — are also its strengths. For the parents and staff at NIH, it comes very close to being an ideal solution to their child care needs.

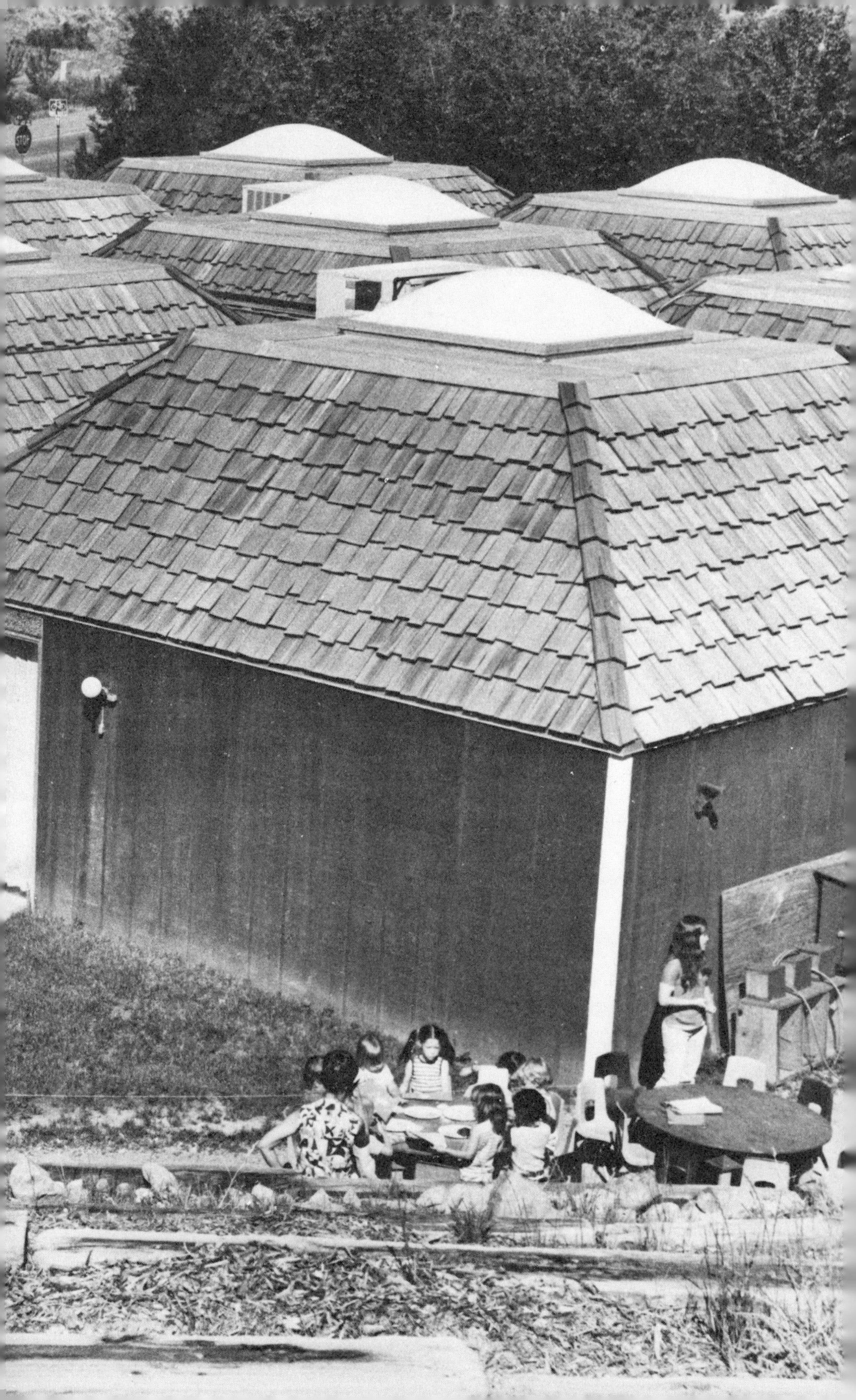
STOP

10
A For-Profit Center

**Mesa: Children's World Play School Learning Centers
Colorado Springs, Colorado**

High on a red-clay bluff, where two winding roads intersect before they climb farther up into the hills of Colorado Springs, there sits an unusual modular building. It looks more like a sculpture than a building; only the hillside playground equipment and the sign with brushstroke letters saying CHILDREN'S WORLD give away its function. A parent there, Margarete Reisz, says, "Children's World is a correct title — it is a beautiful world for children."

When one thinks of the world that adults usually provide for children, one imagines Humpty-Dumpty character cutouts pasted across a wall, or wallpaper covered with smiling lions and frolicking tigers, or round-faced, happy children — a never-never nursery-rhyme land. This children's world couldn't be more different. It has an aesthetic quality that is appealing to children and adults alike. The outside playground is a multilevel environment. In one place a stark, leafless tree stands alone in a sandy open space. Farther up the hill, several trees provide lush shade. All of the construction materials are natural — wooden walls and rough stone walkways. The inside of the building is an extension of the outside. Skylights provide even, clear light. The entire space is open, with areas sectioned off by tall plants and foliage, and there is even a large aviary in the front corridor. In the center of the building, there is a swimming pool. All of the equipment invites physical exploration.

Children's World is a company that operates over fifty-six centers in six states. It is not a franchise because the concept and materials are not sold to individual operators. Children's World Play Schools are centrally owned and operated. New centers are begun by their main and regional offices, and personnel is hired to run the centers. It is a relatively new profit operation — stockholders were paid dividends for the first time in 1975: three cents per one dollar of investment.

Child care is a social system with its own set of values, its own panoply of prejudices, its own likes and dislikes. Within the child care circuit, one of the most pronounced dislikes is the one that people in nonprofit programs have for profit-making centers. A director of a nonprofit center that is also in Colorado Springs put it succinctly when she said, "Children and profits don't mix." In *The Day Care Book*, edited by Vicki Breitbart, Alice Lake writes, "The business of young children is growth and development, and the business of corporations is making money. If you mix the two, can the needs of both be satisfied?"

Critics of for-profit day care explain that their opposition is based on their belief that rich investors will become richer at the expense of children. They claim that for-profit operators put money first, skimping on services to children. Judy Kleinberg, in *The Day Care Book*, writes, "In order to make a profit, many of these programs have large classes, a high teacher-child ratio, little equipment, and poor food, if any at all. The staff is often overworked, underpaid, and offered few benefits and little job-development training. The profit is clearly at the expense of everyone but the owner."

Alice Lake expresses concern about the lack of educators of stature in for-profit enterprises. "Without a strong voice to plead for children, isn't business likely — as much out of ignorance as greed — to trample on [the children's] needs?" Furthermore, the business community is prone to finding a formula, a system, that it can market on a mass scale. A center in Rhode Island might look just like one in Virginia or Mississippi. That leads Alice Lake to a trenchant question: "Will look-alike child care centers inevitably turn out look-alike children?" Joseph Featherstone's memorable label for this phenomenon is "Kentucky Fried Children."

It is interesting that the Mesa center has a newspaper article condemning for-profit centers thumbtacked to a bulletin board in the teachers' room. Perhaps it serves as a warning. For in several important ways, this center has avoided the very real pitfalls of for-profit centers. To begin with, Mesa differs from the three other Children's World centers in Colorado Springs. Although, according to the Children's World brochure, the four centers have the same goals, even on a superficial level they are different: one is in a home, another is in a renovated church, two are in new buildings. On a more fundamental level, their programs vary. They range from a traditional contained-classroom approach to the open, modular plan at Mesa. The four centers, in a way, represent an index of the past twenty years' worth of thinking and learning for their founder, Ann Doss.

Beginnings

Ann Doss was raised in England and moved to Colorado after she was married. In the early 1950s she found herself a widow, with young children to support. In attempting to find care for her children and a job in her profession, nursing, she met head-on the complications of being a single working parent. There was virtually no day care available for her children's age range (infants and toddlers) and for a mother of her income bracket (she wasn't on welfare). Because her need was urgent, she sensed that there must be other people, single parents and families, in her predicament, so she turned her own home into her first center. It was for fourteen children from six months through three years of age.

In starting that center, Ann found that there were no state regulations governing child care. She and several other people banded together and succeeded in getting Colorado to pass a child care act that put facilities that cared for children under state regulation.

Some of the requirements in that act were impossible to comply with or enforce. For instance, it required center directors to have a degree in early-childhood education, but no college or university in the state offered such a degree at that time. "So then," Ann says, "we had to start writing criteria for education courses and selling that concept to colleges and universities." Ann Doss entered one program and earned her own degree. The center in her home began to expand. Slowly she began to acquire more of the property on her block, enlarged her center, and started several more. Eventually she hired directors for each of the centers, and formed a business partnership. But none of the operations fulfilled Ann's dream, which was to design both a building and a program for the special kind of child care she envisioned.

She was determined to create the best possible building, and began her search for the right architect. At first, all of the architects she interviewed thought in terms of a "neat little kiddie place." At last she was referred to an educator and architect from the University of Wisconsin, Byron C. Bloomfield. "Byron was willing not only to take a year's leave of absence from the university, but to take a minimal amount of money for his design. He even put up some investment money to become a partner. Then we formed a corporation. We thought that we could go public with the stock, but that was in the early seventies, when money was nowhere to be found. I literally tramped Seventeenth Street in Denver and went to every bank in Colorado Springs for months before I found someone who would give us the mortgage to finance it. Who ever heard of anyone wanting to build a one hundred and ninety thousand dollar children's center? Aren't church basements good enough?" When it became necessary to seek additional funds, Ann sold her centers to Children's World. She was made a vice president and a regional director of the company, and, with Children's World's financial backing, has moved toward expansion. She continues to construct new centers. It is interesting to note that although Mesa could be considered a model center, Ann did not rubber-stamp that design. The one subsequent center she has built in Colorado Springs is an adaptation and expansion of the Mesa design.

Byron Bloomfield's research, Ann explains, "was on the effect of the environment on children's learning, with special emphasis on the motor-perceptual development of the child." His Mesa design has its roots in the work of Darrel Boyd Harmon, of Texas. Harmon had done a study to find out why grade school children developed learning disabilities and posture and eye problems, and why migrant children of the same age, who almost never attended school, had none of the same disabilities. It was discovered that schools traditionally have one physical setup. There is usually a full wall of windows on one side of the classroom, a blackboard in the front, and a blank wall on the other side. In order for children to focus attentively on the blackboard and the teacher, they have to

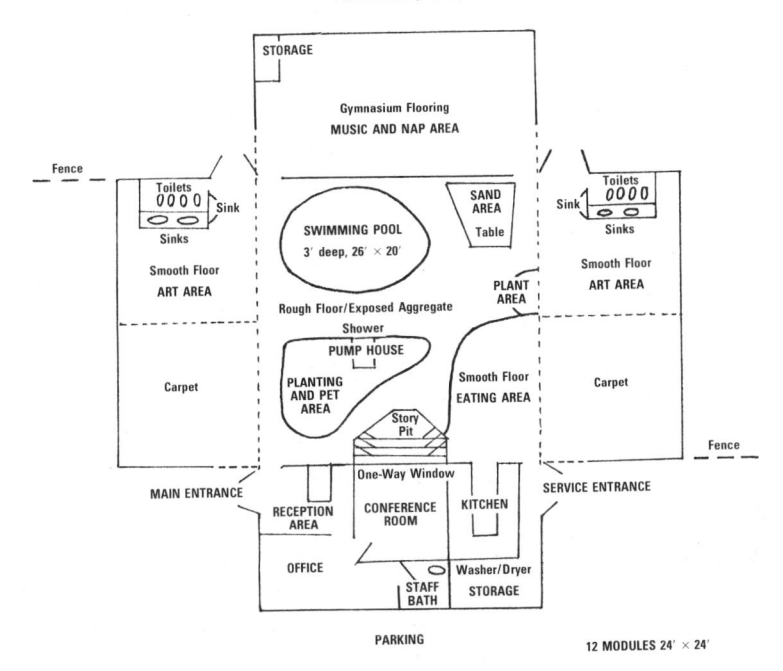

```
                    PLAYGROUND (2 acres)

            ┌──STORAGE
            │
                    Gymnasium Flooring
                    MUSIC AND NAP AREA

  Fence
  ─ ─ ─      Toilets                    Toilets
             0 0 0 0   Sink   SAND      0 0 0 0
                       ─      AREA  Sink  ─
             Sinks        SWIMMING POOL   Sinks
                          3' deep, 26' × 20'
             Smooth Floor      Table      Smooth Floor
             ART AREA                 PLANT  ART AREA
                          Rough Floor/Exposed Aggregate  AREA
                                Shower
                                PUMP HOUSE
             Carpet      PLANTING   Smooth Floor  Carpet
                         AND PET    EATING AREA
                         AREA    Story
                                 Pit
                                                          Fence
                                                        ─ ─ ─
                          One-Way Window
             MAIN ENTRANCE                    SERVICE ENTRANCE
                          RECEPTION  CONFERENCE  KITCHEN
                          AREA       ROOM

                          OFFICE         Washer/Dryer
                                  STAFF  STORAGE
                                  BATH

                    PARKING              12 MODULES 24' × 24'
```

use strong physical control to keep their eyes away from the bright light coming in from the windows. The strenuous task of eye-focusing consumes a great deal of energy. The distance from the desk to the blackboard and the angle of the children's desks create postural and perceptual problems. Furthermore, Harmon found that school-age children do not get enough physical activity. There was a real necessity, he felt, to design spaces to avoid creating a preponderance of learning disabilities.

Space

By the use of a series of skylights, the Mesa building obviates the problem of the bright, blinding glare, dark shadows, and uneven lighting that are common in schools. The skylight domes diffuse the light evenly throughout the building. Ann says, "There is no shadowing on the floor, on the work the children are doing, or on the books they are reading." An absence of windows in the Mesa center doesn't make it dark or confining for several reasons: the skylights give a sense of height, the large open central area creates a feeling of spaciousness, and the glass doors at each of the corners of the building provide an ever-present view of the outside. The building has several main areas: an office-entryway, a large central room with a swimming pool, a carpeted amphitheater in the front, and classroom areas along the sides of the main room. To one side, there is an open kitchen, and in the back, a gymnasium. The only enclosed space in the entire building is a teachers' room, which doubles as an observation booth. Areas are divided by hedges of plants or by low shelving. The inside seems linked to the outside because of the use of materials usually associated with the out-of-doors: plants, water, sand, and stone. These materials give a sense of solitude and quiet not found in some open-classroom plans. Every material, every aspect of the design, has a carefully thought-out purpose. The floor, for instance, has several textures: the roughness of the aggregate surfacing, the softness of the carpet, the smoothness of concrete, and the bounciness of the rubber-spindled floor in the gymnasium, which is also known as the "barefoot room." Each of these surfaces denotes a different kind of area. The aggregate, for instance, means that one is walking from one area to another. Inside an area, there is carpeting. Without having to look, children get sensory messages about where they are. Furthermore, they receive tactile stimulation in a part of their bodies that is usually ignored in most physical-stimulation programs — their feet.

The gymnasium, or barefoot room, is filled with equipment: trampolines, A-frame climbers with long boards that can be attached to create slides, and high walkways. In addition, there are several movable mirrors. "If you have a child walking on the balance beam," Ann says, "that is good in itself; but if he is looking at his feet, he is not using the appropriate posture. If you can get him to focus on something else, then it's better. The thing that a kid likes to look at most is himself. So if you have a mirror, you will get the child to stand up straight automatically."

In the classroom areas of the building, the walls are wood-paneled. Because sound reverberating loudly through open space is common in designs of this kind, the architect put burlap on some of the wooden walls; and that, along with draperies and carpeting, was effective in reducing the sound problem.

Goals

The architect explains the overall goals of the child world environment he helped to create: "Each piece of play equipment, whether inside the building or incorporated into the landscaped playground, has been selected or specially designed to encourage motor-perceptual development as an important basis for cognitive growth." Helen Shelton, the director of Mesa, shares Bloomfield's beliefs. Behavior problems in older children, she feels, often result from too strong a stress on the academic too soon. "If children are pushed into academics," she says, "and sit all day at school and then come home and sit in front of TV, their energy has to come out someplace." Often it comes out in a kind of hyperactivity. Helen feels that physical activity in the preschool years is a prelude to, and the foundation of, successful academic functioning later on. The curriculum at Mesa is well rounded, with arts and crafts, field trips, and units of study. It is more correct to say that this program presents an unusual spectrum of physical activities, both inside and out, that are seen not as supplementary or special, but as an everyday occurrence.

Daily Schedule

Mesa is an open-education center, which means that the children have both free-choice and planned activities. The morning, beginning at 7:00, starts with free choice. The public school and day care children arrive whenever it suits their parents. During the warm months, free-choice time is often spent outside, in the approximately 1½ acres of the Mesa property. The natural shape of the land, which runs up against a bluff, has been left unchanged so that children can climb to a plateau where they can look out over the entire sweep of the building.

On the plateau is a covered, multishaped gazebolike structure that is used by the children in a variety of ways — for resting, dramatic play — or by some, as just a place to get away from other people. A long line of children often gathers at a "cable ride." Here, the first in line stands on a large block, grabs a T-bar handle, and then swings through the air to the other side and back again. Children clamber all along the hillside, to overturn rocks and search for crickets, or climb dead trees. These trees have been stripped of their bark, transported from the woods, and placed in postholes in the playground, making an unusual and very appealing piece of playground equipment. On one side of the center, in a flat area, children ride wheel toys, play in the sandbox, bounce balls, play basketball, or engage in "make-believe" in an open Lincoln Log house. On the other side, in a clump of live trees, others can swing.

At 9:00, the public school children are transported to their schools, and the preschool, junior kindergarten, and kindergarten groups meet in their home-base areas for planned activities. One group may be playing or listening to music or learning some finger-plays; another may be listening to a story about dinosaurs and drawing pictures of their favorite prehistoric animal; still another may be in the barefoot room, tumbling; and in the center of the room, the fourth group will be swimming. Even during the planned activities, there is choice and flexibility for the children. "The only schedule for the children that is maintained tightly is the swimming," says Helen Shelton. "Other than that, I have enough staff [a ratio of 7 to 1] to allow the children choice."

The swimming is the high point of the day for many of the children. Several parents report the wonderful feelings of accomplishment their children have in overcoming an initial fear of water, in being able to submerge their heads, to lift their feet off the bottom, kick, and swim. Gwen Rawley says that her son "would rather swim than eat right now." Swimming is taught by a water-safety instructor.

At midmorning there is "little lunch," or snack, followed by planned activities until lunch. After lunch, the children nap until 2:30. Then the after-school children arrive, and everyone is served a snack at 3:30. The afternoon is a combination of free-choice and recreational activities. At the end of the day, parents pick up their children, often stopping to chat with the teacher, check the child's "mailbox," or read the note, tacked to the bulletin board, telling what each group did that day.

On Tuesdays during the summer, the preschool children have a picnic in one of the parks. Friday is their field-trip day. They visit museums, sanitation departments, and wholesale tropical fish companies, among other places. The older children have more adventuresome trips — hiking in Cheyenne Canyon, for example.

The range of experiences presented to the children at Mesa is in sharp contrast to a criticism of for-profit child care: that it may "trample on the children's needs."

Food

The food program at Mesa also runs counter to Judy Kleinberg's accusation that for-profit centers have "poor food, if any at all." These children are served two snacks and a hot lunch each day. The portions of the food are limited but not skimpy. In truth, the portions may not be enough for some children, particularly those who go without breakfast. The food, however, is fresh and nutritious.

Helen Shelton takes pride in the hot lunches served at the center. She shops for the food at a local wholesale market once a week. However, if one of the teachers tells her that a nearby market is having a special on cantaloupe, she probably will gather several children, put them on the bus, and let them help her pick out the melons.

Ann Doss is likewise very proud of the kitchen facilities at Mesa. Traditionally, kitchens in centers are set apart from the children, enclosed and out of bounds. This kitchen is a three-sided alcove, visible and accessible. It is Ann's conviction that cooking should not be magic; it should be seen. And she feels that, just as they do in many homes, children should be able to go in, stir a pot, sniff, and taste while the adults are cooking, and that they, too, should have the opportunity to cook. The kitchen, therefore, is an area for the children. It took powerful persuasion on Ann's part to convince the licensing authorities that an open kitchen could be safe for children.

Admissions and Grouping

In one other aspect Mesa has avoided the problems of many for-profit centers, and that is in its group sizes. FTE, or "full-time enrollment," is a common concept, heard of frequently in for-profit centers. Full-time enrollment is also important at Mesa; but although the center is technically licensed for 127 children, Helen Shelton says that she doesn't want the enrollment to go over 100, and that she prefers that it remain somewhat below that.

The Mesa center has many options for parents. They can choose full-time (five or more hours) or part-time (three hours or fewer) programs for five, three, or two days a week. In addition, there are before- and after-school, holiday, and vacation-time programs. A child is accepted only after a parent interview, preferably with the child present. He or she is then assigned to a group of the appropriate age range. Groups at Mesa may run as large as twenty or twenty-one children, but Mesa does not have the "high teacher-pupil ratio" that has so often been the target of criticism of for-profit centers. A group of twenty-one Mesa children customarily has three teachers: one head teacher and two assistants.

How It Works

"I don't know how for-profit centers can survive," the director of a nonprofit center in Colorado Springs states. "Well-funded government centers are always needing more money. They can barely make ends meet. How do for-profit centers do it?"

One way they survive has to do with staffing procedures. Often they hire less experienced staff at lower salaries. In this respect, Children's World is no exception. For instance, high school graduates are hired as summer assistant teachers. In each group there is a head teacher with a college degree, and some of these teachers have impressive credentials; others are right out of school. The salaries at Children's World are low — from $250 to $750 a month, with several directors making only $550 a month. The assistants start at minimum wage level. Though their salaries are comparable to salaries in child care centers throughout Colorado Springs, their low pay has created tensions. A teacher, Jennie Allen, reports that most of the staff members at Mesa aren't supporting themselves, but receive additional income from parents or husbands. "The people who have the most difficulty here," Ann Doss confirms, "are the young college graduates who do have to support themselves and are career-oriented. Often they can't afford to stay."

High staff turnover has been a problem at many for-profit centers, and until recently was a problem at Mesa. When Helen Shelton took over as director, the turnover rate was high. But she happily reports that "the staff that I have now is staying with me." Perhaps that is because she is careful about the kind of people she hires — people who really care for children. And perhaps it is because she has become a friend to all of those who work for her.

For-profit centers rarely offer employment benefits, but Children's World does. It provides health insurance and sick leave, and pays one third of the cost of courses in early-childhood education. Children's World is also trying to establish a revolutionary concept in for-profit child care. Ann Doss explains, "We are working toward a stock-purchase plan so that we will soon have employee ownership."

Another way that Children's World manages to make ends meet is by a broad and flexible concept of roles. "We have to be very stringent," Ann Doss says. "I don't have a secretary. And there is never a time when I can't drive a bus, cook a meal, or go in and run a school." Helen Shelton, too, may be seen doing many things during the day — greeting prospective parents, balancing ledgers and accounts, collecting and taking out the garbage, going to the market to shop for food, putting out the mats for nap time, conferring with parents, planning with teachers. Her day is supposed to run from 9:00 A.M. to 6:00 P.M., but on many days she is still cleaning up or working on her books until much later. The teachers' and assistants' hours are not so long. Their week is from twenty-five to forty hours, and they have a break while the children are napping. However, teachers are expected to do more than teach. "We have a janitor who comes into the centers on weekends, but the floors are washed every day by the staff," Ann says. "Cleanliness is part of the staff responsibilities. We are jacks-of-all-trades."

Health The Children's World centers do not have the range of personnel that some government-funded programs do — there is no psychologist, no social worker, no part-time nurse. As a consequence, the centers' family-service programs are limited. The health program consists of requiring the children to have physicals before they enter, and regular immunizations, and each of the centers has liaison with a physician. The teachers check the children daily. All staff members are required to take a first-aid course within ninety days of employment.

Discipline The stated approach to discipline is an adaptation of behavior modification techniques. For instance, a child who pushes, hits, or hurts another child is removed from the group until his or her behavior subsides. In general, there is little cause to use this technique since most of the children are too busy to bother breaking rules. However, there was an observable problem with two teachers who seemed to be locked in combat with several children.

Training It is often stated that teachers at for-profit centers are given little job-development training. At Mesa, training is an expected part of the job. Once a month, the staff meets with the director to map out the schedule and plan the program. In the interim, staff members can attend workshops offered by Children's World for all its centers. Many deal with arts and crafts. For the director, there are meetings with the other Children's World directors and with Ann Doss. Probably the most invaluable training happens informally. Helen says, "If there is a problem, then take care of it right away, not after it builds up." Whenever a difficult situation arises, either Helen or one of the staff members will say, "Let's have a meeting." That usually means that the staff members go out together for hamburgers, and hash over the problem. The difficulty might involve a staff member who is not pitching in to do his or her share, or it might involve a teacher who is having a hard time with a child. "I think that if things are kept on an open basis, then troubles don't develop within the staff," says Helen.

Helen follows the same method when working with parents. "I tell them the same thing I tell my staff; that is, if they have a problem, tell me right away and directly to my face and not in a roundabout way."

Parent Participation

Underlying Mesa's approach to parents is a recognition that parents are busy working people. The parents' activities are intended to be pleasant family occasions, relaxing relief from their workdays. There are breakfasts, teas, and potluck suppers. Helen feels that a social gathering is a good time to get to know parents and find out what's on their minds. "Many times," she says, "if it is a formal meeting, parents will be more rigid and so will the staff; but on a more informal basis, parents will say more about what they're feeling." Ann Doss agrees. "These parents are working parents. Yes, they need to be involved. Yes, they need to feel a good communication going on. But if you say that parents have to attend this meeting and that they have to attend that meeting, then I think you are doing them a disservice."

Parents are welcome to spend time at Mesa whenever they wish. Often they accompany their children on trips. Gwen Rawley expresses the attitude of most of the other parents when she characterizes Mesa as being "open to suggestions." Parents' suggestions are actively sought. Helen sends out a form to parents asking detailed questions about their feelings about the staff and the program. The parents' recommendations are carefully tabulated and are often acted upon.

Helen counters the stereotype of many for-profit directors in her business relationships with parents. The tuition-schedule form states that "all tuition payments are due in advance on the first of every month, or each Monday for parents wishing to pay weekly." If a parent can't pay by the tenth of the month, Helen will say to him or her, "Don't worry about it as long as you can manage by the end of the month, or at least give me something on the account so that I know you are making the effort." She feels that her experience as a parent helps her to be more understanding. "I've been in tight binds myself and I know what it's like." Her understanding does work. She has had very little difficulty with parents on money matters.

Funding The money for the fees comes from two sources: the parents themselves and the Department of Social Services, which pays for its clients' children in a purchase-of-service arrangement. The fees come to slightly less than $1.00 per hour; full-time tuition weekly is $29.00, monthly it is $115.00. If more than one child from a family attends Mesa a 10 percent reduction is allowed for each additional child.

The enrollment figures are the basis for computing Mesa's yearly budget. Ann Doss describes the budget-making process: "I'll start in the spring. I meet with the director and say, 'Here is your attendance, your FTE's for the past year. How do you feel about your school? Do you think you're going to show the same progress? Do you feel that you're going to lose a lot of kids during the summer? How about Christmas vacation? Here's your enrollment picture for this year and here's what happened last year. Now, why don't you put down what you reasonably expect for the next year.'"

Ann compares the director's projection with her own calculations and checks these figures with a budget person from Children's World. "We then arrive at a mutual decision about what we can expect our school to do."

The next step is to project costs for the coming year. The first costs taken into account are the changing ones: building maintenance and repair, salaries (approximately 60 percent of the budget), and so on. Then there are the fixed costs: rent on the building and taxes, for instance. Finally, there are regional costs — which means Ann's salary. All of the centers contribute equally to her salary. "Regardless of whether it's a big center or a little center or an old center or a new center, I spend the same amount of time at each one." Below that budget line comes the final line, "which is the center's contribution to corporate overhead." In some centers, there is a deficit; in some, a profit. The profit is, by decision of the Children's World board of directors, "returned to the shareholders or reinvested in further expansion."

Problems and Changes Ann Doss feels very satisfied with her decision to sell to Children's World. She feels that she has been allowed to go on doing just what she was doing before, except that now she has the advantage of their business expertise and administrative counsel. By the same token, she gives her centers free rein. Each director does her own hiring, firing, and administering. Ann is there to help when needed. It is hard to remain an individual within a corporation, yet Helen Shelton feels Children's World has allowed her to be her own woman.

Finding effective directors for the centers has been one of Ann Doss's problems. She admits to having had some "disasters." It was difficult, she says, to find a person who could run an open-education program, a person who understood that in open education one has to be a "facilitator" rather than a traditional leader. "With Helen," Ann says, "this is her school. She is at ease with this kind of education and is so proud of it."

An open plan created other problems in the planning and scheduling of the program. Thelma Kingston, the music teacher, tells of one director's attempt to "shift all of the children from activity to activity every fifteen minutes." Now, under Helen, the staff has worked out a combination of free-choice and planned activities that works well.

Perhaps the biggest initial problem was the building itself. The noise level was staggering at first. That came mostly from the swimming pool at free-play time. Free play has now been rescheduled for afternoons. Some teachers complain about other aspects — the stone walkways and high open shelves are difficult to clean. The building could have become a monument to design. Some of the people who worked on the design hated seeing the kids and teachers get into the building and "mess it up." But the Mesa staff has now overcome that problem and everyone has accepted the fact that the perfect design isn't perfect — that it has to be changed continuously to keep it an effective environment for children.

For-profit day care is at its best when, in Helen Shelton's words, "you put your children and your staff first." Ann Doss adds, "I think that the greatest motivating force in our centers is our desire to do a good job for children." She concludes, "There will never be a big margin of profit in child care. You can invest in a mortgage and get a twelve percent return; whereas with child care, you are lucky if you make five percent. There has to be a commitment to children all the way down the line."

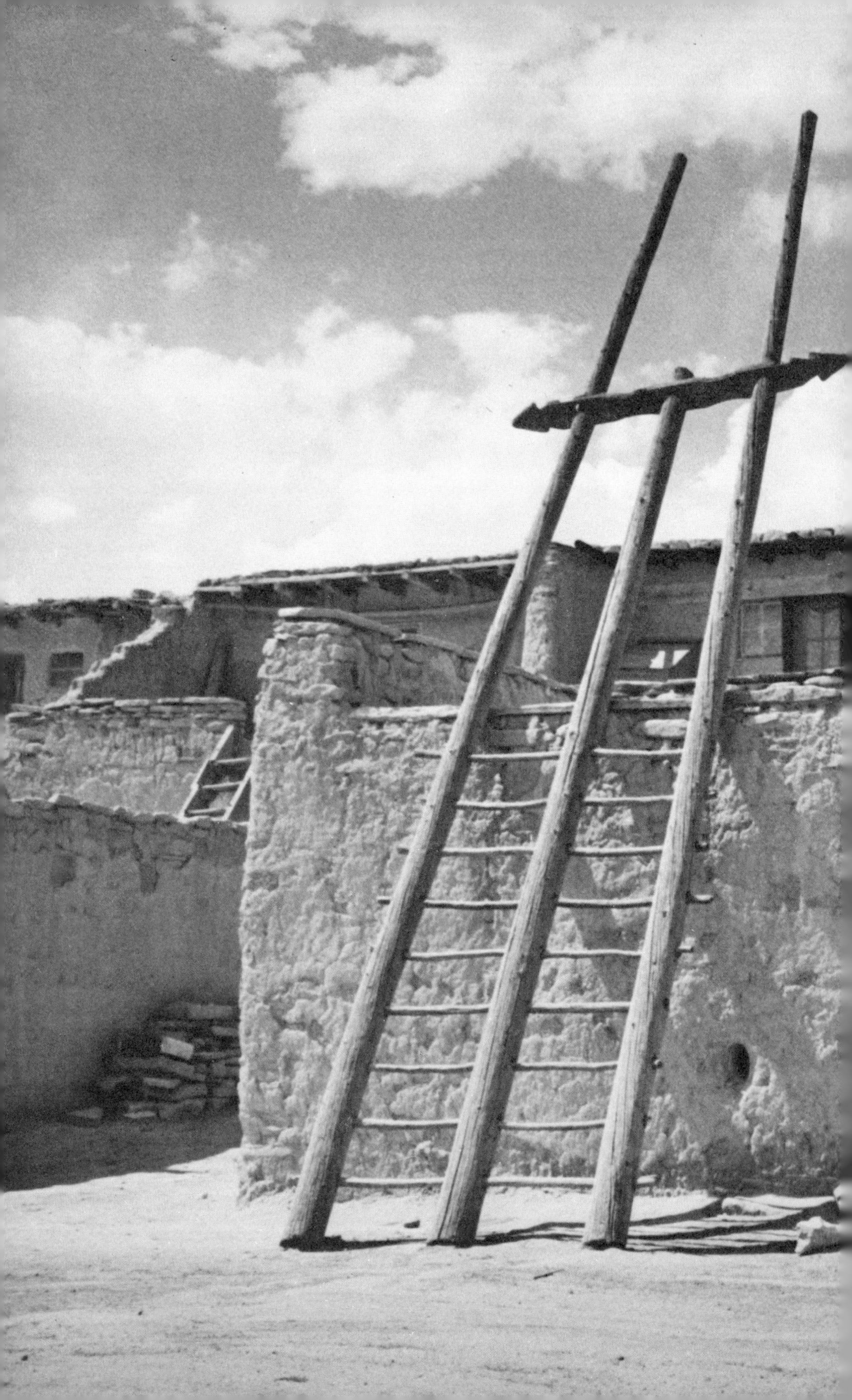

11
A Comprehensive Community-Based Program from Infancy through Preschool

Parent-Child Development Program
San Fidel, New Mexico

The Pueblo of Acoma stretches over miles of spectacular New Mexico scenery. Mountains, mesa, and desert have a scenic beauty about them that has been but little marred by encroaching modernization. The adobe churches and houses seem to grow organically out of the landscape. There's a feeling of timelessness about Acoma, but that is only a surface view. Inside some of those adobe houses, there are exciting and innovative kinds of child care that are responsive both to the needs of people living in the last quarter of the twentieth century and to their deep-rooted love of a cherished heritage.

Beginnings

Prior to 1974, there were no organized child care programs on the Pueblo of Acoma, but as early as 1971 the Bureau of Indian Affairs (BIA) made a commitment to encourage reservations to develop their own comprehensive programs of early-childhood education from infancy through the preschool years. BIA submitted to Congress a request for $10 million, and received the reduced amount of $600,000 to establish two pilot Parent-Child

Development Programs. All reservations were asked to develop proposals for child care programs, and from those submitted, the Pueblo of Acoma in New Mexico was selected as one of the two sites for the pilot comprehensive child care programs.

In preparing the proposal, a small planning group comprised of Acoma residents was established. They made a house-to-house survey throughout the reservation to determine the parents' needs for early childhood programs. Cyrus Chino, a member of the survey team, reports on the findings: "Most parents felt their children needed practice in some of the Anglo * ways and also in our Indian ways. The parents didn't want to lose the Indian culture; they wanted to pass it on to the next generation." The planning team for the Acoma child care services visited programs and invited Anglo experts to help them design their programs, but they were cautious and careful about accepting any advice that seemed to conflict with the basic wishes of the parents whose children would be involved. Cheryl Fairbanks sums up this experience: "We invited experts in and the older Indians brought in the old ways, and there was a meshing of both. You could say there was a coalition between some of the new ways and the old Acoma practices. We wanted to get good people to help us. We got mad about a lot of the consultants because they came and wanted to know about the 'Indians.' We really hired them for something else — for their knowledge of early-childhood practices."

The outcome of the surveys, visits, advice from consultants, and participation of older Acoma residents was the decision to offer parents a wide variety of child care options. The plan called for two day care centers, family day care programs, home-based child care, a resource center, and coordination of health services.

In February 1974, the work of setting up two day care centers began. Two Anglo consultant-trainers were hired. The director of the program and the caregiving staff were selected from Acoma residents. They all began to renovate two buildings. The site for one center was chosen in the town of Acomita; the other in McCartys.

When one sees the attractive child-oriented environments this team created for Acoma children, one finds it

---

* A southwestern term, "Anglo" refers to all people who are neither native American nor Hispanic.

very hard to imagine that they were built from scratch by the people who operate them today.

"We all became plumbers, electricians, carpenters, and toy-makers," says Sandra Simons, the consultant-trainer at Acomita. "Neither building was safe for children when we started," explains Lloyd Vicente, the director of the program, "and it took us about three months to get them into shape." Linda Chase, the consultant-trainer at McCartys, says, "It was neat that we had three months to do the buildings. It gave the teaching staff a chance to get to know each other, to really build a sense of community. When you are plastering, laying linoleum, and doing plumbing and electrical work together, you establish trust and good feelings, which are so important for a teaching community to work from. So when we finally got the kids, we knew each other and we were comfortable working together."

It was during this three-month period of building the day care centers that the new staff began to feel secure about their ability to provide good child care, and to get over initial feelings and misconceptions about what the program could offer to children. Hilda Aragon, a teacher, says, "At first I thought it would be something like babysitting, but when we started working on the center, I really got involved in it."

When the staff members were not working at renovating the two day care facilities, they met together at the community center to make materials and build equipment. From the very beginning the Acoma culture provided themes for the toys, books, and learning games. It was decided that when the housekeeping corners in the day care centers were set up, they would include cradle boards and a dancing area with native costumes and taped Acoma music. Linda Chase explains the role she and Sandra Simons played in the beginnings of the program: "Sandra and I presented ideas and the staff said yes or no. So it hasn't been like coming in and saying, 'This is the way you have to do day care,' but, rather, letting it evolve."

The weekend before the first center was scheduled to open, the staff held open house. Sandra Simons describes the occasion: "It was exciting. The parents came with their kids and we had food for everyone. We had the center set up just the way we wanted it. And the kids loved it! It was great for the teachers to watch the kids respond to the center." Despite the success of the open house, there was not an immediate rush of parents to enroll their children. Lloyd Vicente explains that this was not surprising, since Acoma parents are inclined to move cautiously, to wait and see. "Only about five children came to each center in the beginning," he says. "But with parents talking to each other, the word soon got about that we were doing a good job, and the enrollment started to go up."

Another factor that had an important part in the early stages of establishing the Acoma program was the support and confidence of the board of directors, composed of community people, which oversaw the entire project. Sandra says, "The board of directors trusted us and allowed us the time we needed — time to get kids into the program, time to let teachers grow, without coming in and saying, 'You're accountable on some performance level.' "

In addition to the care offered at the two day care centers, outreach services were launched to include family day care and home-based programs. Here, as with the centers, the primary objective was to build on the solid foundations of the child-rearing practices that already existed in the Acoma community. Cheryl Fairbanks says, "We tried to concentrate on what the mothers were already doing that was good, and then move from there." The family day care program was set up to provide care for children from infancy through two and a half years of age. From the very beginning, the program was viewed as going beyond caring for the physical needs of the child. The Acoma proposal called for "a setting for a continuing dialogue between parents and caregivers about good-quality child care . . . and an education program which will provide immediate applicable information on child care and development for family day care mothers." Training programs for family day care mothers were established as well as regularly scheduled home visits by staff members.

In keeping with the desire to offer comprehensive child care programs with options for parents, home-based services were offered to mothers who wished to have an educational program for their children in their own homes. Acoma selected the Verbal Interaction Project, designed by Phyllis Levenstein, of the State University of New York at Stony Brook, for its home-based program. Its emphasis is on stimulating verbal interaction between the child and the parent. Toy demonstrators visit the mother and child in the home and demonstrate activities for language development. Then the toys and books used by the demonstrators are given to the mother.

The home-based mothers, day care mothers, and day care center staff are all encouraged to use the Resource Center, which contains books, materials, play equipment, and activity cards. The center also has workshop facilities, where all those involved in the various programs attend meetings and training sessions. A health coordinator, whose principal job is to maintain health records on all children in the program and to refer families to appropriate health services, rounds out the picture of the services offered under the Acoma Parent-Child Development Program.

Comprehensive child care programs that involve families appear to be a coming thing. It seems an almost natural evolutionary process — a center is set up by people with specific, defined notions of child care, and the staff quickly makes the discovery that effective care interlocks with a host of other services. Responsive staffs reach out to encompass or make linkages with these services. From another direction, those responsible for funding are looking with increasing favor on those programs that are comprehensive in nature. With all of the approaches to this kind of inclusive care, there is the inherent danger that a community will become the recipient of a "transplant plan," which may not graft well in the new location. In fact, if the plan has few or no organic ties to the community, it may be rejected by the community "body." The beauty of the Acoma Parent-Child Development Program can be credited in large part to its having been built on a natural system of child care that was functioning informally in the community. The plan has capitalized on the strengths and skills of the people who were already taking care of young children. It has linked and extended these existing strengths through training and the sharing of experiences.

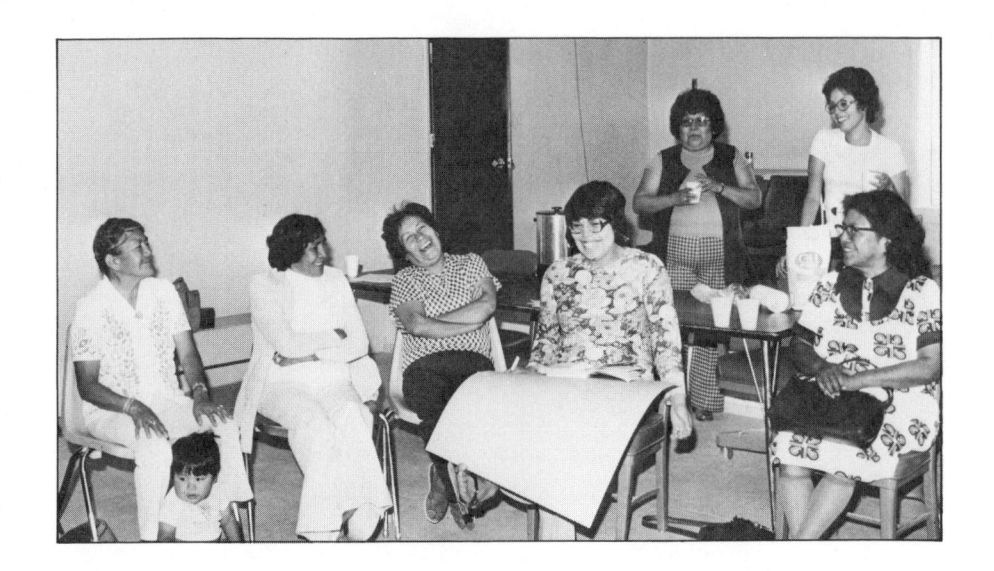

Goals

The Acoma comprehensive child development program has many specific goals for the children it serves, but there is one overarching goal — *positive self-image*. Linda Chase says, "Our primary goal is to provide positive experiences, which are going to build the kids' self-confidence. Preparation for school is a secondary goal. We are trying to provide the kids with a sense of independence, competence, self-worth, and to do so in a way that lets them retain a sense of their own culture." A teacher at the McCartys Day Care Center says, "It seems to me that if you build a child's self-confidence, you are doing the most to get him ready for school."

Lloyd Vicente explains that the central concern with the goal of positive self-image came from the findings of a survey conducted as a part of the original proposal for funding. This survey revealed that many Acoma children had a hard time with school because of low self-esteem. They were shy, and afraid of what was usually their first experience away from home and parents. It took over a year for most of the children to adjust to the new environment. Recognizing this problem, the day care staff has deliberately set about devising ways to build the children's self-esteem.

In one training session, Cheryl Fairbanks encouraged the family day care mothers to think about positive self-image. "Have you ever felt good about yourself," she asked, "and then someone said or did something to make you feel bad?"

Several of the women nodded in silence, and one

spoke up: "I cooked a delicious dinner for my family. I spent a long time on it, and I felt good about myself. But no one said anything about the dinner. They just ate it and didn't say anything. And then I felt bad." Another woman said, "I had that happen, too."

"Can you think about times when, without meaning to, you may have made a child feel bad?" Cheryl asked.

After several stories had been shared, Cheryl told the women how important it is to make children feel good. "Loving children affects the way they look and grow, and think and feel," she said.

Of the children in the day care centers, Linda Chase says, "We give them lots of hugs and kisses, and frequently call them by their names. We respect them and provide them with activities they can be successful at." Rebecca Lucario, a caregiver, says, "I think it gives the Indian child a better image of who he is if you use things from his culture. It gives him something he can relate to. When I was a child, we always learned about things that related to white people." From the outset, the Acoma culture has been incorporated into the learning. All of the teachers speak Acoma; traditional costumes, dances, music, games, stories, and foods are all a part of the daily curriculum. Acoma motifs are used in puzzles and learning toys. Acoma festivals and legends are a vital part of reading-readiness experiences.

Admissions Admissions criteria based on family need were established by the planning group before the day care centers opened. In reality, however, the centers operated on a first-come, first-served basis, with no fees charged to anyone. This relaxed situation worked until recently, but now enrollment has exceeded the maximum number of funded children, and admissions will be more structured.

Selecting Caregivers A board of directors composed of community people interviews and hires caregivers. "We are looking for responsible people who will be good with kids," says Lloyd. Linda, who went through the process of being interviewed and hired as a consultant-trainer for one of the day care centers, recalls, "When the board did the interviewing and hiring, the members had a very humanistic perspective in terms of the kinds of questions they asked. There wasn't any 'Have you had classes in this or classes in that?'"

The board of directors does have many questions designed to determine how prospective caregivers feel about children, what age groups they prefer to work with, their willingness to continue training, to attend meetings at night, to go out into the community, and their ability to speak Acoma. This does not mean that educational background is ignored. The two consultant-trainers are certified in early-childhood education, as is the teacher in charge of the home-based programs. But the central concern in the selection process is the teacher's attitude and willingness to learn. Working from this base, the teachers learn the more formalized teaching techniques on the job and in staff-training sessions. These selection criteria also apply to the support services of the program. Custodians, cooks, and bus drivers are all considered part of the teaching-learning process. Arlene Pasquale, a caregiver, explains, "Although we have different titles, we all do the same thing."

This approach has served the program well and has produced a group of caregivers who are sensitive to the needs of Acoma children and who are continually growing professionally. Linda Chase sums it up: "As the teachers went through training, some of them experienced incredible changes and growth. That is really what teaching and learning are all about. But the caring is what we were looking for in the beginning."

Grouping

Eighty-two children are served by the Acoma program. There are thirty-one children in the two day care centers, ranging in age from two and a half to four years. The children are grouped heterogeneously in a well-planned program that provides for the variety of ages and individual differences. The staff feels this mixed-age arrangement allows for a great deal of beneficial peer teaching and peer caregiving.

In the family day care services, there are thirty-five children ranging from infants to two-and-a-half-year-olds. Another sixteen children are served in the home-based program.

Space and Daily Schedule

Both of the day care centers are open Monday through Friday from 7:30 A.M. to 5:30 P.M. Daily schedules at the two centers are similar; Acomita will serve as an illustration.

The Acomita Day Care Center is located in a four-room

adobe house set back against a ridge of red rocks at the end of a small village. The four rooms are a visual treat. The entrance room is painted bright yellow with orange and yellow curtains. It has a two-story platform at one end for climbing and playing. Fat ropes are suspended from the ceiling for rope-climbing. This is also the block room, and there is a good supply of hand-sanded building blocks. The second room has a book corner with cushions, a science area, and space for dress-up and dancing. Mobiles made of colorful shapes with each child's name printed on them hang over the book corner and contribute to the festive air of this room. Feather wands, beads, and buffalo headdresses hang in the dancing area, where there is a record player. An aquarium and a parakeet enliven the science area. The third room serves as an art and dining area. The walls are decorated with Acoma pottery designs and pictures of native Americans. The fourth room is the kitchen.

The children who arrive early engage in free-choice activities until 9:00 A.M., when breakfast is served. After breakfast the staff sets up activities both inside and outside the building. Children are usually allowed to join whichever activity interests them. Some remain in the art room to paint, make collages or sponge prints, or do cutting and pasting. Others put on bright-colored plastic smocks and rush outside, where the water table is filled with green sudsy water. Another group joins one of the caregivers in the shade of the large, roofed sandbox, where they sing songs to guitar accompaniment. This brightly painted sandbox was made from wood donated by the local lumberyard and built by the staff. The children and caregivers made a field trip to collect fine yellow sand to fill it.

In the latter part of the morning, the children settle into a "quiet time," with puzzles, learning games, and picture books. Some of the older ones practice writing their names and others form a group around one of the caregivers to listen to a story.

At lunch time all of the children and caregivers gather for a family-style meal. The children serve themselves, handling the task of pouring their own milk and juice from small metal coffeepots with tight lids that make pouring easy and reduce spilling. Tacos, beans, rice, and fruit are favorites with the children. Often they have bread they bake themselves in the outdoor oven, which was built under the direction of Grandma Sanchez, the center's resident grandmother. As at breakfast, the children set up the tables and help with clean-up.

During nap time, the caregivers plan schedules, organize activities and trips, and share ideas.

Outside play usually follows nap time. The playground is well stocked with homemade equipment. Most of it has been locally scrounged. As one mother commented, "They put junk to work!" An old-fashioned wagon wheel has been made into a merry-go-round. The parents and staff have created a climbing hill that has a slide built into it. There are painted tires arranged for hopping games, old railroad ties for climbing, a big adobe oven, and a vegetable garden.

The children may come inside when they like and engage in free-choice activities. Often they dress up and do Acoma dances.

The day's schedule is varied by trips away from the center. The children are taken on visits to farms, sheep camps, the airport, the zoo, and lakes for swimming. The favorite trips for everyone are those to the village feast day celebrations.

Discipline

Discipline in the two Acoma day care centers is labeled "problem-solving." Caregivers try to help the children achieve self-control by talking through any antisocial and negative feelings. They help the young children to identify their own emotions and to deal with them in ways that don't hurt themselves or other people. Sandra Simons explains, "We're saying to the child that it is cool to have feelings, to be angry. But there are ways of acting out those feelings that aren't destructive or harmful. At the same time, we strongly reinforce the fact that we do care about each other and about ourselves."

The staff considers adult modeling an important aspect of discipline. They have worked on this approach in teacher-effectiveness courses. The staff has also involved parents, and several parent nights have been devoted to the discussion and sharing of ideas about discipline. Lois Waconda, who is director of the home-based program and who has a child in one of the day care centers, talks about her reactions as a mother to the center's approach: "At the beginning, when my child came home and said she was angry, I stepped back and said, 'Where did she learn that?' It was real parent education for me. It wasn't the teachers coming out and telling us. My kid and I, we thought it through."

"Respect" is a key word in the discipline approach — respect for each other, respect for older people. Grandma Sanchez is an important influence in the children's learning basic respect for all people.

Many of the parents freely admit that they were brought up with strict discipline and little or no discussion about feelings, and their initial tendency has been to treat their children in the same fashion. But these parents do recall a very different kind of approach used by their grandparents — an approach much closer to the one being used in the day care centers today. Lloyd Vicente says that the present approach is actually a return to the more traditional system. "I think we as Indian people have gone through stages. My grandparents used to get really angry if my mother scolded or spanked a child. They said, 'Talk to them. Don't spank them. What's the matter with you?' I think we're coming back to that traditional approach."

Parent Participation

Parents have been active from the very beginning of the Acoma Parent-Child Development Program. They remain so, and it is interesting to note that more than half of the board of directors, which oversees all aspects of the project, must be composed of parents. Important decision-making, involving hiring, firing, and the approval of training programs, is under the board's control. The Acoma program also provides training for parents in child development, and offers workshops in nutrition, prenatal care, and health.

There is a monthly meeting for family day care parents in which child-development practices are discussed. Lois Waconda reports on these sessions: "We try to find out from the family day care mothers what they want and then look for someone who knows about that subject, and we try to get that person to talk to us. If we can't, we study up on the subject ourselves." A family day care mother describes the understanding and sensitivity of the staff: "When they began to work with the day care mothers, they didn't come in and say they had all the answers. They concentrated on what the mothers were doing already and then opening it up to all kinds of other things."

The Acoma program offers parent-effectiveness training courses and distributes a monthly newsletter to all parents. The two day care centers hold periodic meetings and encourage frequent informal visits. The staffs of the centers feel especially close to parents who gave so much time and creative effort to renovating the buildings and producing the toys, games, books, and furnishings.

Many parents appreciate the advantage the program has for them as working parents, but they feel there is more. They all see other values for the child: independence, preparation for later schooling, learning to share and socialize. Ezilda Sanshu, a mother, praises the program: "It's preparing the child for what it's going to be like in continuing education. It was very hard for someone like me. I was born and raised here, and the only time I went away was when I went to elementary school. It was really hard, but this way I feel they are preparing the child."

Food

Good nutrition is an integral part of the Acoma program. There is a consulting nutritionist from the Indian Health Service who does menu-planning for the day care centers. She maintains a good relationship with the cooks at the centers because she is willing to plan meals around traditional foods.

To integrate nutrition into the daily life of the centers, the staff involves the children in a variety of cooking experiences, and each center has a vegetable garden. Jack Lucario, a caregiver at McCartys, works with the children in the garden. "Can you figure out why we cover these beet seeds with soil?" he asks four-year-old Jeremy. "So the birds won't get them," Jeremy answers. "Yes, and why else?" Jeremy can't think of another reason, so Jack says, "Stick your finger into the soil and tell me how it feels." Jeremy makes the discovery that the soil is damp and the best seeds will be protected from the hot sun.

This involvement with gardening has also helped the staff to introduce many new foods to the children. None of the children liked beets, says Sandra Simon, "but when we planted them and went to the garden and picked them, washed them, sliced them, and the kids were involved in the whole thing, they all ate beets."

Health The health coordinator of the Parent-Child Development Program oversees the health records of children in the day care centers, day care homes, and in the home-based programs. She visits both centers and the homes, and does referral services for children and their families. She also runs health workshops for parents and caregivers and maintains a community health resources directory.

All children must have a full medical examination before entering the day care centers. Screenings for ear and eye problems are done periodically in the centers. There is some hesitancy on the part of many Acoma parents about using the available medical and dental services. Lloyd Vicente explains, "I think the clinic is an intimidating place for many parents. That's why they hesitate to go." The children in the day care centers are taken on field trips to the medical and dental clinics to make them feel more comfortable in these strange settings. Lois Waconda works hard with the parents and family day care mothers to get them to take their children to the clinic.

Training Training is viewed as an essential and ongoing part of the Acoma child care services. Courses are offered twice a week through the All-Indian Pueblo Council by the University of New Mexico, and credit toward a college degree is granted. Staff members of the day care centers and parents involved in the family day care programs are encouraged to take these courses. Five staff members are currently enrolled.

The consultant-trainers of the two day care centers use the "Exploring Childhood" materials developed by Educational Development Corporation for staff training. In addition, there are weekly classes for curriculum development called "Programs for Children." The family day care

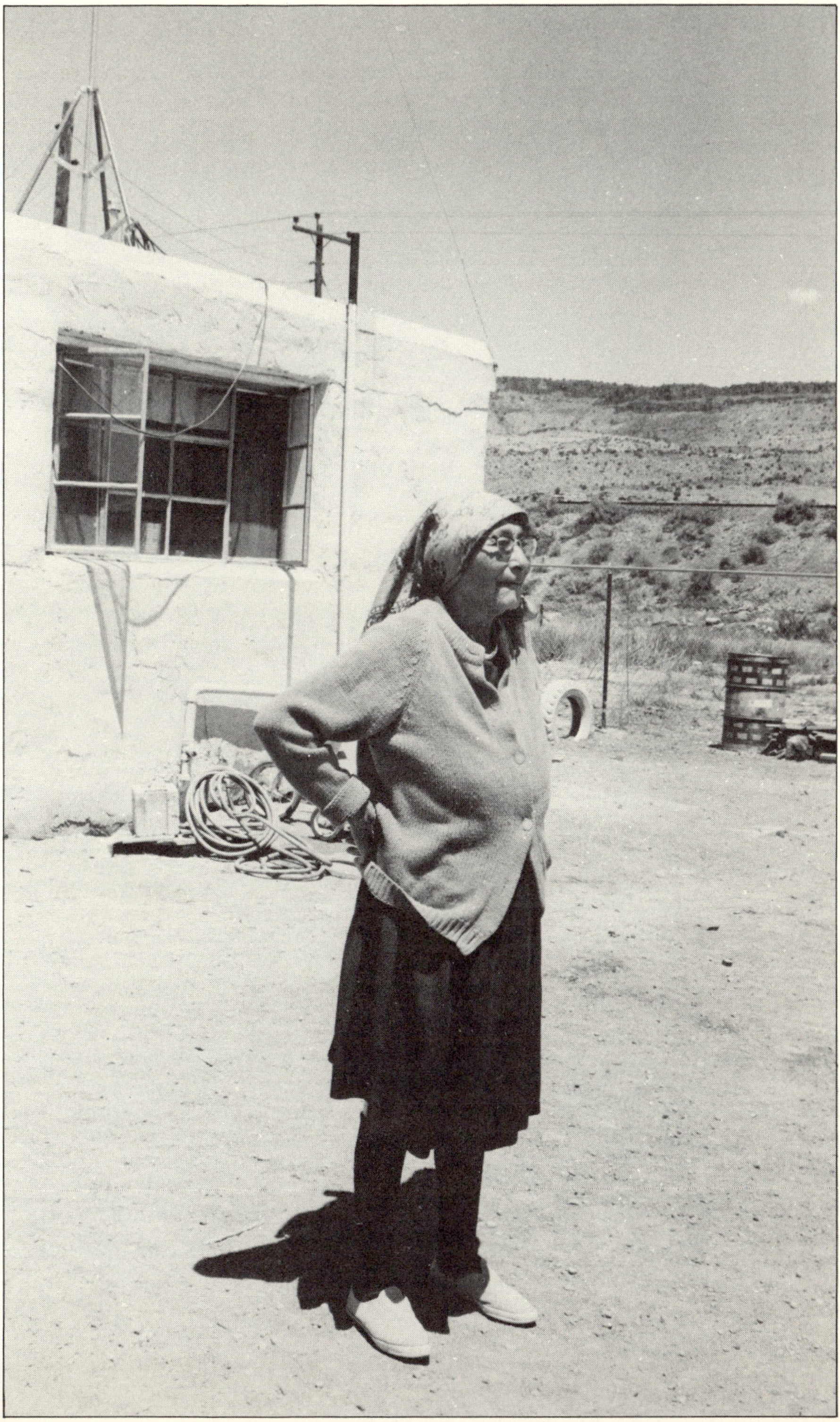

mothers have biweekly training sessions, which are focused around such topics as first aid, dental hygiene, language development, and how children learn.

While the formalized training constitutes an important part of the learning life of the Acoma programs, the informal, on-the-job training is perhaps the most valued. Sandra Simons says, "We are training all the time. We're modeling all the time." At the day care centers, nap time becomes caregiver-training time. All members of the staff talk enthusiastically about the great training value of the experience of working together to design and build the two centers. Rebecca Lucario says: "At first it was difficult for me. Toys were just toys and didn't have real educational value to me. It was difficult for me to think on a child's level. But I changed, and began to look from the child's view."

Grandma Sanchez is another person in the training process who provides a strong link to the Acoma culture. She is a good source for both staff and children, enriching and enlarging the learning process. In describing what she does, Grandma Sanchez says, "I teach about what was. I teach the language of the sun, the moon, and the stars."

Problems and Changes

The "wait and see" attitude of parents that characterized the first year of the Acoma Parent-Child Development Program has shifted to positive support and active participation. Both the day care centers and the home-based programs have become meaningful parts of the community, and have created a new sense of community pride in the things the parents have been able to do for their children. Parents have a new awareness of their role as educators. They are pleased to see their children learning the Acoma language and becoming involved in their cultural identity. The programs have also provided jobs in the community, and they are jobs that are respected and satisfying.

The two consultant-trainers (who are the only non-native Americans in the programs) have always viewed their role as the sharing of expertise and knowledge that would some day be no longer needed. The native Acoma staff has moved rapidly toward developing its own leadership, and one of the two consultants is ready to leave. But Cheryl Fairbanks, one of the original planners of the program, still sees additional training as the key to the continued success of the program. "We started out just to train the teachers, but then the cooks and the janitors didn't understand what we were trying to do. I feel that everyone, including the director and board of directors, needs to be in on the training."

Some problems persist. Each year the board of directors is subject to change when a new governor of the Acomas takes over, since part of the board is appointed by the governor. There is still a need for greater cooperation between health services and the child care programs. The Acoma Parent-Child Development Program is a pilot project dependent on the allocation of funds from sources over which the local community has very little control. But all of these seem manageable hurdles to a staff and a parent group that have built a remarkable program of child care in a short time. Their enthusiasm runs high, their success is visible, and at this point the program is firmly grounded in tribal support.

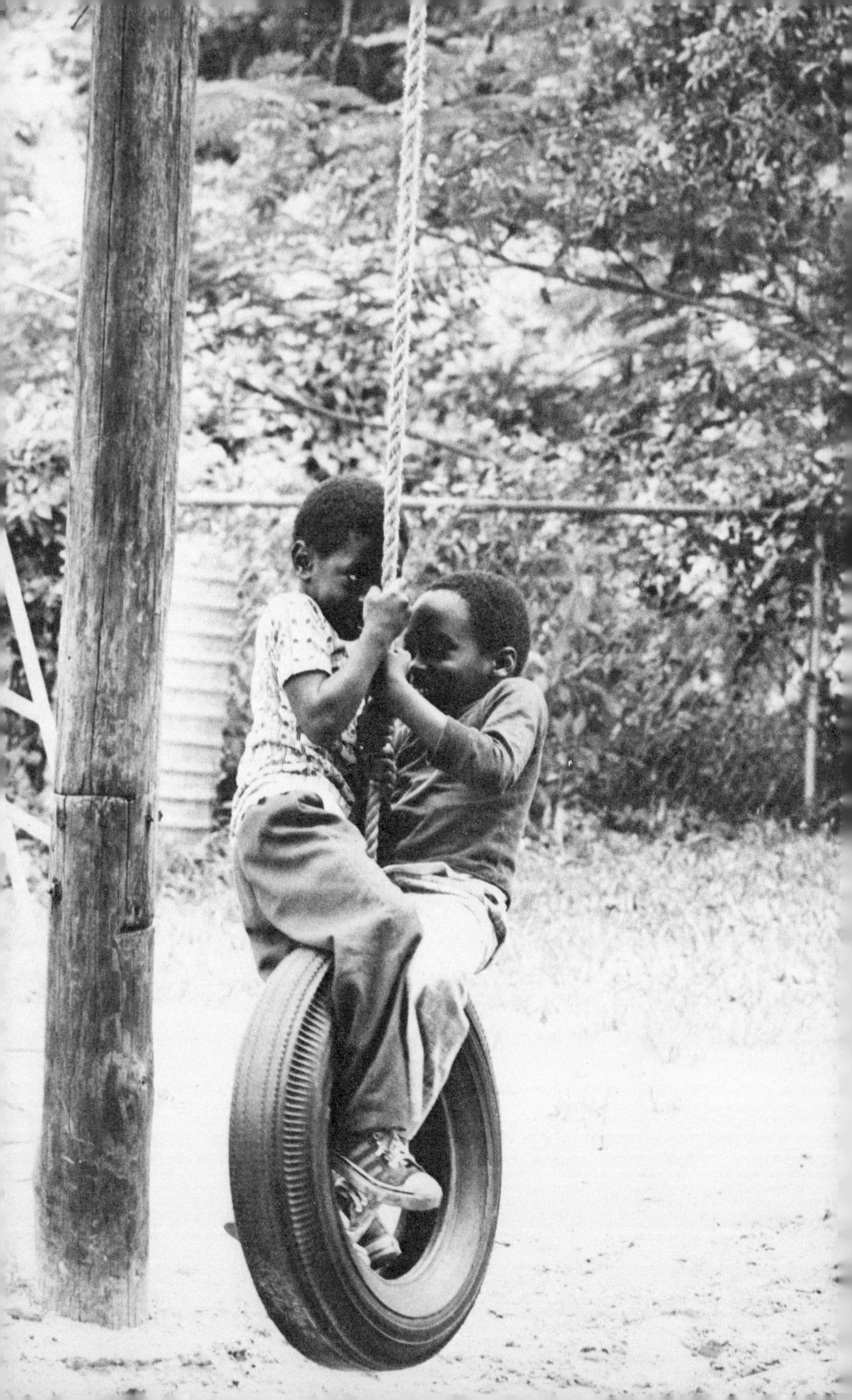

12
A Center in Transition

**Penn Nursery/Day Care Center
Frogmore, South Carolina**

Ten five-year-old children sit around a table waiting for their teacher to bring paper and crayons. One child starts chanting, "I feel good." Another joins in: "I feel good." Soon the whole group is chanting together, "I feel good. I feel good!" The children's radiant faces, their proud alert bodies, carry the same message. They do, indeed, look as though they feel very good.

These children are at the Penn Nursery/Day Care Center in Frogmore, on Saint Helena Island off the coast of South Carolina. Part of the reason they feel good today goes back a hundred years into the history of their homeland, an island of blacks who have been free for over a hundred years.

Like many others on Saint Helena Island, John Gadson, the current executive director of Penn Community Services, likes to tell about this history and about the history of Penn Center:

> There was a group of people working for the Union government who, when the Civil War started brewing, began to wonder what would happen in the South to the economic system when there was no more slave-master relationship. After the Union Army and Navy took the island without a fight, most of the slavemasters left their plantations, with a lot of blacks on them and a good cotton crop growing. The Union government paid wages to the slaves, and a whole new system of farming came out of it. It was called the Port Royal Experiment. At the end of the war,

the experiment ended and most of the white Northerners left. One person who stayed on, a Boston lady by the name of Laura Towne, started teaching. She communicated with the Quakers in Philadelphia and got them interested in her work. Someone in Philadelphia took three little one-room barracks and shipped them down to Frogmore. When they got here they were connected into a three-room school and named after William Penn. So that's where we get the Penn name, after William Penn, the lover of freedom.

From its very earliest days, Penn Center was committed to the idea of offering high-quality elementary schooling and vocational training to blacks. Its goal was expressed as "developing the hand, the heart, and the mind," and this continued to be the aim until 1948. At that time, Penn dropped its vocational training and elementary school and became a conference center. It was here that the major strategies of the civil rights movement were planned. Dr. Martin Luther King, Jr., and the Southern Christian Leadership Conference found Penn Center to be the ideal retreat for conferences.

"In the late nineteen sixties, Penn began conducting programs for leadership development," John Gadson continues. "These were people who came out of the civil rights movement, and the first question they asked was about Penn itself: 'What are you all talking about? You talk about black leadership and your chairman of the board and your director of programs are white.' When that question came up, it shook Penn pretty badly. Good people were being attacked — not the old racists anymore, but good Penn folks. The end of that was that the director resigned, and so did a large number of the white staff, and I came in after that. Of the five directors Penn has had, I'm the first black."

Penn Center's programs have changed with the change in leadership. The center still operates as a conference site, and it is an idyllic setting for that. Its grounds are spacious, with woods and lawns studded with ancient, moss-draped oak trees, interlaced with marshes and inlets of the sea. But other subjects are now also studied at Penn: economics, history, culture, land retention, land use, education, and child care.

Beginnings Child care for preschool children has a long history at Penn Center. One of the caregivers, Mrs. Corinne Brown, has been with the program since it began, twenty-eight years ago. "It started with interested parents who saw a need for a nursery school," she explains. "A lot of working parents were keeping their older children out of school to care for younger children. So, in nineteen fifty, we selected key people from each plantation [the island is divided into plantations rather than districts] and formed an organization. The parents were in complete control, and Penn Center was our sponsor." Penn provided a building, and the parents established a program. It was a full-day program to accommodate the hours of working parents, and was operated at the astonishing charge of only $2.00 per child per week.

Until three years ago, the day care program at Penn ran on a very informal and flexible basis, with Penn and the community group sharing the minimal expenses involved. Good custodial care and a strong emphasis on teacher-directed activities to prepare preschoolers for entrance into the public school system were the two main objectives. Because of increasing costs, problems of licensing, and more complicated bookkeeping procedures, the parent group asked Penn Center to take over the actual operation. This was also the time when government money was available for child care, and Penn Center was set up to receive funding and assume responsibility to the funding agencies.

Goals

John Gadson was interested in making the long-established custodial nursery program the best center in South Carolina. "We always had a good program," he says, "but we never had anybody who had a strong background and experience in child development." John felt a sense of mission in trying to develop a center of excellent quality. "If we didn't do it at Penn, no one else in South Carolina would for a long time," he predicted. In his search for a new director who would be knowledgeable in child development and capable of training local caregivers, John made contact with Gardenia White, who had spent many years in New York City working in early-childhood education and as a day care consultant. Gardenia was an inspired choice. She not only had the skills and years of experience, but she could readily relate to the local community since she was born and raised on Hilton Head Island, only a short distance away from Penn Center.

It is easy for a center that has been around for a long

time to become rigid, set in its ways, to resist growth. Even programs that are born out of tumultuous social change can become shadows of what they once were, stiff and lifeless sets of routines and practices. Penn Center has overcome this tendency, for today it is a center in transition. Many of the long-standing attitudes that characterize Penn are still in evidence. A sign in the center reads, "Give me a fish and I will eat today. Teach me to fish and I will eat for a lifetime." This expresses the pride in independence and the appreciation of learning that are at the core of Penn's purpose. But the center is also moving in new directions. Its goals are still strongly weighted toward preparing the children for school, but the younger teachers have other goals, too. Annie Lee Johnson, a teacher, says, "We try to help kids be aware of themselves as human beings, help them with social contacts with their peers and adults, help them in sharing, and help them develop skills."

Gardenia White talks about goals in relation to parents: "I haven't met any parents who haven't wanted the same goals for their children though they may go after them in different ways. A lot of parents say they want their children to learn to read and write, but they also say, 'I want them to grow up to be good people.' That's what everybody wants. They all want their children to grow up to be able to think for themselves, make their own decisions, be capable of dealing with society, and therefore they must learn academic skills and how to think. It's all of that combined."

Funding The Penn Nursery accepts children from two to five years of age and has a total enrollment of forty-four. Some are children of fee-paying parents; others are funded by the state Department of Social Services. To qualify for free care, a family must be on welfare or have an income low enough to meet the eligibility requirements of the department. Both John Gadson and Gardenia White dislike having the funding of poor people tied into the welfare system. "I have seen the most antisocial people coming out of departments of social services," John says. "They are departments that seem to make people bad. They develop a mental set that is hurting us, because we are forced in our minds to think of children in two groups — those on welfare and those who aren't." Gardenia adds, "It starts out negative at the top of the welfare system and comes all the way down like that to the children. It is assumed that the money is going to be spent the wrong way and that you are wasting it on people."

Both John and Gardenia feel that problems with child care are more pervasive than just the economics of funding. They feel that centers should be accountable, but they deeply resent the funding sources' interference with the day-to-day operation of their center. Gardenia sees the role of the state funding agency as "making sure that the place is safe, healthy, and that the people who operate it are kind people, who are not going to endanger the lives of children. I think they should make sure the money is properly spent, but these requirements are enough. I don't think that anybody in the Department of Social Services knows much about child-rearing. They never come in and ask what you are doing and why you are doing it. They say what you must do, or they are going to withdraw your funds." John adds, "We do need minimum suggestions and helpful rules to follow which allow people freedom to set up their center in their own way as long as they meet minimum requirements. Don't try to make two centers operate the same way — that's what they try to do."

Daily Schedule

The daily program at the Penn Nursery/Day Care Center begins in the early morning when a school bus circles the island, picking up children. The teachers take turns riding the bus with the children. At 8:00 A.M., a hot breakfast is served. Then the children are all grouped together for a "sharing time," during which they sing or listen to a story. After sharing time they are divided into single-age groups, and work on a variety of teacher-directed activities. Most of the activities are aimed at reading and math readiness, but this time is broken up with art and dancing, and, on some days, trips. There is a midmorning snack followed by outside play, which usually lasts until lunch time.

There is an initial shyness about the children in the Penn Nursery that may be typical of rural children in general. But this shyness in no way seems to hinder a genuine friendliness on their part, that is, they are shy but not afraid. One parent credits much of this lack of fear to the social benefits the children derive from the center. They change, the parent says, from children who stand back with their thumbs in their mouths to children who are eager to try new things. That change is very much in evidence. When a teacher puts on a record for dancing, the new children may not join in, while the children who have been at Penn for a while quickly step in and dance.

At lunch the children are served a nutritionally balanced meal and are encouraged to try a variety of foods. The caregivers have lunch with the children and eat the same food. One of the caregivers describes the food: "We take basic food and regionalize it. We have chicken, peas, rice, and vegetables, and make sure the children eat a balanced meal." The children also help in setting up and cleaning up after lunch. Nap time follows lunch. When the children awake from their naps they help with the task of storing all the cots. This transition time, like others observed when there was a shift from one activity to another, is handled in a distinctive style by the children. They organize themselves with one of their favorite song games, giving the activity an orderly flow. "One, two, buckle my shoe," they sing while rearranging furniture for a new activity. "Face to face, and back to back," they chant, turning to and from each other as they pass the cots along for storage.

After the transition from nap time the children go outside to the playground, or they may have a large-group activity inside. Some parents begin picking up their children around 3:00 P.M., and the bus leaves at that time.

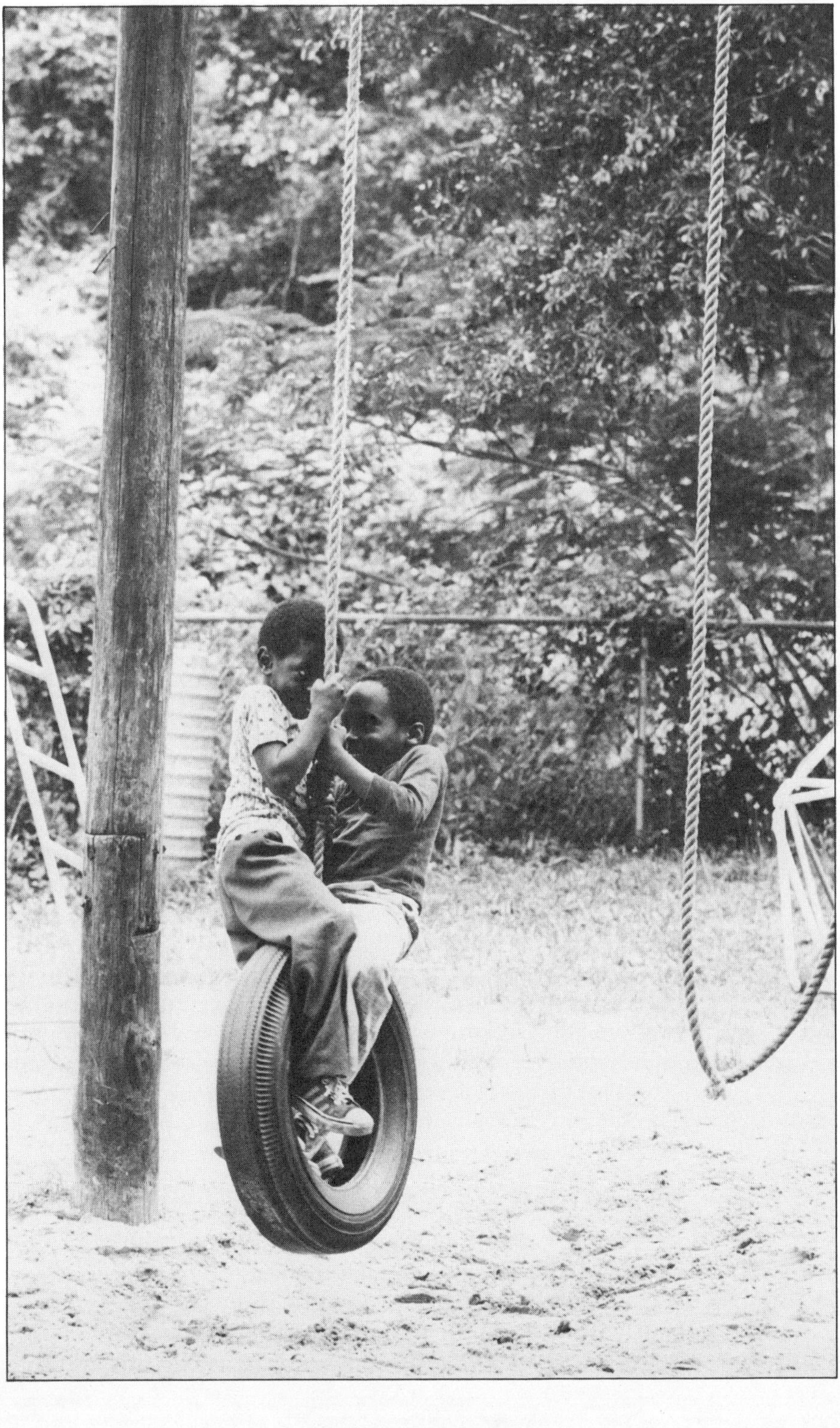

However, the nursery remains open until 5:00, for parents with longer working hours.

Health The curriculum includes health, safety, and nutrition activities as well as the activities to stimulate reading and math readiness. A nurse from the Department of Social Services checks the children twice a month, and there is an excellent health station on the Penn Center campus, which offers free medical services to children and parents.

Parent Participation Historically, there has always been an involved parent group connected with the Penn Nursery/Day Care Center. One parent, Norma Johnson, speaks of the high regard the parents have for the center: "The people at Penn have the reputation of knowing how to produce kids who play and learn to the best of their abilities and who will learn quicker because their minds have been motivated so that they want to learn." There is still a vital and active group of parents who support the center, but with the recently enlarged group that has resulted from welfare funding, there is less involvement. Irvina Faulkner, another parent, says, "I wish more parents were involved, because I really believe that all parents want more than custodial care for their children. They might not know how to say it, but I think they want it. They know it makes a difference, coming here. I've seen it in my own children." The staff speaks about the shyness of some parents and their reluctance to communicate with the center. However, there is evidence that this is breaking down. The Penn staff has a particular approach to working through such problems. John Gadson explains: "In developing people and working with people, it takes time — step-by-step kind of time. My philosophy with all of Penn is that you don't have to hurry to get there. It may take you two days if you do the right things with people, but it is better to take the two days than to do it quick and wrong."

The active parent group meets once a month, and supports Penn Nursery in several ways. It helps the staff define goals for the children, and contributes both time and money. The parents engage in many fund-raising activities: fish fries, raffles, dances, and dinners. They contribute time and talent, also. The fathers built most of the playground equipment; mothers made curtains for the entire school; parents volunteer for field trips with the children. Each year the parents of the graduating children give a special gift to the nursery — the water fountain, heavy-duty playground equipment, a new refrigerator, and other items were such gifts. The day after graduation, one parent, Jean Smalls, brought a cake for the staff and said, "Thank you for the wonderful job you've done with my child." Another parent remarked, "After my child graduates, I am going to give a month's day care money for another child. I will never forget this place."

Staff training is one of the new directions in which the Penn Nursery/Day Care Center is moving. Gardenia White was hired to help bring about change. Effecting change is one of the most difficult tasks of any trainer, but Gardenia has managed to begin this process without alienating people. By forming good personal relationships with the staff, and not setting herself up as an indisputable authority, she keeps channels of communication open. She does demonstration teaching and asks the teachers to observe her and discuss honestly what they like and dislike about what she does. In this way they are learning from each other. The results are impressive and there are no feelings of resistance in the staff relationships.

Training

Gardenia functions as both director and trainer. Sometimes she finds the dual role a complicated one. "As director I would say to a teacher, 'You can't let anything interfere with the running of the day care center' but as a trainer I know that things do interfere. To be a trainer you really must have these people as friends and be available to give counseling." To Gardenia, training ties in very closely with hiring. She is looking for teachers who are committed to child care. She is also looking for people who enjoy being with children. The teachers always seem to be having fun with the children at Penn, whether it's Mrs. Brown, making a clay figure for a child to play with, or Miss Johnson, down on the floor, demonstrating how to do the crab walk.

Gardenia says, "I also like to hire people who have some political awareness, people who are willing to do creative things for their own growth and development." She holds training sessions once a week and is available to the staff every day as a resource person. In her training program, she hopes to move the staff toward more child-initiated activities, "to get them to feel more loose and let children do more things on their own."

Problems and Changes

The small size of the white clapboard house the nursery occupies presents a problem. Some of the caregivers regard it as their biggest problem. They have experimented with permanent learning areas and found that they were difficult to maintain. This is particularly true at nap time, when almost all of the floor space is needed. However, they have not abandoned the idea of learning centers. A teacher explains, "If there is something you want to do on a particular day, you create a center for what you want when you want it." In this way the staff has gained some flexibility within the limited space.

The Penn Nursery/Day Care Center staff members regard the guidelines that come with funding as another problem. A teacher says, "I think that it is impossible for us to meet them and still do a good job. It is impossible because we get so frustrated and upset with the restrictions that we can't be the kind of models we should be for the children. The Department of Social Services representative came to visit our center last week. She came during nap time and made an awful comment about how dirty the kitchen floor was. It *is* dirty during nap time, which comes right after lunch. We use every bit of available floor space for the cots, and we always wait until after the naps to clean the kitchen floor so that we don't disturb the children. If she came after nap time she would never find the floor dirty. But she really made people angry, because she didn't even ask why, or anything. Those are the kinds of things we deal with every week. It makes for frustration and anger, and it goes on and on." The director of the center says, "If I could have the perfect child care center, I would give the power to the director, staff, and parents. And I would like to be able to call on consultants to help with management or other problems we might have, but when their job is finished, they should withdraw."

The Penn Nursery/Day Care Center is a center in the process of change. The staff still responds to the parent body's desire to prepare their children for successful entry into school, but new emphases are apparent; they reflect the changing attitudes of parents and the impact of the training program conducted by the new director. And they call for a much more closely knit relationship among staff, children, and parents, who, according to Gardenia White, all want the same thing: "To see good things happening with kids."

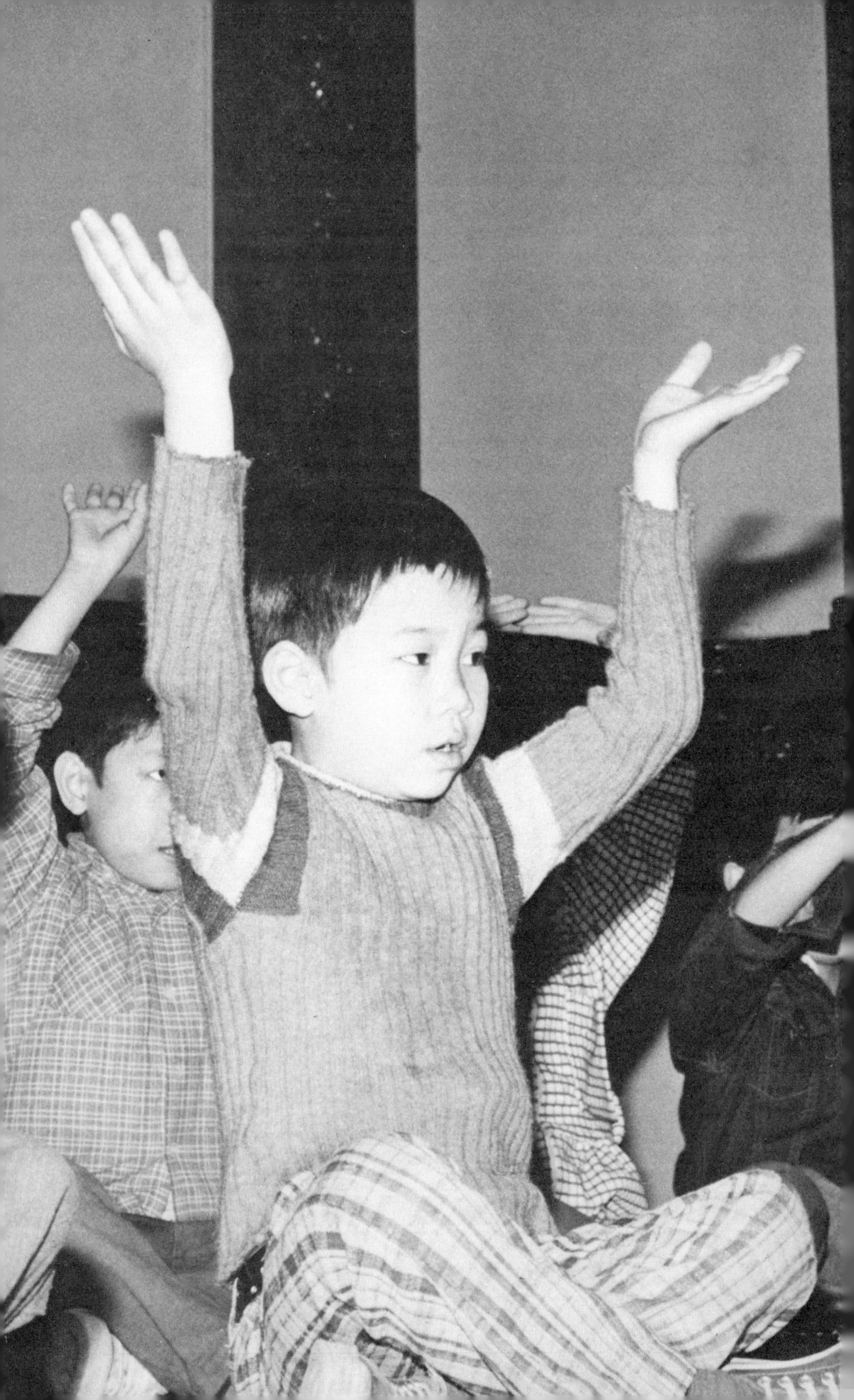

13
An After-School Program

Chinatown Planning Council
P.S. 42
New York, New York

New York City's Chinatown has been spreading; on one side it has moved into Little Italy, on the other it is edging into the predominantly Jewish Lower East Side. This latter area is almost like a tableau of recent immigration history. The street floors of the buildings contain Jewish stores marked by Yiddish signs. But above the stores, often in crowded tenement apartments, live Chinese people. Most of them have immigrated under the recently liberalized immigration laws. They left Hong Kong and Taiwan and came to America with a single purpose: to better themselves economically.

However, once the Chinese were settled in America, they found things weren't as easy as they appeared from afar, particularly if they had children. Child care was scarce. Without relatives to help them, some parents had to quit working, thus reducing the family's income. This was deeply disturbing to them because it thwarted their desire to achieve upward mobility, which demanded of them hard work. Single parents sometimes had to go on welfare, a step they were reluctant to take. The parents of school-age children often resorted to the "latch-key child" system; the child came home to an empty apartment after school and spent the afternoon watching television. Living space for most of these families was so limited that there was often no room for children to play or do homework. The parents were fearful of leaving the children at home alone, but even more afraid to allow them to play in local parks, which are well known as hangouts for winos, drug addicts and pushers, prostitutes, and street gangs.

Beginnings Just at the time this new influx of Chinese immigrants began, in the late 1960s, Allen Cohen took the job of director of the Chinatown Planning Council. Up to that time, the council, a social-service agency, had been mistrusted and disliked by the Chinese community. Al Cohen was determined to turn things around. He wanted to know what the Chinese themselves wanted and needed. A neighborhood survey told him that child care was one of their highest priorities. His first efforts were directed toward establishing full day care programs for preschool children, but he found himself entangled in the city's massive bureaucracy. He was sent from one agency to another to get the necessary clearances and licensing, until he finally felt "like a Ping-Pong ball." Eventually, Al wound up a day care political activist, and a realist.

At this point he shifted his efforts to the creation of an after-school program. Ironically, the process was relatively simple. He petitioned the Agency for Child Development (ACD), the New York City agency through which federal child care money is funneled, and it agreed to fund one after-school program provided that the Chinatown Planning Council could secure space and 1 percent of the operating budget. The matching money was obtained from the first group the council asked, the Chinese Garment Manufacturers Association, a major Chinatown employer. Al reasoned that a public school building would be the most practical setting for an after-school program. He approached a local principal with the idea, and the principal agreed to the use of his school. An official from ACD asked Al when he expected to start. Optimistic because of his apparent success, Al boasted, "Give me the money and I'll start tomorrow." But the official's response was, "You can't — it takes months." Both claims were exaggerated. Four weeks after Al's initial discussions with ACD, in July 1969, the first of the Chinatown Planning Council's after-school programs opened.

Al Cohen describes the beginnings: "We had a trickle of kids coming in, and we were a little bit anxious at first. The Chinatown Planning Council was not well known at that time, we didn't have a good reputation, and a lot of people were afraid of us. We made a sign to advertise the program, and the kids dribbled in over the summer. By September we had a full enrollment of thirty-five kids."

The following year the program was expanded to 100 children. The Chinese parents had waited to see what kind of program it would be, but when the word spread through the community that it was, indeed, a good program, they began to apply in large numbers. The council decided not to expand the initial program further, but, instead, to set up similar programs in other public schools. This process of setting up new programs has continued, and today there are seven such programs, serving from 75 to 100 children each. The programs are filled predominantly with Chinese children, although there are a few Hispanic and Italian children.

The After-School Program at P.S. 42 opened in February 1971. It did not have a smooth beginning. Because P.S. 42 was an old building, ACD refused to accept it as a suitable location, citing such violations as inadequate lighting. "I said to ACD," Al recalls, " 'What do you mean, we can't start a program there? Eight hundred kids are in that school and the Board of Education says it's safe and sanitary.' We pushed them on it and they finally let us use the space, with the agreement that the school would redo the lights."

There were also problems of space within the school. The principal said there was no room for an office for the director of the program. Even though the Chinatown Planning Council was paying rent for the use of the building, the director had to improvise an office in the corridor. The attitude of the principal reflected the misgivings that many school people feel about community-based organizations. Karen Lieu, director of the After-School Program at P.S. 42, says, "We had a lot of resistance because of the strike they had in the public schools several years ago. We represent the community, so I would say that much of the resistance came from the teachers and their union. They felt that it was community versus school. Maybe they thought we were trying to take their jobs. Maybe they thought that if we had the power of the parents behind us, we would go against some of the things they wanted to do."

Relationships with the public schools have eased over the years. Allen Cohen cautions, "You start out with a very narrow base, using public school space. You use only this room and that room, and you have to pay for everything. But eventually you work out the relationships."

Goals It is conceivable that these after-school programs could have turned out to be merely extensions of school, giving the children a nine-hour school day rather than a six-hour one. Or they could have been prolonged study halls, providing a place where the children could do their homework with assistance and supervision. Or they could have been repositories for children whose purposes were seen in negative terms rather than positive terms: "keeping the kids off the streets," "keeping the kids out of trouble," or "keeping the kids from flunking in school." Some after-school programs have fallen into this pattern.

The After-School Program at P.S. 42 is none of those things. And the primary secret of its success is that it is staffed entirely by Orientals. It is they who decided the directions and shape of their own programs. At P.S. 42 they have defined their goals as giving the children the skills they need to succeed in America while understanding and respecting their own Chinese background. Yee So Leong, a parent, explains that the duality of cultures can be difficult for the children. "The old culture is like a piece of stone under the ground. The children don't see it and they don't feel it at first, and they have a hard time picking it up. But my husband and I still feel that our children should learn about our culture."

Many teachers in the program define their goal as helping the children adjust to the new society, which involves not only improving their knowledge of language and culture, but also encouraging the positive self-image of the young children, who are usually afraid and very shy. Their major goal for the older children is independence. All of this is in keeping with the charge to staff in the *After-School Handbook*, which states, "The primary goal is to provide secure, warm, healthy, and creative experiences for the children of working parents."

Admissions Following the first year of the After-School Program, when children had to be recruited, there have been more applicants than there are places for them.

To conform to the funding regulations, the program has

income-eligibility requirements for the families. Parent interviews to determine eligibility are handled by Gilna Yuen, who speaks Chinese, Spanish, and English. After she processes the applications, final approval is made by ACD.

The irony in this situation is that the combined income of families in which both parents work sometimes shoots above the eligibility level, and the children are no longer eligible for the after-school care. However, such care is essential if the mother is to continue working. Gilna remarks, "The parents say, 'Right when we are trying to better ourselves, then we are told we can't keep our child in the center.' " In addition to those children from families who meet the income-eligibility requirements, the After-School Program attempts to include children who are in "emergency situations," or are having "crises in the family."

After the criteria are met, admission is on a first-come, first-served basis. Waiting lists are discouraged. When the enrollment reaches 100, interviews are stopped until there is an opening.

Because of the special needs of the children and parents in this program, more than usual care is given to the selection of staff. The funding agency requires that group teachers have state certification in early-childhood or elementary education. Karen Lieu says she is looking for something more than written qualifications. "I sit down and talk with the candidates to see what they are like as people. I want to know, are they really concerned with children? Do they have ideas of their own?" The assistant teachers do not need to be certified, and are usually young Chinese college students who care a great deal about children.

Selecting Caregivers

Since the major difficulties these children (and their parents) face are language and culture adjustments, the After-School staff is expected to be able to handle this aspect of the program as well as the educational requirements. Al Cohen states, "It is a policy of the Chinatown Planning Council to hire bilingual people." A few of the teachers speak Spanish as well as Chinese and English.

There are very few male teachers at P.S. 42 during the regular school day, but the After-School Program has a policy of having one male caregiver in each classroom. Karen Lieu feels this is especially important because "many of the children's fathers work in New Jersey and Pennsylvania in restaurants and come home only once a week."

Parent relationships are another deep concern in the selection of staff. The ability to speak to the Chinese parents and their children in their own language, to communicate with them in a nonthreatening and supportive fashion, is essential to the close ties the After-School Program seeks to establish with the families. Lois Chin, a teacher, expresses this special sensitivity this way: "Just being Chinese, I am more sensitive. I won't put them [the children and parents] down, and I can say that when I was a child, the same things happened to me." A three-month probationary period allows the director time to observe and determine how well new staff members fulfill this important function.

Grouping In the P.S. 42 After-School Program there are 105 children, ranging in age from six to twelve years. They are divided into five groups of twenty to twenty-five children each. In providing a program that is appropriate to both the age and developmental level of individual children, the staff has found that multiage grouping works best for them. There is usually a three-year age span in each group, and placement in a group is made on the basis of social and language skills.

In the space of a few minutes, the time it takes for the after-school children to have a snack in the downstairs all-purpose room, their school-day classrooms are transformed by their after-school teachers. Bookcases are pushed out from against the wall to create room dividers, materials are brought out from storage cabinets, and the After-School Program begins.

    The children who are learning a second language don't just sit down to workbooks or language lab lessons. They make their own books. In faltering English at first, they dictate stories. They illustrate these stories and they make up their own comprehension questions for other readers to answer. One child devised a clever system. Whenever he didn't understand a word or phrase, he drew a picture of a puzzled-looking bear with a question mark above his head. This bear became the subject of his stories. And as his eagerness to communicate led him speeding into rapid comprehension of English, his stories grew more complex and detailed.

Daily Schedule

The youngest children, the six- and seven-year-olds, learn about reading from such things as a picture recipe for making dough. In the course of following the directions for the dough recipe, they count tablespoons and they measure cups of flour. The eight- and nine-year-olds learn still more about weighing and measuring by using milk cartons filled with water to answer their teacher's questions written on index cards. The emphasis on learning skills through experience is maintained even with the oldest children, who are ten and eleven years old. In planning a camping trip, they gathered information they needed on animals, first aid, insects, weather detection, and food preparation. Then they made quiz cards, which were used as a question-and-answer game that two children can play together. In addition, they wrote reports containing the information they learned, and dittoed and collated them into a collection called *Handbook for Camping*. They also wrote essays on their expectations of the trip. One of the children, Tsz-wan, wrote:

> I expect to learn about the wild and free animals who live in nature. I expect to learn how to pet the squirrels without startling them. I expect to learn how and what makes the plants in the world grow. I expect to learn about nature because I want to see and feel all the beautiful things that are not manmade and not a thing that takes energy and pollutes the world. I expect to learn how to fish in a real pond or lake.

Mei-mei expected this:

> In the camping trip, I expect to learn how to cook better, how to fish and to do better housework because I won't have anyone to fold my blankets and other things like that in the camping house. I also want to try to take care of myself.

The teachers of the seven- and eight-year-olds devised an ingenious way to teach about the traditions of the Easter holiday. They had the children make their own dyes for eggs. The children crushed, smelled, and tasted beets, spinach, blueberries, and coffee beans. They cooked these foods in water to make dyes. Several of the foods were not familiar to the Chinese children, so in the course of making Easter eggs, they also learned something about the American diet.

The After-School Program can be divided into four components. One is the experiential learning of skills; the others are homework, sports, and Chinese activities. The children in each group have some part of their afternoon schedule devoted to each of these components, with the exception of the Chinese activities. These are scheduled only once or twice a week instead of every day. Andy Mai teaches classical Chinese dance to all the age groups once a week. With intermingled joy and concentration, the children watch Andy's every movement, and then mime him boldly and imaginatively.

Sports seem to be a favorite part of the program. The hockey games are enthusiastically played and wildly cheered by the children. Unlike most bleak public school yards in New York City, the outdoor space at P.S. 42 is decorated with bright murals, completed during one summer by the children in the After-School Program. Each has a distinctive style. The youngest group decorated theirs with colorful foot- and hand-prints. The oldest group designed a painting of the playground after studying perspective with their teacher, who is also an architectural student. One of the other murals depicts Picasso-like drawings — on trips to the Metropolitan Museum of Art the children had become attracted by Picasso's work.

Discipline

When the younger children first come to the After-School Program, there are seldom any discipline problems. They tend to be very shy, quiet, and passive. Lucy Wong, teacher of the youngest group, says, "We rarely have to raise our voices. The biggest problem is getting the children to speak up. They are afraid to speak and afraid to express themselves. If someone takes something from them, or if another child hits them, they are afraid and they don't say anything. We try to draw them out and say that it's all right; that they can tell us and we will find a way of working it out. As the year goes on and they see it is not threatening to voice their feelings, and that it does not have negative consequences, they feel free to talk about what goes on at school and what goes on at home."

The teachers relate this shyness to both the strict discipline the children are apt to experience at home and to their adjustment to a new culture. The public school teachers, according to Lois Chin, don't attempt to teach the children to express their feelings. She says, "The children are very disciplined at home, and I think most teachers stereotype the Chinese — assume they are always quiet and submissive. It starts in the home and just goes on in the school."

As some of the older children become frustrated with school, they have no outlets, no avenues for redress. The After-School Program tries to fill this lack by providing the children with a place to let off steam, to work through some of their frustrations with a staff that is sensitive to their problems and supportive of their special needs. Lois Chin, who teaches eight-, nine-, and ten-year-olds, explains: "If they don't function well in the regular school, they take it out on us when they come down in the afternoon. The teachers in the public school punish and embarrass the kids — make them stand in a garbage can or hold a cup over their heads. My approach is to talk to them, calm them down. But sometimes when they've had a very bad day, they just freak out in the afternoon. I try to balance the morning with the afternoon." This approach works well. Those children who are often troublemakers during the school day surprise their regular teachers by being cooperative and industrious in the After-School Program. Aside from the explosions following a rough day in school, discipline problems in the After-School Program are far less frequent than in the regular school. Karen Lieu reports that some of the schoolteachers have begun trying the reasoning approach used in the After-School Program to deal with discipline problems.

In the After-School Program the teachers involve the children in a lot of problem-solving and discussion as well as decision-making about what should be done when individual problems arise. They also communicate with the parents and try to get them to interact with their children in this way. It seems to work.

Parent Participation   The After-School Program provides parents with a feeling of security about their children. Of almost equal importance to them is that the children receive help with their homework from bilingual teachers who are friendly to parents. As the parents have become more involved with the program, they have come to appreciate other aspects of the curriculum.

From the beginning, the director of the Chinatown Planning Council has stressed the key role he feels parents must play in maintaining an effective center. Says Al Cohen, "The first thing we have to do is involve parents in the program, if it is going to survive. We say to them, 'This is your center and we want you to become involved. We want you to sit in on the hiring of staff and we want you to help decide what to have in the program, and to review any policy changes.'" Al, however, admits that this ideal involvement has been a slow process, but in many ways it has been fulfilled over the years. Today he can state, "We are the backbone of any demonstration in the city where day care is the issue. I can turn out two thousand parents within two days on this issue because it means so much to them."

Karen Lieu explains why the parents have become involved with the After-School Program while shying away from the regular school. "Most of the parents couldn't speak English. They were afraid to come to the school building. But we tried to make them feel a part of the After-School Program, to make them feel they had a right to voice their opinions." To bring this about, the After-School staff had the advantage of speaking the parents'

Chinese dialects. They also made the first overtures to the parents, with home visits and invitations to visit the program. They provided translation services for the parents and offered help with bills and medical problems.

Once a child is accepted into the program, a parent is required to pick up the child personally at the end of the day. David Lee, a teacher, says, "Even though it is sometimes only a matter of our saying hello and good-bye to the parents, just to see them and recognize them is beneficial. We want them to know that we are concerned and want to share things with them." Apparently it works. Yee So Leong describes the relationship: "It's very comfortable. The teachers are very close with the parents, and they do spend extra time with the children." Steven Lee, another parent, says, "I only came here two years ago. My wife and kids didn't speak English. Now the kids get help after school with homework and speak good English. The kids catch up very fast. I don't have to worry so much at home. This day care center is the most important thing to the Chinese community."

Many parents speak of the nice balance the After-School Program provides between American and Chinese culture. Steven Lee says, "I want my children to have a bit of the American and a bit of the Chinese, and I think the center has a good balance between the cultures." Another parent remarks, "English is important and I feel you have to change a little bit to fit this country; but I still love and feel strongly about the Chinese culture. It's not the language so much; it's the ideas, such as helping each other."

While the Chinese parents have developed a close warm relationship with the program's staff and are active in the Parents Advisory Committee, most of them are still hesitant about voicing opinions about the curriculum. Lois Chin explains: "The parents have such respect for the teachers and feel we are such professionals that they think whatever we do is fine. Even if I told them something outrageous, they might not disagree with me." Despite this reluctance on the part of the parents to speak out on curriculum matters, the teachers are well aware that the parents favor a strong emphasis on academic subjects. Al Cohen says, "I think if the parents had their way, we would do the education bit the entire time. But we say the kids need to have music and art, recreation and exercise. We want to develop their bodies as well as their minds. They don't fight us, and the longer they're in the program, the more tolerant they are." Karen Lieu says, "It's funny, when ACD gives the program a thousand dollars and you ask the parents about a trip with the kids, they say they want to spend it on books. They will pay any amount as long as it's for books or educational supplies."

Food

The staff makes sure that the children have fruit, meat, bread, and milk each day. They also use cooking activities as part of the school program and in this way introduce the children to good nutrition and a wide variety of foods. In keeping with the Chinatown Planning Council's policy of community development, food is often ordered from neighborhood restaurants run by parents. "This way, buying food from them, we are helping the parents and they are helping the program, and that way they will also put a lot of meat in for the children," says Karen.

Health

Although health care was not part of the original program, the staff does include health education in the curriculum. It also cooperates with the Chinatown Health Clinic, which runs screenings and diagnostic tests for the children.

Funding

The ACD funds for the After-School Program are a composite of 75 percent federal, 12.5 percent state, and 12.5 percent city monies. The estimated unit cost per school-age child is $45 a week. The program is limited to families who meet the income-eligibility requirements, but most of the neighborhood families have incomes low enough to qualify. Some minimal income is produced through fund-raising at bazaars and social functions. The parents are not solicited for funds, but are encouraged to give time and talents for program activities.

Training

Teachers in the program are required to have a bachelor's degree in early-childhood or elementary education, with state certification. However, each classroom has an assistant teacher who does not have to meet these requirements. This allows the After-School Program to employ young assistant teachers who have special training in art, architecture, physical education, and music. The director of the program has a master's degree in early-childhood and elementary education.

The core staff of the program provides an intensive period of orientation for new teachers and assistant teachers when they join the center. Weekly staff meetings are all considered training sessions. Workshops on special subjects are held throughout the year. These are generally given by a teacher with a specialty to share. As Lois Chin explains, "Each of us has a special field, and is strong in it." These workshops have included such themes as children's literature, music, art, sports, first aid, racism and sexism, and teacher attitudes.

The staff is young, well trained, and eager to continue the process of learning. Lucy Wong expresses her feelings as a member of the group: "I think that our staff is unique. We are a close-knit group and that helps with the free flow of ideas. We feel free to share."

Problems and Changes

Despite its rapid growth and popularity in the Chinese community, the program still faces the problems that beset it in the beginning, though they are less severe. The continuous influx of Chinese immigrants results in a constant renewal of the language and adjustment problems. But the staff is more experienced, and there is a growing base of community support from those who have preceded the new arrivals.

An old cultural problem related to sexism persists within the Chinese community and spills over into the After-School Program. Karen Lieu explains: "The old Chinese valued the son more than the daughter. It is still a problem. For instance, the parents are very hesitant about letting their children go swimming. They will sign a permission slip for their daughter, but when it comes to the son, they may not sign." The After-School staff, through its sensitive handling of the parents, shows its respect for these attitudes, but at the same time it tries to help parents move toward new understanding about sex roles.

Space in the public school system is also a lingering problem. Al Cohen says, "Even though we are renting space and paying the custodian, we can't have fingerpainting, we can't have a lot of messy activities, because the custodian gets upset." But the relationship has improved, especially with those custodians who receive extra money for taking care of the After-School Program. The director of the program, who was first relegated to a temporary office in the corridor, has now moved to a well-lighted, attractive room that is large enough to serve, as well, as a family center for parents of children in the program.

There are incipient problems with the teachers' union, the United Federation of Teachers, which eyes the After-School Program with a degree of distrust. Some of these feelings stem from the position taken by the Chinatown Planning Council in recent union strikes. The union has also denounced the After-School Program for not paying union scale for positions that are called "teacher." There is real concern on the part of the After-School staff that, with the shrinking job market for teachers, the UFT may soon try to take over its programs. The staff will strongly resist any such move because it is firmly committed to an attitude described by Karen Lieu: "Day care is unique, and very different from public school. I think it should stay in the hands of the local community group." David Lee adds, "If it were incorporated into the public school system, it would lose its individuality. It needs to be kept separate. The more freedom day care has, the better it can work with children and their families."

The public school teachers' attitudes about the After-School Program and the dual use of their classrooms have undergone significant changes. Karen recalls the problems when the program was initiated: "Starting the program, I was very emotional. And I used to cry a lot, but not anymore. We just go on doing what we think we should, and a lot of the public school teachers now appreciate what we're doing. In the beginning, the teachers complained about many things — that the classrooms were left dirty, that the kids were taking things. They didn't realize they were talking about the same kids they were teaching in the day school. It was always *your* children and not *our* children." Today the concern is much more in terms of *our* children. Many of the public school teachers have good rapport with the After-School staff. They discuss the problems they have in common and share anecdotal records about the children. Often there are specific referrals from the public school teachers, who have come to appreciate the After-School Program as a support for children.

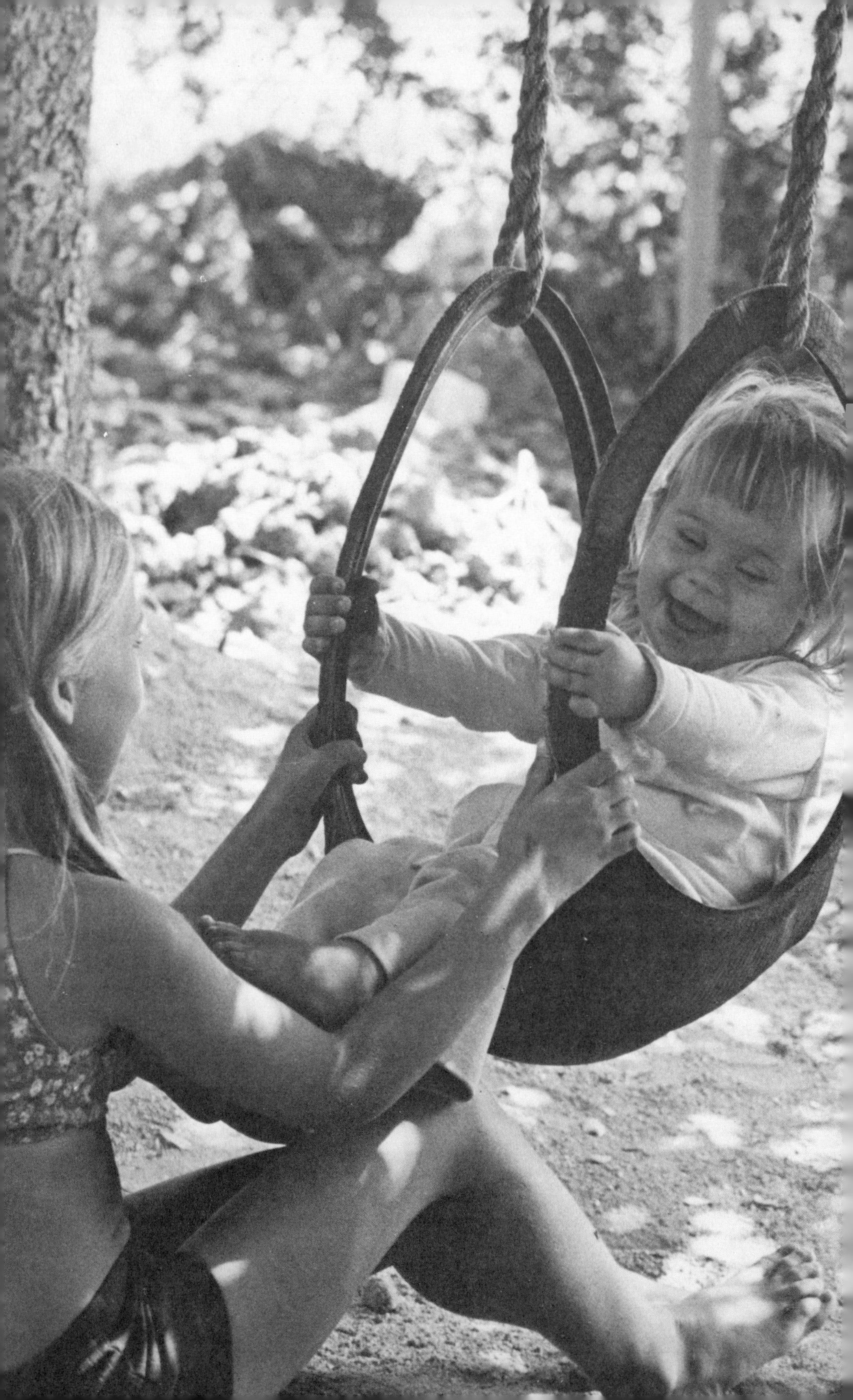

14
Family Day Care

Pasadena, California

Family day care is the care of a child in another person's home. It is the most commonly used kind of child care; estimates indicate that as many as 75 percent of all children in day care are in family day care. Both the image and the reality of this type of child care in America are somewhat dismal. As one family day care mother herself put it, it is an image "of a harassed woman with six screaming children caged in an upside-down playpen." Family day care has been branded as "children's parking lots" by New York Congresswoman Shirley Chisholm. It is seen as children kept in front of a television set; as women being exploited to take care of children for less than adequate pay; and as the multiplication of the injustices and problems of being a mother. The image is so bad that one family day care mother said that she didn't advertise that she was a day care mother because of all the bad publicity she'd heard. "Depending on whom I'm talking to," another day care mother stated, "I often say that I have a nursery school in my home."

But family day care can have another side. It can offer parents a "home away from home" for their children. It can offer them a choice in the kind of child care they want. It can provide an extended family for children. Or it can offer truly individualized child-rearing, as June Sale of Pacific Oaks College, a Pasadena-based college of education, says. And it is economically feasible because it doesn't require massive funding.

This kind of positive child care exists in many family day care homes in Pasadena. There is Liz Wilson's home, where the children call her "Mother Liz" and her husband "Daddy Herb." Going into their home, one would probably find Mr. Wilson sitting in his armchair after work, giving a bottle to a baby; later he takes two of the older children with him to gather the eggs in the chicken house, to pitch hay to the horses and goat, and to have fun riding in a wheelbarrow.

The same kind of family feeling exists at Amparo Gomez's home. She and her husband eat breakfast with the children when they arrive, often sharing tortillas with them. The children call them "Abuela" and "Abuelo," the Spanish for "Grandmother" and "Grandfather," and the children's parents feel that they, too, are part of the Gomez family.

Debbie Sakach, another family day care mother, affectionately helps a young child swing alone for the first time, then quietly sorts out the facts in a dispute between two three-year-olds over whose turn it is to ride the tricycle, or talks about a five-year-old's fingerpainting with him. Her home feels like home. Debbie's teen-age son works alongside the younger day care children as he pieces together a new bicycle for himself, but stops to help set up the plastic swimming pool when it is time for the children to swim.

In all of these homes, family day care mothers see themselves as warm and caring mothers to the children. And they also see themselves as professionals. As Liz Wilson says, "It used to be that you were a baby sitter and that was all anybody thought about it or allowed you to think about it. But I feel that now we are making it a profession. You know, we have to go to school, we take classes, we study, we read books until one or two o'clock in the morning, trying to find out what is best for kids."

Teaching goes on all the time in these homes in Pasadena, but it is done while the family day care mother maintains the feeling of a home. At her dining room table, Amparo Gomez gets into a discussion about "what is two" after reading a book to Marco, three years old. Liz Wilson uses her dining room table to play a game she made up to teach the children colors. And at Debbie Sakach's house, one child's finding a lizard in the swimming pool becomes a learning experience for everyone. The children try to figure out where to house the lizard, reasoning that it would jump out of a small box. Debbie's thirteen-year-old son remembers an aquarium he has upstairs and runs to get it. The children then tackle the problem of what to feed the lizard. A final problem erupts between two sisters. The older one, who caught the lizard, won't give her younger sister a turn holding it. "Try to solve the problem between the two of you," Debbie suggests. A few minutes later, the girls come back with the solution: "Jody can be the first one to hold the lizard tomorrow," the older sister says. "Is that all right with you, Jody?" Debbie asks. And when she hears that it is, she tacks up a note: "Jody will hold the lizard first tomorrow."

The teaching that occurs in these family day care homes is both preplanned, as in the making of games, and incidental, as in the episode with the lizard. It is meant to broaden the children's experience. The children are taken on trips. The local librarian comes to read to them. And, in some homes, special teachers are brought in to teach such things as painting and dancing.

In many instances, when child care becomes overly professional, it loses its close ties to parents, becoming less responsive to their needs. This has not happened in most of these Pasadena family day care homes. Pasadena has been able to develop a unique form of family day care. And the question must be asked: How has this been possible?

June Sale feels that Pasadena is a community small enough to have its people be accountable to each other. Phyllis Lauritzen, who runs a program for training prospective family day care mothers, feels that a great deal of credit is due to a group called the Consortium. The Consortium, organized by the Planning Council of United Way, meets once a month. Among its members are many of the local leaders in child care, and others in all the fields related to child care — medicine, health, education, and family day care mothers. "We are all trying to relay what the needs of children are," Phyllis Lauritzen says. "And sometimes it's difficult. Maybe you see the need and nobody else does. You have to keep hammering away at it. But because the Consortium does have a lot of people who are knowledgeable and who are leaders, we can do it."

Perhaps the major factor in the uniqueness of Pasadena's child care is an organization of the family day care mothers themselves. It is called WATCH, an acronym for "Women Attentive to Children's Happiness." In 1971, Pacific Oaks College conducted a study of family day care. At the end of the study, there was a meeting of the twenty-two women who had participated. One of these women, Amparo Gomez, said, "I feel so good, seeing all these women together and knowing that there are other people just like me. Why don't we form something, like a union?" Staff members at Pacific Oaks wisely pulled back, offering help when needed, but not taking over the new organization. From that beginning, WATCH has grown to over forty members.

The goals of WATCH are:

— to help in the rearing of happy, well-adjusted children by providing a choice of environments;

— to establish close communication between the natural family and the day care family;

— to promote education of the community and family day care personnel;

— to raise the image of family day care.

During the first few years, WATCH experienced the growing pains that can occur when many different people try to come together as a group. The organization had to undergo shuffling and reshuffling, until it developed its distinctive form and leadership. But there was also the joy felt by the members in being able to share concerns, to bring questions to the group, and to benefit from each other's experience. At the present time, they are bringing in outside volunteer speakers to their once-a-month evening meetings. The topics for these meetings have included "Talking With Parents," "Messing Around and Feeling Good About It," and "It's Terrible Tax Time." Attendance at all meetings can earn the day care mother credit at Pacific Oaks College or a Family Day Care Certificate. WATCH now maintains a toy supply for lending. WATCH members have developed a buddy system. If one member is feeling tired or at the end of her rope, she has someone to call to talk things over with. She can even take her children to the other person's house and share the care of the children. Or, with her buddy, she can arrange time off for herself.

Another benefit of WATCH is a monthly newsletter called *WATCH Windup,* which features a lead article about some aspect of child care, information about legislative issues, as well as many practical ideas.

In addition to WATCH, Pasadena now has another program that benefits family day care. Under CETA (the Comprehensive Employment Training Act), prospective family day care mothers can be trained and helped in becoming licensed while receiving a stipend. In a six-month program run by Phyllis Lauritzen and Doris Byrd, the prospective day care mothers visit, and eventually have placements in, established day care homes. They meet community people who will be resources for them in the future. And they make equipment for their own homes: blocks from milk cartons, stools and tables from industrial paper tubes, flannel boards and blackboards. They also make small block accessories from wooden dowels, and dolls and animals from scraps of material. One ingenious idea is using people who have been convicted of minor crimes and sentenced to render service jobs to repay society; they now build furniture for the day care homes. The same spirit seen in the family day care homes exists in this training program. The participants share experiences. One mother's comment about her own child's difficulty in learning to talk led to a heated discussion about how children learn. Another mother's statement about her child's eating habits initiated a forum on nutrition.

Pasadena is not a day care utopia. All of these achievements have taken long, arduous hours of work, particularly volunteer work. The mothers volunteer their time to attend WATCH meetings and to make that organization work. June Sale and Yolanda Torres, also from Pacific Oaks, volunteer their time to consult with WATCH members. Phyllis Lauritzen volunteers far beyond her allotted paid time to make her training program function effectively. There is much more work than there is money to pay for it. But the people do plunge in and do the work, reaping the benefits of better care for children.

Debbie Sakach — A Group Family Day Care Home

Debbie Sakach's home at first glance looks like just that — a home, perhaps with several neighborhood children who have come over to play. It takes only a few minutes to see that it is far more; that this is a family day care program in which a great deal of thought has been given to how the rooms are furnished, what activities are offered, even how the children are spoken to. However, the presence of a program in no way diminishes the comfortable feeling of the home.

Beginnings Debbie came to family day care as the mother of four children, two of them preschoolers. There were three reasons that led her to seek work in child care: she had acquired a large house with lots of space; her mother, who lives near Debbie, had lost her teaching job; and Debbie herself wanted to earn extra money so that she could improve her new home. She applied for a day care license, and obtained it within six weeks.

In order to become licensed, they had to comply with minimal requirements: the yard was fenced; knives and detergents were put away safely; space was provided for ten children; the family had tuberculosis tests. Debbie and her mother were fingerprinted. A member of the Department of Social Services paid an initial visit, and arrangements were made for inspections every six months thereafter.

Preparing for the licensing became a family project. Debbie's husband put in the fence; she and her mother fixed up the house and yard. Even though she didn't have the license yet, Debbie decided to take care of a child and use the money to buy sand and other things she would need.

Once Debbie decided to go into day care, she sought out others who were working in the field. "I talked to every day care mother I knew of and I asked each of them how they handled this and how they handled that, because there was no book to read. I got a variety of opinions and I learned from their good as well as their bad experiences."

Once licensed, Debbie began to get referrals from the Department of Social Services. She was also permitted to advertise in local papers. Family day care allows the licensed caregiver the right to accept or reject children. The licensing agency does, however, specify the number of children and the ages that may be accepted. Debbie has what is known as a group family day care license; the age range is set at three to eight years, and the total number of children is limited to ten. Since her two preschool-age children were at home and would be part of the group, she began by choosing children who were approximately their ages. "I added one child at a time until I reached my capacity. I had to grow with it, because I'd never done this before."

> In California, grandparents live far away. The kids don't have the true sense of family we had.
>
> — Debbie Sakach

Goals

Much of California is populated with people who come from other parts of the country; people who have left their home towns and moved away from their family ties. Debbie Sakach and her husband grew up in Ohio, and though her mother lives nearby, she is very aware of what it means to live far away from grandparents, aunts, uncles, and cousins.

"My personal goal," says Debbie, "is to provide a home substitute for children whose mothers are working." She wants her home to feel like an old-fashioned place where everyone becomes very attached to one another; a home that is "large enough to have fun and small enough to be a family." Her general goals for the children are the same as those for her own children: to grow well, to learn to live with each other. She therefore puts a great deal of emphasis on helping children become able to solve the problems that arise between them. Her specific goals for each child are based on what she learns from the child's parents. She asks the parents what they want for their child and then she tries to provide it.

Admissions

It is through her admissions procedures that Debbie first finds out about the parents' goals. She has developed a set of questions that help her get to know a family quickly. She asks the parents to describe their child and to tell her what they hope to find in a day care home. She looks for parents who, she feels, will fit into the kind of family she has and who want what she has to offer. If the parents' expectations diverge widely from her approach and attitudes, she advises them to go elsewhere.

The interview takes place in Debbie's home, with the child present. "I think most mothers can tell if they want their child to be in your home," Debbie says. "Selecting a child care home is like buying a house; you finally see the one you want." When a child is accepted, there is a two-week trial period, after which both Debbie and the parents decide whether to continue.

Whenever possible, Debbie likes to introduce the children into her home gradually. Constance Jordan, the mother of two children, reports, "I started leaving the kids with her on an hourly basis while I went to job interviews. They got used to the situation, to the other kids, and to the procedures. At first I just left them in the mornings. Then later I left them for lunch and picked them up in time for their naps. After that, I left them through their naps. When it came time for me to actually start work full time, they were ready."

Selecting Caregivers Debbie's group family day care license requires that she have people to aid in her program. She started out by having her mother help her, but when her mother took another job, Debbie had to find additional help. She turned to part-time college students who, she found, were good as long as she was present and helping. She now has a college student assist her three mornings a week during the summer, and in the afternoons during the winter. But the college student is not experienced enough to take over her group when she has to be away. So she found a mother who wanted part-time work. She says that mothers already "have developed skills by raising their own children," and that she feels good about leaving the children with them. As she selects children, so she selects helpers who will fit comfortably into her family and with her way of doing things. And, again as with children, she allows the helpers to be themselves. "I show them my way of doing things, but I don't expect them to do it just my way."

Grouping Initially, Debbie grouped children around her own three- and five-year-olds, but as happens in a family, the age groups gradually expanded. Now she has children from three to eight years old. She has found that "usually the children will stay within their own interest groups, but they cross over a lot. If they feel insecure, they may want to play with someone who is younger. If they are feeling really bold, they may want to play with someone who is older."

The parents particularly like the broad age range. Penny Hutchenson says, "My daughter has experiences with younger and older children. She is an only child and wouldn't otherwise be able to do this."

Debbie has recently admitted a child with Down's Syndrome. Her presence in the group seems to bring out the most positive aspects of interage grouping. The children

Family Day Care

enjoy her; they like to bring her a bottle or toys. Debbie has helped the other children see that this child should do things for herself. The children watch with pride as she practices walking and swinging by herself.

The summer and winter programs do vary with the size of the group. In the summer, Debbie has her full complement of ten children every day; during the winter she has about half the group in the morning, and the rest — the older ones — after school.

Space and Daily Schedule

The day care children in Debbie's program have the use of her front yard, her fenced-in back yard, and the bottom floor of her house. The upstairs is off limits for all but her own four children. In this way, she manages the tricky task of bringing other children into her family. Her own children can go upstairs to their rooms to be alone; there they keep the possessions they don't want to share. Because they do have their own toys and their place, Debbie feels that her children more readily accept the other children into their home and family.

Debbie's day as a family day care mother begins at breakfast. While she organizes her own family for the day, children and parents begin to arrive. There is not the usual doorbell or knock to announce their arrival — they just walk right into the house and talk with Debbie as she cooks breakfast. "It's their home," says Debbie. "Having them walk right in makes it a little more homey for the parents and children."

Debbie's husband is very much a part of the family day care home. He sees the children every morning at arrival time. Because his office is only a few blocks away, he sometimes joins the group for lunch and tries to be home before the children leave. The single mothers in the group feel that this day care father relationship, however limited, is especially important for their children.

In the morning the children have a combination of free-play and planned activities in the fenced back yard. The picnic table is often set up for such activities as finger-painting. Some children choose the tire swing; some climb into the treehouse; others go to the sandbox. The younger children often choose wheel toys and ride on the patio and down the driveway. On hot days, Debbie's two teen-age boys set up a bright yellow slippery-slide. The children change into bathing suits and run down the slide, spray hoses, and splash in the plastic wading pool.

The vacant lot next door is often not vacant. It is where the children go to explore and try out their homemade butterfly nets. Debbie uses not only the immediate home surroundings, but introduces the children to the community through trips. A few of the places included in her long list of trips are the local zoo and firehouse, museums and libraries, pony rides, and even a tour of McDonald's.

During the school year, Debbie has arranged for people in the community to help broaden her program. Last year, a college student came in to teach tumbling. She has taken advantage of a library service offering story-readers to groups of six or more children twice a month; the children can also borrow books from the library.

In family day care homes there is often equipment to be repaired and heavy yard work and painting to be done. Debbie sees service and repair people as adjuncts to her program. She has searched for people who like children and who are eager to respond to the children's many questions about their jobs.

The children usually have lunch outside in the yard. On cold or rainy days, Debbie arranges a winter picnic on a large sheet in front of the fireplace, with fireplace-toasted marshmallows for dessert.

The children are divided into two groups at rest time: nappers and non-nappers. The nappers sleep on floor mats in the large dining room. The non-nappers can either choose a toy or game from a container labeled "Quiet-Time Activities" on the toy and materials shelves, or they can play quietly outside in the yard. As the younger children wake up they join the older ones in activities.

The house begins to fill with parents between 5:00 and 5:30. One child leads a parent to the climbing frame to show how high she can climb; another proudly shows off a new fingerpainting. This is also a time for Debbie to share the highlights of each child's day with the parents. "I insist on three to five minutes of each parent's time at the end of the day," says Debbie. "Parents need to know what their children did that day and to become re-acquainted with them. If I sense a parent is really in a hurry, then we fit in three minutes on a walk to their car. I don't let anyone get away until I talk to them."

In disciplining children Debbie also maintains a comfortable, familylike approach. She perceives the admission process as an important factor. "I try to select children who will go well together. Since I am bringing children into my home, I want them to be children who can get along." That probably contributes to her having few discipline problems. The selection process extends through the first two weeks of child care, allowing both Debbie and the parents a chance to confirm or revise their initial impressions.

Discipline

Debbie considers discipline problems that do arise as something to be shared with parents. When one of the children suddenly started hitting, she tried offering him more physical activities. And she discussed the problem with the child's mother. Together, they tried to figure out what was wrong, but nothing seemed clear until it occurred to them that it might be that the mother had a new job and was spending less time with the child. When the mother took more time before dinner and at bedtime to be with her child, he began to stop the hitting.

Debbie cites boredom and the lack of problem-solving skills as the major reasons for discipline problems. To minimize boredom, she provides many activities that give the children a balance between vigorous active play and quiet-time involvement. She finds that "letting the children solve as many of their own problems as possible without intervention" works very effectively as a self-disciplinary device.

Debbie believes that many aspects of child discipline problems relate to, and sometimes stem from, adult expectations. She now has revised her expectations about sharing for children under three years of age. "When someone has a toy and doesn't feel like sharing it, we just say, 'Alexis doesn't feel like sharing now. Maybe in an hour she will, or maybe today she won't feel like sharing at all.' The children basically accept that because they know that sometimes they don't feel like sharing either."

Accepting children's behavior without getting upset is perhaps the key to her relationship with children. "I think if your acceptance is limited, you cannot enjoy children."

Parent Participation Debbie believes communication with parents to be of major importance. "Everything needs to be talked about. Any kind of skill day care mothers can develop along these lines is useful."

Debbie tries to develop a "sisterly" relationship with the children's parents. The relationship begins with a parent interview in which she is careful to make her own values and goals clear to them. She tells them that she does not believe in a rigidly structured program, that she provides lots of activities and materials for individual interests, and that she is interested more in the quality of the children's play than in keeping them spic and span.

When the child is accepted into the program, Debbie makes her expectations clear both in writing to and by talking with parents. This includes what time the children arrive, when the children are to be picked up, and when parents are to pay her. Debbie feels that a lack of clarity with parents can be the source of misunderstandings and conflicts. So she is very careful about this.

The most valued part of Debbie's relationship to the parents is the few minutes she shares with them at the end of the day. During this time she makes a point of telling each parent something about his or her child, and she is quite thoughtful about which highlights of the day to report. "Some days you can tell that a parent isn't in the mood to hear about a problem," she says.

After a short time, most parents do feel a "sisterly" relationship with Debbie. One parent says that after having her child with Debbie for a few days, she "knew it was home. It felt good." One mother frankly admitted that she felt guilty about going to work until she found a place for her children with which she was comfortable. Another feels it is very important to get a day care mother who doesn't sit the children in front of a television set all day.

The words "openness" and "freedom" are used frequently in parents' descriptions of Debbie's program. "Debbie is much more open than the other places I tried." "I like the freedom my child has there." At the same time, they praise the educational and developmental benefits their children receive. One of the parents sums it up this way: "I'm glad that she continues her education. She is always going to classes, such as child-development classes, to learn about different types of activities for the kids. They are never bored." Another parent says, "I prefer a home like Debbie's, where the children get the nurturing that is impossible in a center."

Food

Debbie has carefully thought through the way she handles the practical details of her program. She decided that each child should bring his or her own lunch, but she would supply morning and afternoon snacks. Many parents like preparing lunch: "That way I have a handle on the nutrition. I can balance the breakfast and the dinner from there."

Health Debbie has special authorization from parents for medical care of the children in the event of emergencies. In her daily routine, she keeps a close check on children for colds, fevers, swollen tonsils, and so on. If a child gets sick during the day, he or she can lie down, until a parent arrives, in a small room Debbie has set aside for this purpose. She uses individual drinking glasses (with names for those who can read, colors for nonreaders), which helps reduce the spread of colds and other contagious diseases. She also gives the children vitamins, with the parents' permission.

Through the Los Angeles County Family Day Care Association, Debbie has low-cost liability insurance, which covers the children for accidents both on her property and on trips.

Funding Debbie's standard fee is $30 per week. This includes the snacks she provides for the children. When two children from the same family are in the program, the rate is $50 per week for both. Occasionally, Debbie uses a barter system. "I have one mother who is going to college to finish her degree, and we trade off. She helps me take the children on outings and that helps to pay for her child's day care." Sometimes Debbie has offered a reduced rate "if the child is someone I really need to match another child with, and the parent cannot afford it." But this is rare, since the fees charged to parents are all she is paid for her long hours of work.

Debbie asks parents to pay in advance on Monday for the coming week; that precludes long-term debts or nonpayment by parents. She pays $2.10 an hour to the college students who assist her on a part-time basis, and $3.00 an hour to the mother she employs as a substitute.

Because of this rather meager budget, Debbie has worked hard to locate and use free resources in the community. As a member of WATCH, she has the use of a toy lending library as well as information about free or inexpensive materials in the monthly newsletter. Debbie is also looking into the possibility that children in family day care may be eligible for the free-lunch program. By keeping informed about, and using, the established community services, she feels she can contribute to keeping down the cost of day care.

Training

Most of Debbie's training for a job in family day care has come from the practical experience of raising her own four children. Her experiences with summer campers and Cub Scouts have also proved valuable. But it is her association with WATCH that has been her main source of learning. Through workshops she has received training in child development as well as in such practical matters as handling her income tax and home management.

Debbie misses having someone in a supervisory position. "I don't have modeling for myself," she says. She would particularly like to have someone help her learn more about communicating with parents. She feels that being able to listen to parents is such an important skill that she wants to learn how to do this better.

Problems and Changes

Family day care is, by its nature, a lonely job, and Debbie's biggest problems stem from that fact. It has been difficult for her to find help. Before she found a substitute, someone she could trust the children with when she was away, she experienced those "tied-down, no one to turn to, no way to get away" feelings. Until she found others to help her clarify her thinking, she suffered from feelings of isolation.

In some parts of the country, family day care does have a local support system. The Department of Social Services is responsible in Debbie's area, but very often these people look for what is wrong, and take a judgmental stance rather than a helpful one. Debbie has had to seek her own help, find her own resources, build her own connections. Because she is committed to doing so, and because there are organizations like WATCH in her community, she has been able to get some help when she needs it. She wishes for even more help someday: a central resource place for family day care mothers to come and to bring the children, a place to talk with child-development specialists about children.

Another problem stems from the negative attitudes, on the part of some professionals, about family day care. When family day care mothers seek help from professional child care agencies, they sometimes find themselves ignored or put down. Debbie and other WATCH members see one of their missions as having themselves accepted as peers among professionals.

It is, interestingly, in the matter of acceptance that Debbie has changed the most. "I thought that I was a very accepting person when I started my home," she says, "but now I find that I am even more accepting of children's behavior. I don't get upset. I expect them to be children."

It is a balanced sense of acceptance that Debbie has developed. On one hand, her respect for others prohibits her from trying to make people over; rather, she attempts to listen to them and help them attain what they want for themselves. On the other hand, however, Debbie is not complacent when things don't seem to be working. This ability to say that something isn't going well is "one of the main ways I have changed," she reports. She has now learned to ask a parent to withdraw from her home a child who doesn't seem to be fitting in with the group. "It hurts to do it," she says, "but I try to do it in the least hurting way possible."

The skill of accepting people, but not accepting their problems as inevitable or unresolvable, is perhaps central to the success of Debbie Sakach's family day care home. She is always reaching out to know more. "Keeping my home going is possible," she says, "because I keep feeding myself. I do a lot of reading, and try to expose myself to the current philosophies." Debbie has been able to create a home for children that is alive with activity and yet still comfortable and calm.

Amparo Gomez — A Family Day Care Home

"I started out because of my daughter's confidence in me as a mother. My daughter volunteered me," says Amparo Gomez. | **Beginnings**

The Gomez home is not large, but it works well for the children. Both Amparo and Debbie Sakach sense the same needs in the California children they serve. Amparo says, "The children learn the give-and-take that really is family style." That, she feels, is very essential to children of working parents and from small families. She firmly believes that childhood should be "a time of play and a time to be happy." What she wants most for children is the "opportunity to be themselves. I've always wanted my children to . . . not be the best, but to be the best they can be." The goals for her day care children are the same as those she has for her family. | **Goals**

In the Gomez home, the principal caregiver is Amparo; her husband, who is semiretired, spends a lot of time with the children. Amparo describes the children as "flocking to him" and "clustering around him." She says, "He spoils the children. They'll play with him and he loves to play with them, but they're never disrespectful to him." The children's parents say the same kinds of things: "As soon as I tell my son that Abuelo is going to be there," Eladio Saine states, "then my son wants to go. Sometimes he comes home in the afternoon and he will call me Abuelo rather than Papa. So I know he is very attached to him." The Gomezes are like grandparents to most of the children they care for.

Grouping In maintaining this familylike atmosphere, the age groups are mixed in Amparo's house. She is licensed as a family day care mother, which means that she can take up to five children. The group varies from day to day, however, because Amparo takes part-time as well as full-time children, an arrangement that the parents appreciate because it allows them more flexibility. Of mixing ages, Amparo says, "They learn from each other. For instance, an only child can see what a baby is — what they were like; the little ones learn from the older ones."

Amparo keeps children only through their fourth or fifth year. She feels that when they get older, her home isn't large enough to contain their energies.

Space and Daily Schedule The children's day care day begins with breakfast. "Because working parents often have to rush the child in the morning, the child may not feel like eating," Amparo says, "and it results in an unhappy child in the morning. So I like to have them eat breakfast with us." Breakfast around the large dining room table is a relaxed family time. Mr. Gomez always lets the children gather around him for pieces of tortilla from his plate.

Breakfast is followed by free-play time. "Children are naturally curious," Amparo says, "and they ask me many questions. I always try to answer them to the best of my ability, but I don't want to push education on them."

With regard to daily planning, Amparo readily admits, "I don't really plan each day because sometimes the things that you enjoy the most are the things that happen spontaneously with children. They have more fun when it's their idea and you fall in. You don't need expensive toys — you can improvise."

Amparo is flexible about lunch time. She says, "Some bring their lunch, and I make lunch for the others. But sometimes it's better for me to fix lunch for everyone." After lunch, the children all take naps. Amparo stresses the importance of a rest in the afternoon. "I often take a nap myself," she says. By 3:00, almost everyone is up.

The afternoons are filled with activity. "My kids are drop-outs from 'Sesame Street' — they aren't content to just sit. Sometimes we go out on walks and the children see the house numbers or flowers or other things. They'll ask me questions, like 'What color is that car?' 'How do you put the numbers together like one hundred?' 'Why are there three numbers?' And I explain it to them. When they are little they just hear you, but when they reach an older age they begin to put everything together. That's the way they learn. They watch and they learn. But at times they show you — they pick up something and tell you about it and *you* learn things! When Abuelo is home, he loves to play with the children. Sometimes I see them running around and I'm always out there cautioning them, and he'll say, 'Leave them alone. They won't get hurt.' And they don't. I think, being a mother, I'm more protective and cautious about them." This has led her to lay down safety rules prohibiting climbing too high or running out near the street.

Amparo is insistent that parents pick the children up between 5:00 and 5:30 P.M. "I get tired and am ready for some time to myself," she says. At pick-up time, Amparo and the parents talk about the day — about how the children learned colors, how some counted cars, or about how someone else had a fight but it was settled.

As part of learning to live as a family, problems do occur. When one does, Amparo's first measure is to reason with the child. She finds that explaining the consequences or the "why"s to children not only helps solve problems, but helps prevent them as well. But there are times when she finds it necessary to use "more stringent methods." With such problems as biting or hitting, she may separate the child from the group or have him or her sit in a chair for a period of time. **Discipline**

Parent relationships have been remarkably pleasant and easy for Amparo. She credits a great deal of this success to the selection of parents who go along with her lifestyle and have values that are about the same as her own. She reflects on the seven years she has been a day care mother: "I trust the parents and I guess they respond to my trust in them." She is very perceptive and sensitive about the feelings of young parents toward their children. "It's kind of scary for young parents, leaving their dearest, most prized . . . I don't know whether to call it *possession* . . . in the whole world in the hands of another person." She works very hard at making the parents feel confident about leaving their children in her home. **Parent Participation**

Over the years, Amparo has had parents who are psychologists and educators, and she feels free to ask their advice about problems that arise with the children. If it seems appropriate, she passes this advice along to other parents. She also frequently asks parents what they would advise in certain situations. "I learn from parents, and they probably learn from me." Amparo and her husband come to seem like relatives to these parents — older, wiser people who help them with their children and to whom they can turn.

Training "I had my training with my own children, and they turned out pretty well. But I'm older and I can look back at the mistakes I made, and improve; I can see the frustration I had when I was a young parent. I can put myself in the parents' shoes." Amparo tries to keep abreast of current trends and attitudes about child care. She is a member of WATCH and finds it a very valuable resource for both day care mothers and parents. But she stresses the importance of common sense and experience. She says, "You can read a book, but the experience is what counts."

Health As part of her comprehensive program, Amparo is willing to care for sick children. She keeps children with colds or fevers in a separate room, where they can lie down with a book or engage in some other quiet activity. She gives them juice and administers medication if the parents request it. Through the county licensing agency, she has accident insurance, which covers the children while they are in her care.

Funding Amparo charges from $25 to $30 per week for each child, payable at the end of each week. This includes care from 7:00 A.M. to 5:00 P.M., and whatever food the child needs (breakfast, lunch, and snacks are provided for some of the children). The reason for two weekly rates is explained: "They say you're supposed to charge everybody the same, but you can't, because some people are professionals and get paid more; others do work that doesn't pay much, so the day care mother has to gauge that."

Amparo points out that her weekly rate amounts to only about $.50 per hour per child. She finds herself caught between her desire to keep down the cost to the parents and the rising prices of necessary materials and services. "People say, 'You should do this for altruistic reasons.' Fine, but when you go to the market, you can't take out your altruistic card and say, 'Look, I'm a day care mother. I need groceries.'" She deplores the fact that families will spend a lot of money for a new car but begrudge the money spent for child care.

Amparo says that she hasn't had any real problems. "That's one of the beauties of a day care home," she admits. It is her own home and she can do things in her own way. Amparo's age did concern some parents: "I was a little hesitant at first," Julie Saine says. "But to me she seemed just as capable as a younger woman, if not more so, because of her experience." Amparo is able to take care of as many as five young and active children because she plans carefully, parceling out her time during the day so that she doesn't get worn out. The difficulty comes when her own daughter asks Amparo to take her children for the weekend so that she and her husband can go away. "Of course I say yes, and I take them," Amparo says. "I don't mind it, but one thing spills into the other, and sometimes I get tired, naturally — the duty of being a grandmother and a day care mother."

Amparo has a sureness, a confidence in herself that undoubtedly communicates a sense of security and stability to the parents and children she works with. She is not, however, set in her ways, stubborn, uncompromising, or rigid. Perhaps this is because her security is tempered with a joy in people and eagerness to hear what others have to say. She has all the attributes that make her grandmotherly and professional in the very best sense of both of those terms.

Problems and Changes

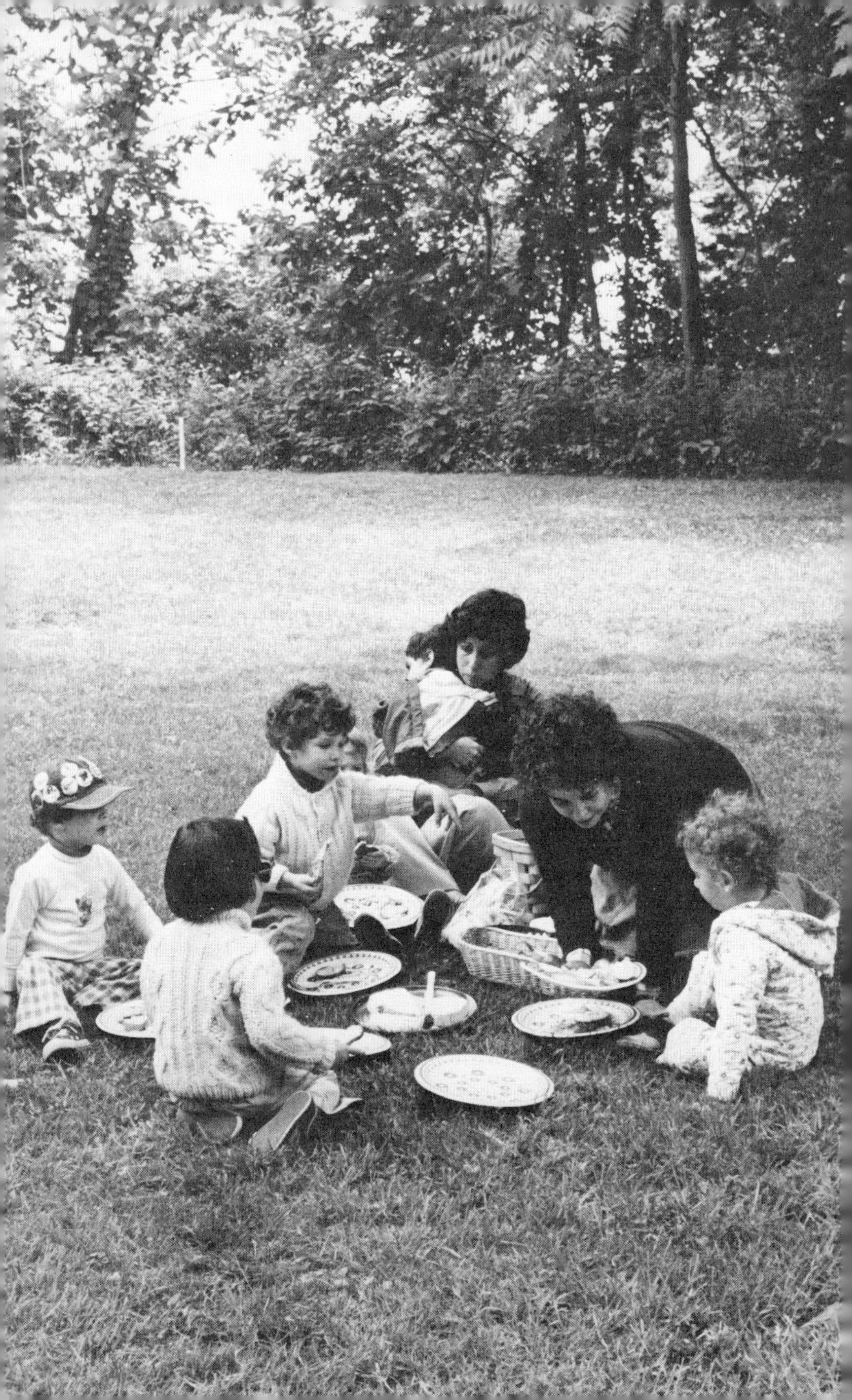

15
An Experiment with Informal Child Care

**The Day Care Neighbor Service
Portland, Oregon**

One aspect of child care seems to remain constant: most children of working mothers are cared for in their own homes or in the homes of neighbors. Peter Sauer of the Bank Street College Day Care Consultation Service describes the scene that occurs in his New York City neighborhood twice daily: "At eight-thirty in the morning and at five-thirty in the evening, hundreds of children may be observed crossing streets and avenues, riding in strollers, being carried, riding behind a parent on a bicycle seat, towed along by the hand from one house to another by teen-age baby sitters or grandparents." He calls this "the West Side underground child care system," noting that it is totally "separate from the smaller, isolated universe of formal day care centers."

The opinions about this form of child care, usually called baby-sitting, don't vary much. In *Child Care — Who Cares?*, the editor, Pamela Roby, writes that parents report that baby-sitting is the least satisfactory arrangement. Most arrangements of this kind, according to Margaret O'Brien Steinfels in *Who's Minding the Children?*, are "the result of desperate situations — both for the mothers who must work and find care for their children and for women who must work and find child care their only [job] possibility. With both, what is best for the children can often only be a secondary consideration." These homes have been called barren, overcrowded, dangerous, filthy. "Sometimes," Ms. Steinfels reports, "they don't even provide custodial care."

This realm of child care is for the most part condemned and ignored. The professionals in child care simply don't know who these people are and where these homes exist. Alice Collins and Eunice Watson, however, have been working in this area for the past several years, though they entered it through the back door. As social workers and researchers in Portland, Oregon, they had a grant from the government to "develop a new kind of child care." Their original plan was to create a day care exchange — by offering incentives, they would induce day care mothers to come to the exchange for training, which could lead to licensing.

"You can't begin anything in day care without the neighborhood knowing about it," Alice Collins says. "So we began to get calls from people saying, 'Can you help me find a baby sitter?' To the first few calls, we said no. After a while, we said yes." She and Eunice Watson began to call women who were doing family day care to ask if they had room for more children. Eventually they found that there were certain people in the neighborhood who knew everything that was going on in child care and could help find baby sitters.

Both Alice Collins and Eunice Watson began to see this as a recurrent pattern: there were certain people in the neighborhood to whom others turned for help with their child care problems. These were the people mothers called when they wanted to find a baby sitter, saying, "Can you help me find someone to take care of my kids?" They were the same people baby sitters called, asking, "Can you help me find some kids to take care of?" These helpful people were, likewise, the ones neighbors came to talk to when they had problems with their children or with their families or friends. Alice and Eunice dubbed these people "friendly helpful neighbors." They also became aware that the friendly helpful neighbors were in touch with very large numbers of people.

In their book, *Family Day Care*, Watson and Collins describe such a person:

Mrs. Smith's children are in their early teens. [Mrs. Smith] is no longer busy all the time keeping house and looking after them, but she feels she should be at home when they are, and besides, she likes her home and has no special job skills or career goals. Her husband prefers her to be home, too. She does have an interest in helping others and is especially interested in children. She has always been a kind of baby-sitting resource for her friends. Mrs. Smith is likely to "watch the children" when a neighbor has a beauty or medical appointment or wants to do a few hours' shopping. There are always extra children in and out of the house. Neighbors drop in on Mrs. Smith, too, for a cup of coffee or a chat about the good and bad things going on at home; to use the washing machine when theirs has broken down; or to get a new recipe or describe a successful one.

Once or twice when a neighbor has gone on a trip or there has been a serious or prolonged illness in a neighbor's family, Mrs. Smith has made a regular arrangement to look after a young child every day and been paid for it. Now, when the increased costs of teen-age needs has put some strain on the family budget, she wonders if she could pick up some extra money by daily baby-sitting for one or two children. This would bring in a little income, let her remain at home, avoid the expenses attached to going out to work, and do some good for children, whom she enjoys for themselves.

Learning and meeting the licensing requirements is no problem for Mrs. Smith nor for the people who want her to look after their children, and soon she is "baby-sitting" a two-year-old of a mother, who, having just been divorced, is taking a secretarial course. News that Mrs. Smith now is an "official" baby sitter moves with rapidity over the neighborhood grapevine. The nurse tells the dietitian at the hospital, whose sister-in-law is looking for someone to take care of her baby. A neighbor mentions it to a friend dissatisfied with her present arrangement. Mrs. Smith begins to get requests for care of children of strangers as well as those of friends.

She wants to go on as she always has, taking the children along when she goes to the store or does other errands, keeping them in the house or outdoors as the weather allows. In short, she does not want to change her lifestyle, but it makes her feel a little out of it and maybe selfish to just do what she likes at home while she knows about the need for good child care and her ability and pleasure in giving it. . .

Since she began baby-sitting, a number of Mrs. Smith's friends and acquaintances have remarked, "I wouldn't mind taking on a couple of kids myself if I knew where to find them." So, when Mrs. Smith begins to think about how to help someone when she cannot, she may suggest a person she knows is interested in doing baby-sitting.

She tends to think of someone giving the same quality of care she does, since she is apt to think of the needs of children rather than the simple expedients a harried mother might resort to when temporarily desperate for someone to care for her children so she can accept an urgent job offer.

Mrs. Smith is just one person, just one of many friendly helpful neighbors. These people are not all parents of teen-agers, or middle-class, nor do they have all the other qualities of Mrs. Smith. Alice Collins and Eunice Watson became interested in finding out what these people had in common. Art Emlen, with whom they worked, insisted that they do this systematically, writing down a list of qualities and independently rating these people according to that list. As Alice tells it, "Eunice and I didn't speak to each other for three weeks. It was the hardest job I've ever done. And we were convinced that it was useless, that we would end up with nothing. And we came out with so much that was valid that it was embarrassing."

They found that all the friendly helpful neighbors had intact families with school-age children. But the characteristic they found the most important is the one they labeled "freedom from drain." Alice Collins explains: "We learned from our research that these were people who, for no apparent reason, had an excess of human kindness, an interest in other people, a healthy interest, not a neurotic interest, and who naturally took care of other people in a very grown-up way . . . not because they needed people to love them, but especially because they were interested in the children in their area." Freedom from drain, Collins and Watson have found, has very little to do with these people's economic situation. It is a personal characteristic. "I never talk to a group of people about friendly helpful neighbors without their knowing exactly who the helping person in their neighborhood is," Alice reports.

At that point, Alice and Eunice did something very unusual: they decided to work with this natural system. Alice admits that the decision surprised her colleagues. "People always say that as long as the friendly helpful neighbors were doing so well by themselves, then why did we need to get in?" The answer she and Eunice give is that, by joining people like Mrs. Smith and adding their professional skills to the neighbors' natural ones, they could help with recruiting and matching adults and children, and in sustaining day care arrangements. Together, they felt, they could make a useful team that would improve day care for more children than either they or the friendly neighbors could reach alone. They went to their project director at the U.S. Office of Child Development and asked permission to change the nature of their project. Permission was granted. For the following four years, they created Day Care Neighbor Services in three varying neighborhoods as defined by school districts: one in the northwest section of a large city, another in its more recently developed southeast, and the third in two trailer courts in a nearby county.

In the beginning of the project finding day care neighbors in the very first neighborhood was difficult. Alice Collins recalls, "We spent the whole summer planning how we would do this, and the only thing left was to get out and find the day care neighbors. But somehow, we didn't get about that very fast." She attributes their hesitation to the fact that "in social work, we are taught to wait for people to come to us. It is really hard for us to go out."

Eventually they took an approach they call an "anthropological one." Eunice describes it: "Every neighborhood has its own characteristics, and even if you just go and look around as you walk around the block, you will see patterns of where kids are and where they're not. You can get very good at observing patterns. Then you begin to sense a little bit of what the neighborhood is about. And you begin to see what central place people are involved with, whether it's the local grocery store, the self-service laundry, or the school. You have to put yourself in that neighborhood and pay attention to what you see and hear." Alice summarizes: "You simply sit on a rock and try to be as inconspicuous as possible and watch what is going on and talk to anyone who will talk to you."

Their method of finding the friendly helpful neighbors was to talk to people, asking them about day care in their neighborhood. They discovered, however, that the standard answer to "Who works in this neighborhood?" was "I don't know anything about my neighbors." If they asked, "Who gives day care?" the answer was usually "Nobody." The best approach, they discovered, was to introduce themselves as people interested in child care, not for their own children, but in general, and ask such questions as "Whom would you ask if you needed to find a baby sitter?" or "Is there baby-sitting around here?" or "Do people have a hard time finding baby sitters?" Local restaurants, drug stores, small markets were often the best places to go to find people to talk to; school secretaries, ministers, and public health nurses were particularly helpful.

It took a while for the suspicion to wear off. At first, they were told that they might want to talk to Mrs. Whosiz on such-and-such a committee. According to Alice, "That almost never paid off. By and large we stayed away from the obvious official kinds of day care people because they didn't know anything about the kind of day care we were interested in except that they thought it was all bad."

Collins and Watson refer to their manner of recruiting day care neighbors as "an admittedly long, drawn-out process." When they found a prospect, they telephoned. If that person was responsive, they made an appointment for an interview. The purpose of this interview was "to gain a general impression both of the neighborhood day care system and the potential day care neighbor as a person in her own community."

"During the interview," Alice says, "we didn't ask the person right off the bat to be a day care neighbor because we felt it would be smarter to interview her and then come away and decide what we thought. I interviewed one woman who I was absolutely sure would be a marvelous day care neighbor . . . if her kid hadn't come home from school right then and I hadn't had the chance to see her with her own child. We were slow and careful about making choices, which was one of the things that upsets people who are interested in this notion. It takes time."

Alice Collins feels strongly that selecting the day care neighbors is a professional job. "It takes a professional with a professional set of antennae that pick up what people say and what they don't say, what their actions are and what their actions aren't." They were looking for giving people who enjoyed being around children, who seemed to be the center of a network of people. They guarded against people who were looking after kids to answer their own neurotic needs or mainly to provide a source of revenue. "There were people who said, 'I just love kids and I love my house full of them,' " Alice reports. "Forget them."

"If they had too many kids around them," Eunice adds, "they often weren't treating them as individuals at all. They just liked the idea of having kids around and telling you about it, but as you were sitting there, the kids were doing stuff that told you they didn't like kids at all. The other thing was that if they had too many children around them, they couldn't relate to adults. We were looking for people who could also relate to adults."

Once they had decided which people were good prospects, Alice and Eunice went back and asked them if they would be day care neighbors, explaining that they would pay them $25 a month. The day care neighbors were asked to keep records of whom they talked to and helped, but otherwise they were told, "Don't do anything different. Just tell us what you do." Alice recalls the typical reaction this prompted. "Without fail, they thought this was a wonderful idea. They said, 'This is what I'm doing anyway, and I'd be glad to talk to you about it.' And a week later, they'd call up and say, 'My husband won't let me do it.' 'My children won't let me do it.' 'I can't do it.' And each time they did that, I fell apart, but Eunice said, 'Never mind, they'll do it.' And so they did."

As social work consultants, Alice or Eunice met with the day care neighbor once a week at first, but as soon as they had developed a relationship, the sessions were reduced to twice a month and then once a month. In that way, the social workers could each work with twelve to fifteen neighbors at one time. They maintain that it was absolutely necessary to meet with the day care neighbor in her own home at her convenience, and to be ready to accept interruptions — the neighbor was always getting telephone calls and having children and adults drop in.

The kind of relationship they developed was a careful one. As professionals, Alice and Eunice were committed to not disrupting or taking over what was happening within the neighborhood network. One of the first things that always happened, according to Alice, was that the day care neighbor asked her or Eunice, as a social worker, to talk to someone who was having a problem. "We consistently said no," Alice reports. They wanted to enable the day care neighbor to deal with the problems herself. However, they would spend as much time as was necessary talking with the day care neighbor about what tack to take. They were also careful to keep the relationship with the day care neighbor both friendly and professional. Eunice tells of one woman who tried to develop a mother-daughter relationship with her, which she says she was quick to change into a more sisterly feeling.

"Our purpose," Alice says, "was to help the day care neighbors deal with problems they ordinarily could not have dealt with alone, and to give them the support and recognition that would help them continue to reach out. One of the things in our society is that people usually don't reach out. Before we teamed up with them, most of the day care neighbors helped only people who asked them." As an example, Alice recalls a day care neighbor's telling her how bothered she was to see a mother who lived nearby continue to send her child to a "perfectly dreadful day care situation." When Alice asked the day care neighbor why she didn't say something to the child's mother, the reply was that she really didn't know this woman. Alice said, "Well you don't, but I bet you know someone she knows and could find a way to be introduced to her." In a short time, Alice says, the day care neighbor had an introduction and was helping the mother find somewhere else to send her child. Alice feels that the day care neighbor would not have reached out without the support of a consultant.

Also, Collins and Watson agree that they helped the day care neighbors work with a wider range of people. For instance, they report that day care neighbors would do anything for a mother who needed to find a baby sitter to go back to work; but they would have nothing to do with a mother who called and said, "My baby is six weeks old and driving me crazy. Could you help me find some part-time care?" Alice says, "It was part of our job as consultants to get them to see that this mother needed day care as much as anybody else — to see that this mother has a universal kind of feeling." They also found themselves dealing with the day care neighbors' prejudices — perhaps against poor people, or people on welfare, or minority people — and helping them learn to see other points of view.

The Day Care Neighbor Service, as a research-demonstration project, concluded with some very definite research findings. The social workers discovered, for example, that arrangements last longer and are more satisfactory between strangers than between friends. "Between friends," Alice explains, "it gets kind of uneasy when something goes wrong." They found that when there is an arrangement between strangers, with a third party such as the day care neighbor who facilitates it, all the parties know more clearly what they are getting into.

They also found that the day care neighbors were recruiters of good caregivers. "They knew good people," Alice Collins says. "They didn't refer parents to the people they didn't think much of. We had one lady who wasn't very good. She called each of the day care neighbors in turn and said, 'It's so hard to find kids to take care of. Will you help me find some?' Each one of those day care neighbors called us afterward and said, 'What'll we do with this lady? She needs the work, she needs someone to take care of, but honestly, it shouldn't be kids.' " Alice reports that this was one situation in which her intervention helped. She could suggest that this woman work with older people, a job everyone agreed was more suitable. Alice states that day care neighbors "made consistently good matches between day care givers and day care users." She attributes their ability to make good placements to their being "good people themselves, with good judgment and strong egos."

The day care neighbors' primary job was helping people find day care. But they also kept their fingers on the pulse of the whole neighborhood. They acted as marriage counselors and chaplains and child-rearing experts. It is interesting to note that Collins and Watson found the Day Care Neighbor Service a tremendous boon in deterring abuse of any kind. Day care neighbors were, in fact, the first people to sense or see neglect. They were able to step in and work with a mother who was locking her children out at night, and with a husband who was drinking his salary and not bringing food home for his family. In the latter case, in Alice's words, "The day care neighbor in the trailer park noticed that the father brought home only little bags — bags that weren't big enough to contain much food. So the neighbor went over there and asked the mother, 'Are you getting enough to eat?' This mother, who was young and shy, admitted that she didn't have enough food. The day care neighbor took her to the store immediately and bought her some food. When the father turned up that night, she ran him off the place. Eventually, the father persuaded his family to take him back and promised to change. The day care neighbor sat at her window and made sure the promise was kept. And you have a happy ending."

Alice continues, "Nobody else saw that neglect. Nobody would have known about it." She and Eunice Watson think that it is the partnership between the naturally helpful neighbor and the social worker that makes this kind of service possible, a service that moves out to help where help is needed.

The major problem with the partnership arrangement is that a day care neighbor can't nominate herself for the job. Sometimes when a day care neighbor moved, another neighbor called up and asked if she could do the same job. "She wasn't necessarily the right kind of person," Alice says. "How do you say no? This gets to be a problem in a closely knit neighborhood. I don't know the answer."

At the end of four years, Alice Collins and Eunice Watson ended their project. Their training in community organization had convinced them that demonstration projects should not linger on and become permanent fixtures; they should be absorbed into existing programs. Fortunately, they found several organizations that wanted very much to take on the Day Care Neighbor Service. The United Fund agreed to put up 25 percent of the funds. When Alice and Eunice went to the state to secure the other 75 percent, they were turned down. "The state," in Alice's opinion, "didn't believe in day care, didn't want any part of it. The man who was in charge was interested in foster care and was scared to death that if he took on day care, foster care would get less money."

Nobody else has as yet picked up the Day Care Neighbor Service. The project's originators recognized that one of the major obstacles to the development of day care neighbor services was the difficulty professionals had in accepting the fact that day care neighbors existed, as opposed to having to be created or trained by professionals. Furthermore, they have found resistance to the idea of a professional consultant working in partnership with an untrained neighborhood person. The arrangement is neither familiar nor attractive to some professionals.

The idea has, nonetheless, aroused genuine interest and enthusiasm all over the country. The people in information and referral agencies will undoubtedly come into contact with people who are friendly helpful neighbors.

Perhaps some information and referral service staff could be assigned for consultations with the natural community resource people.

Says Alice Collins, "The fact that we have found that these networks exist is a contribution to child care." Her experience has shown that those who work with these networks can expand the services available within a community and can promote better child care and prevent abuse and neglect. "For me, the outcome of this study was my increased conviction that the right way to work is in consultation with networks."

HARDING HIGH SCHOOL
•tours
•exhibits
•keynote speakers
•program sessions for

16
A Local Support System for Child Care

The Child Care Corner
  The Southside Child Care Committee
  The Child Care Resource Center
  The Toy Lending Library
  The Group Family Day Care Project
Minneapolis, Minnesota

There is a sad irony in the histories of most organizations whose business is to help the child care system. Whether these organizations are in the large cities of the East, the rural farms of the South, the prairies of the Midwest, or the deserts of the Southwest, many of them have had a remarkably similar development. They were conceived in idealism. Their goals were altruistic — perhaps to untangle a bureaucratic mess, or to gain some community control, or to bring together disparate elements of the child care community, or to give parents information about child care services. These organizations began as friends to the child care community, but many have become foes. It is as if they had turned into monsters that bit the hands of those who originally nurtured them. Once established, once their power had been consolidated, many organizations ceased trying to represent their constituencies and attempted instead to control them. The mere mention of the word "agency" makes many child care workers blanch. They tell stories, agonizing stories:

• In a southern county, an agency that is supposed to give parents information about child care simply hands them a list. Dialing the first five places, one parent finds that the list is outdated. Three of those places haven't existed for well over a year.

• A working mother applies to a public family day care agency for child care for her baby. The day care group gives her the name and address of a day care mother with room for a baby. It turns out that the day care mother speaks no English. When the mother asks if she can be referred to a day care mother with whom she can communicate about the baby's needs, she is told to take the home she has been assigned or to look elsewhere on her own.

• In an eastern city, a funding agency issues an edict that all children have to be present at their centers by 9:30 A.M. That means that a parent who works a later shift and wants to be with his or her child until 10:00 can't be accepted into these centers.

• A midwestern agency gives welfare mothers a test to determine their vocational aptitude and finds that one mother is suited to be an airline stewardess. This mother, who has three young children, has no interest in leaving her children and becoming a stewardess. She wants to study child development. The agency won't authorize or pay for child care, however, unless the mother takes the stewardess-training course.

• An agency in an eastern city plans to close many child care centers under its jurisdiction rather than renegotiate expensive leases it has made directly with landlords, thereby depriving hundreds of families of child care.

The common strand here is that a bureaucracy has ceased being responsive to children and families, perhaps even counting them as "slots" rather than as real people. It is a bureaucracy that has become so entrenched that it is difficult for a center, a family day care mother, or a parent to have any say in what happens to them. It is a bureaucracy that often serves its own purposes. Furthermore, it is a bureaucracy that siphons off money to pay expensive salaries, money that otherwise might go directly to child care.

Are there any solutions? It is naive to think that child care can exist without some kind of superstructure or organization to support it. Whether it is a person who baby-sits for one child or a center that cares for a hundred children, each has needs beyond what it can provide for itself.

In Minneapolis, Minnesota, there is a group of working people involved in child care services that calls itself the Child Care Corner. It is, in fact, four separate child care groups, whose members think that the solution to bureaucratic neglect lies in their studying the nature of power and of organizations, seeing what the dangers and pitfalls are, and then designing organizations that are less likely to fall into patterns that are expensive, self-seeking, and self-serving.

The backgrounds of the people at the Child Care Corner are significant. They have had experiences on all levels, working for organizations of different kinds, in politics, in unions, and in the child care system itself. From their diverse backgrounds and experience, they have forged a series of unwritten principles by which their organizations — the Southside Child Care Committee, the Child Care Resource Center, the Toy Lending Library, and the Group Family Day Care Project — operate:

- They assume child care is a community matter.
- Their policies are determined by their community board of directors.
- They reach out actively into the community of formal and informal child care to find out what the needs are.
- Their own actions are in response to the needs they find.
- They always offer people choices. In fact, using them at all is a choice that people can make. They don't take over child care groups; they are available as resources.
- They attempt to stay small. If a need for another function arises, they help other people fill it themselves rather than enlarge their own empire.
- They operate on the lowest possible budgets.

Their principles are surprising. Imagine a group wanting to stay small when it could grow grander and bigger. Imagine letting other people do a job when the group could easily expand and do the job itself, and imagine intentionally trying to keep to a low budget. These tenets, however, surprising as they may seem, are the key to the formation of unusually successful child care organizations.

One senses the success of the four organizations as soon as one enters the Child Care Corner in South Minneapolis. Jim Nicholie tells of his first impressions: "I remember when I first came here from California, I looked all around to find out what was going on in child care. This was one of the places I came to. I walked in the door and said, 'What are you doing?' It didn't look like an office. You didn't get met by a secretary as you do in so many places. You don't get handed a brochure. It's a much different feeling. You walk in, and Billie Lockett [the director of the Resource Center] or whoever is there says hello and shows you around. You feel welcome and you feel that it is easy to come back, even without a specific reason."

The buildings themselves are the type of nondescript utilitarian buildings that served as dry cleaning or grocery or drug stores before the advent of shopping centers. Set on a corner, they are one-story, square-shaped, distinguished only by large panes of glass with the faded signs of by-gone businesses and the newly painted signs of the Child Care Corner. One building houses the Toy Lending Library and the Group Family Day Care Project. The first thing one notices in this one-room building is the carpet — a patchwork of bright colors, pieced-together samples from rug stores. The message right away is "We use what someone else might have thrown away." All along the sides of the room are shelves filled with what also might have been cast-off toys or books, but have been carefully repaired to look as good as new.

This building connects through a rear door to another building — the home base of the Child Care Resource Center and the Southside Child Care Committee. The front room is a meeting office and reference room. There is a large conference table next to a shelf of child care books and filmstrips. The back room is used as a drop-in center for young children. It has an enclosed platform for climbing that reaches almost to ceiling height. Next to the platform is a square space, framed by low pieces of wood, for block-building, or playing with trucks, cars, or animals. At the far end of the room are a sofa and a door leading to the as yet unfinished small back yard of dirt and concrete. The basement room has been recently renovated as an arts and cráfts space for elementary school children.

The Southside Child Care Committee

The brief description of the buildings only begins to suggest the multitude of activities that goes on in them. It all began in 1973 with one VISTA volunteer. Margaret Boyer explains: "The people from South Minneapolis wanted to have input and some control in child care in their area. They worked with an organizer from the Greater Minneapolis Day Care Association. Then they applied for a VISTA volunteer. And that's how the Southside Child Care Committee started. The VISTA volunteer and the committee became politicized in their frustrations with child care. They had a really hard time attracting and holding people in their committee, and they realized that you have to offer services to people as well as using them for political action."

The Southside Child Care Committee has kept its political focus. It has one staff member, Margaret Boyer, and a yearly budget of $9800. Most of its work is done through volunteer committees. The Needs Assessment Committee does research about the kind of child care that already exists and the kind that should exist in the community, and it analyzes where the decision-making, funding, and administrative power lines lie. There is also the Outreach Committee. One current project calls for committee members to take political candidates and reporters to visit centers, parent co-ops, and family day care homes; this is an attempt "to raise their consciousness about what child care is and what its needs are," Margaret says. "We are going to have a grand finale with a press conference, and try to get commitments from the candidates."

The Outreach Committee also has brunches, "to get parents and people from different centers together. Right now the goal is to have them share information." At one such meeting, the people found that they had many issues to talk about, ranging from what to do when the weather is hot and humid and the kids are going wild, to how to make their centers places of good quality, how to improve the program, and how to handle cuts in funding.

Funding is one area in which the Southside Child Care Committee and the Resource Center combine forces;

they hold workshops on proposal-writing. Southside also has a committee of community people to review proposals for their neighborhood. Margaret is a nonvoting member in this group, which she characterizes as "a strange conglomeration of people — a minister from a conservative church, family day care providers, people from centers and from parent co-ops." The Proposal Review Committee reviews all proposals (thirty-six of them in 1976) and makes recommendations to the funding agency, the Greater Minneapolis Day Care Association. Though Southside began as an area committee for the Greater Minneapolis Day Care Association, it is now connected to it only voluntarily, and its recommendations are in no way binding. Despite that, all of Southside's recommendations were accepted without changes, which Margaret credits to the meticulous accumulation of knowledge and to the finding and casting out of any parts of a proposal budget that might have been padded.

Political work, Margaret says, is arduous, often not very rewarding. "Sometimes it feels as if you're hitting your head against a brick wall. It is really hard to feel that you're accomplishing something."

The Resource Center

Margaret Boyer is glad to work side by side and often in conjunction with the service organization Southside helped to found several years ago, the Resource Center.

The Resource Center grew out of the efforts of a group of parents from the Southside Child Care Committee to provide child care in their own community. Billie Lockett tells what happened: "At that time they started looking for a licensable space. They weren't able to find it. From not being able to find the licensable space grew the idea of the Resource Center. At first people just volunteered. I was taking leave from my job at a child care center and I came in and volunteered. In April of nineteen seventy-four I was hired as the first staff person."

It now has two full-time staff members, Billie Lockett and her secretary, as well as one part-time person and two students from the Neighborhood Youth Corps. Originally the Resource Center "hustled" its funding from many sources — donations from local churches, businesses, and foundations, and a grant from the state. In 1976, it received a sizable state grant ($29,000), and expects to raise $8000 from churches and foundations.

The Resource Center holds approximately twenty-five workshops a year on such topics as "Infant Stimulation," "Nutrition," "How to Make Homemade Toys," and "How to Start a Center." These workshops are accredited through the state Welfare Department, and are run by community people. They are held at the Resource Center or in centers or homes throughout the city.

Passing on information and knowledge is an important function of the Resource Center. Its staff puts out a monthly newsletter that has a circulation of over fifteen hundred and costs $4 for individuals and $6 for groups for a one-year subscription. Everyone at the Child Care Corner contributes to the newsletter — the Southside Child Care Committee has a page, for instance. It carries information on what's happening in the child care world in Minneapolis and editorializes on such controversial issues as child abuse or children's rights.

The Resource Center also circulates information by maintaining a library well stocked with classic and current books on child development and child care. It has, in addition, films, filmstrips, and slide-show presentations made by local people. There is a children's library for the neighborhood children, where they may borrow books or spend the afternoon sitting cross-legged on the floor or sprawled on the sofa, reading.

The playroom in the Resource Center is a drop-in spot where parents can bring children for a few hours. Two mornings a week, neighborhood mothers hold play groups. The mothers run their own play groups, taking turns planning activities. They keep a journal in which they write how they felt about the activities they planned, what worked, and what failed. "Play Group," according to Billie, "is a place for the mother who is not working. Usually these mothers are left out of the child care scene."

The Resource Center has free planned activities for children, such as "Black Folk Tale Day," a magic show, and arts and crafts classes. Arts and crafts classes are held on Tuesday mornings for five weeks during the summer. There are classes for children from three to five years old, and for children from six to nine. The average attendance is about twenty-two children per class — at a cost of $1 each for all five weeks.

The arts and crafts space in the basement was started in response to a problem. "The play space," Billie says, "was set up for toddlers. Elementary school–age kids were going back there and being very destructive. We felt that was our fault. Being a small staff, we weren't taking any time with these older children. We weren't offering them anything to do. So we expanded to the basement and set up the arts and crafts center. And we hired a part-time person to run the summer program and to be present after school."

Family day care homes and centers can plan field trips to the Resource Center. Activities or movies are provided for the children, giving the adults an opportunity to browse through the adult library or talk to other child care people.

One of the main functions of the Resource Center, and the one that it is best known for, is what is called Information and Referral. All during the day, the phones are ringing with requests from parents.

• "I just lost my baby sitter. Can you help me find child care by this afternoon?"

- "I have three children and I'd like them all to be in the same family day care home."
- "I want a center that provides transportation."

Parents also walk in, children in tow, saying:

- "I just got a job and am going to start Monday. Can you help me find someone to take care of my six-year-old son?"
- "I want to go back to work part time, and I need a place that will take kids for a few hours every day."

Billie Lockett and her secretary are not fazed by even the most difficult request. They explain the types of child care available and ask for the parents' preferences. Then they do the footwork, calling several places to find out if they do have room for the child in question. If the mother has come to the Resource Center, they hand the phone to her so that she can make an appointment for a visit. If the parent has telephoned, they call back with the information and the telephone numbers of the places they have found that do have space. From their conversations with the parent, they have gained an idea of what kind of place she or he wants — but it is a principle at the Resource Center to give parents a choice. They talk to parents about how to select child care, and suggest several places for them to visit. In addition, they give each parent a booklet they've written called *Which Way Guide to Child Care in South Minneapolis*. This guide spells out ways for a parent to judge a program in relation to four main areas: (1) parent involvement in the program, (2) the physical setting and its impact on children and adults, (3) the program content in relation to stated and implied goals, and the strategies used for their implementation, and (4) the general social and emotional interaction among parents, staff, and children.

Billie asks parents to telephone her to report about the visits and let her know what selection they have made. If a parent doesn't call, Billie calls the parent. "A referral," she says, "can take up to two hours. The most important thing to me is that people walk out of here and feel good about us and send other people to us."

The details of each referral are written on a form and filed. The Resource Center keeps many files. For instance, it has what it calls a People's File. This contains the names of skilled community people who can participate in folk-singing or craft workshops. The people in the community have access to the People's File. The Resource Center also maintains a list of baby sitters — people who will go into homes and take care of children either full days over a few weeks for a child who has the measles or for a few hours if a mother needs to go out.

The list of the center's services goes on and on. It opens its play space to groups that need child care during meetings and conferences. It has helped many other organizations set up and run their own child care programs. Two such groups are Eden House, a treatment center for men who are addicted to drugs, pills, or alcohol, and the Harriet Tubman Shelter, a crisis center for women and children who have been battered. Billie Lockett and Margaret Boyer are also working with Winnaki House, a drug treatment house for native American women. They have set up child care there, so that the children of these native American women are no longer put in white suburban foster homes. "The mothers," Billie explains, "were very afraid that their children would lose their identity and their closeness with the family. I'm sure that it will encourage more women to get help, knowing that they are not going to have their children uprooted and feeling confident that the welfare system will not step in and say, 'Oh, you're a naughty mother for being an alcoholic and I'm going to take your children away.'"

The Resource Center does not limit its activities to the usual child care boundaries — the world of licensed family day care and the licensed centers. Its staff digs around to see what needs to be done — it wants to be just as attentive to the neighborhood mother who stays at home as to the mother who goes to work. And it delves into realms that are usually overlooked by the child care establishment; for example, senior citizens. The Resource Center has a member of a local senior citizens' organization on its board of directors, and Resource Center staff members have gone to the senior citizens' group and conducted workshops. At Christmas time, it holds a toy-making workshop. The senior citizens make toys for their grandchildren or for children in local centers.

Every summer, the staff of the Resource Center goes on a "neighborhood walk." In Billie's words, "One or two of us knock on people's doors in the neighborhood. We talk about what they would like to see us do — and then we bring it all back. From the walk last year, we got more play group mothers; we got volunteers to help with the newsletter; we got board members."

The Resource Center staff did such a good job of stirring up interest in its work that it was bombarded with requests from all over Minneapolis. In accordance with Billie's belief that the organization should not build an empire, but should help others to found similar organizations, in 1975 the staff at the Resource Center helped to form another Resource Center on the north side of Minneapolis. Because Billie also believes in working cooperatively, the two Resource Centers have many projects in common. "One thing we do to cut costs," says Billie, "is put out a newsletter together. We also have monthly joint staff meetings where we try to share information. And we do joint fund-raising."

The Toy Lending Library

Billie saw still another need in her community. Family day care providers didn't have the money to buy much in the way of toys and equipment. Billie realized there should be a central place where providers could come to borrow toys. One of Billie's funders suggested that she write that service into her proposal, and assured her that this request would be funded. Billie said no. She thought that an organization of family day care providers should be the sponsor. She asked the Hennepin County Family Day Care Association if it was interested in starting a toy lending library. The association and the Resource Center wrote a joint proposal for revenue-sharing money and were funded. A Kiwanis Club in Willmar, Minnesota, a city about 200 miles away, agreed to help the Toy Lending Library get on its feet. They started a "truckload of toys" drive that lasted for four days. On the final day, the Kiwanis Club arranged to fly the Minneapolis people to Willmar. "We got on the radio station," Billie recalls, "and people started calling in, donating bikes and all kinds of other things. We had a good day. We brought a truck loaded up with toys back with us and that's what started the Toy Lending Library." At its outset, the Toy Lending Library ran into a problem. It was difficult for family day care providers to leave their children and come to the library to pick up toys. They didn't have the time.

Often, they didn't have the transportation. Zoe and Jim Nicholie of the Group Family Day Care Project thought of the solution. They could lease a van to be shared by all of the child care groups in the Child Care Corner. One of the van's first uses could be delivering and picking up toys for the Toy Lending Library.

The Group Family Day Care Project

The Group Family Day Care Project grew out of personal and professional needs for Zoe and Jim Nicholie. In the first years of their marriage they had gone to school and then worked together. When Benjy, their first child, was born, they began to drift toward a more conventional pattern. Jim held a full-time job; Zoe stayed at home to take care of Benjy and do part-time work. "At the end of that year," Zoe recalls, "we were having severe problems communicating." In attempting to understand what was going wrong, they realized, in Zoe's words, "that for the first five or six years of our marriage we had worked cooperatively together on jobs and that we really did work well together."

Sharing one job and sharing the care of Benjy was their agreed-upon solution. But jobs that could be shared were hard to come by. They felt that they would have to create rather than find such a job.

At the same time, a new family day care license was adopted by the state of Minnesota. Called the Group Family Day Care License, it entitled a provider to care for, within certain specified provisions, up to ten children. The first year that this license was in effect, more than a dozen such group family day care homes and parent cooperatives were founded in Hennepin County. "We just knew," Jim Nicholie states, "that providers who were going to take care of six to ten children in their houses would need some support and help. We also just knew that there would be things coming down the pike that would affect group family day care; that is, legislative decisions would be made about funding and licensing. We thought these decisions should have some basis in real experience." Zoe and Jim decided that here was an opportunity to create a job that they could share, a job that would be of social use. It would be a two-pronged project that analyzed and studied the quality of these homes and that also offered services.

Their first move was to contact all of the people licensed to run group family day care homes in Hennepin County and ask them if they were interested in participating. They received in reply a resounding yes. Then they applied to the state for monies that had been set aside under the new license for a demonstration project. Their proposal was a contractor-type; the Group Family Day Care Project outlined goals and contracted with the state to reach these goals by a specified time. The group providers agreed to serve as an ad hoc committee-of-the-whole to meet monthly to determine the policies and directions of the project. There are now four staff members, Zoe and Jim, a fix-it person, and a driver for the van.

The service part of the project revolves around the van. With the van, the staff members take toys fom the Toy Lending Library to the group family day care homes and also provide transportation for field trips. "In the first six months," Jim says, "we started out doing field trips in the mornings. The provider would call up and schedule a trip and we would go to his or her home and pick up the provider and all the kids and go to a place that they had decided on. After a while, we found that there was a need in group family day care for the school-age children to get out in the afternoons and flex their muscles."

"We found," Zoe explains, "that the after-school time was a particularly hard time for the provider." The provider had the difficult job of finding an activity that would satisfy the energetic older children but was quiet enough so as not to awaken the little children from their naps. The van now picks up the school-age children from several homes and takes them on a trip with Jim or Zoe as the adult in charge. The Group Family Day Care Project provides these trips two afternoons a week, which means that every child in the homes that are part of the project goes on two such trips a month.

Linda Kelly is the fix-it person on the project's staff. She admits that a woman fix-it person is at first surprising to people. Her job is repairing toys and equipment, finding "scrounge" materials, and designing and building toys and environments. To begin with, Linda didn't know where to find scrounge materials. "I just started calling people [firms that might have rejected or salvageable materials] in the Yellow Pages, A to Z." She now has established local contacts. She knows what days the scrap bins at a lumberyard are likely to be full, when wallpaper companies might be willing to give away sample books, and she has regular days for picking up paper from printing companies. The scrounge materials that Linda collects are then distributed by the van.

Though the van is leased to the Group Family Day Care Project, it can be used by the other three programs at the Child Care Corner. Margaret Boyer of the Southside Child Care Committee uses the van to take political candidates on a tour of local child care facilities. Billie Lockett from the Resource Center uses it to bring people to workshops or meetings.

The four organizations that make up the Corner feel very strongly that they should stay separate and autonomous. Each should have its own community board of directors; each should be funded separately. And funding does not come easy in these times. Staff members at the Corner have to spend a great deal of time hustling money. But in this area, as in others, the organizations help each other, even to the point of writing joint proposals and letting each other know of any new-found source of money. Separateness does not mean exclusivity to these groups. It means cooperation. The very closeness of their quarters makes sharing inevitable. If Billie Lockett is out of her office giving a workshop or raising funds, the others in the three groups all know how to take down information for a referral. If Kathy Olson from the Toy Lending Library is out, the others know how to check out toys.

"This sharing makes our small budgets go farther," Jim Nicholie says. "We are all on very tight budgets. Sometimes there will be just one person in the office, but that doesn't mean that people who come in won't be helped; we all know how to help."

There are monthly Corner meetings to bring each group up to date on what the other groups are doing. These meetings are opportunities for members to discuss problems that may have arisen. Working together doesn't mean an absence of problems; there are times when the people on the Corner disagree.

In general, the staff members on the Corner find that their separate but cooperative positions work well. "When we get sick of dealing with each other," Jim says, "we can retreat within our own jobs."

Billie Lockett says, "Many times we talk about how we

don't want to be a clique that makes decisions for child care. We don't want to sit here on this Corner and say what is going to happen to everyone else."

The members maintain that their major problem has been reaching out to the "everyone else." Though they have made many inroads into their community, into the world of informal child care, they are not in the least satisfied. "We find that centers and providers use us a great deal," Billie maintains, "but one of the things that we are really lacking is use by community people. We are constantly working on getting more neighborhood connections."

Looking in on the Child Care Corner in Minneapolis on any one day gives one the feeling that the organization has brought together all of the elements of child care: it works with parents; it works with children; it works with the professional world of child care; it works with the community. Somehow, it all seems symbolized by the fact that as Billie Lockett talks on the telephone to a local parent, helping find the right child care center, her own daughter sits contentedly beside her and draws.

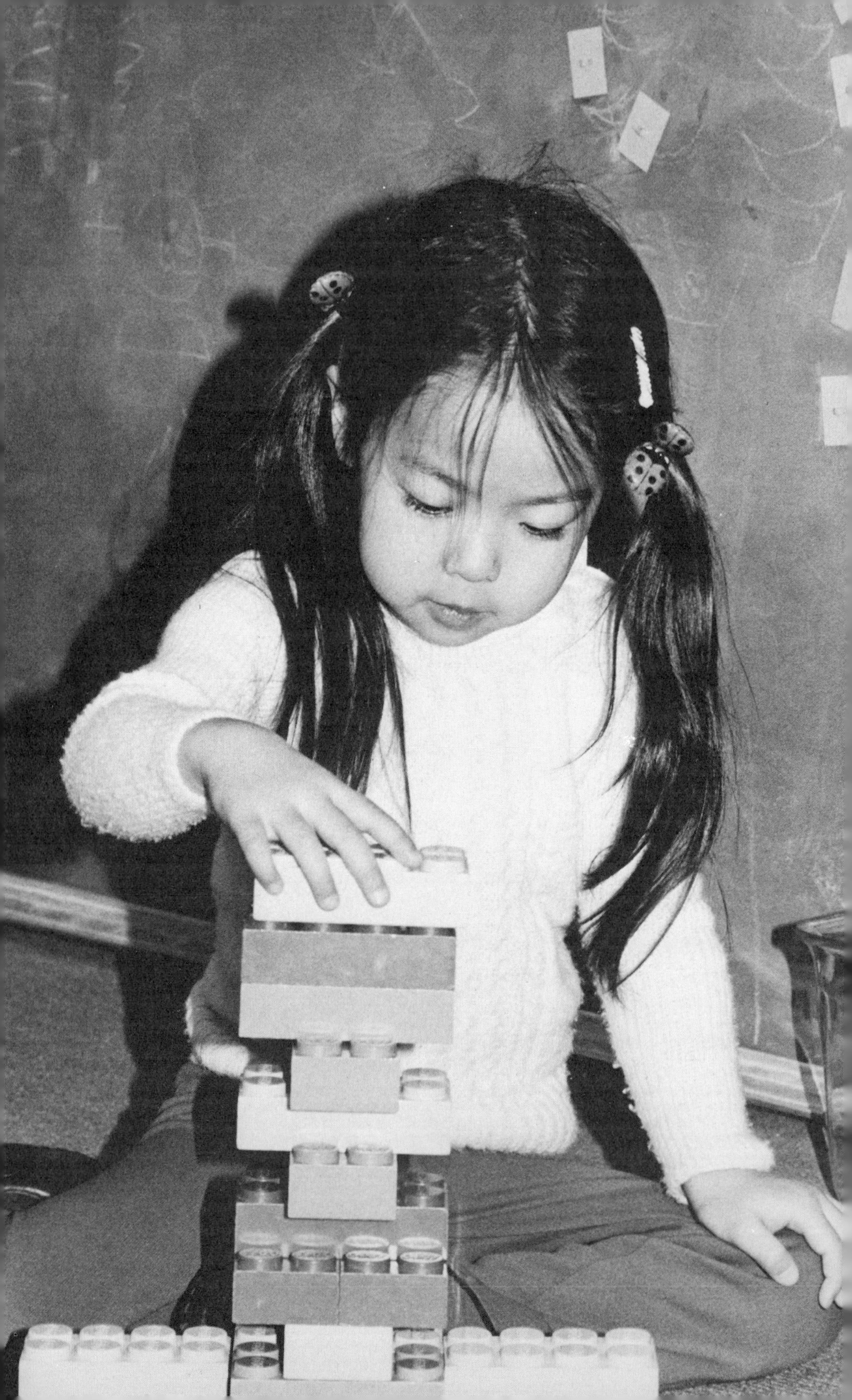

17
Patterns

This book has been a journey for us, not only geographically, but intellectually as well. All the while we were investigating specific programs, in specific places, we were traversing the realm of social organization. We were attempting to chart a course in this realm by asking ourselves: What makes a good child care program? Can we map any factors that are common to all the good programs in spite of the vast diversity among them?

In our first visit, to the Children's Pumphouse in New York City, we were struck by the personality of the director, Irma Garay. She was like a magnet who drew the program together and held it as a unit. Her force could be strongly felt.

In our next trip to investigate family day care, in Pasadena, California, we found the same phenomenon. Wherever we went, whomever we talked to, June Sale, a consultant to the family day care association, was mentioned. She was talked about in the same kind of terms we heard Irma Garay referred to — words of genuine admiration and respect.

We began to hypothesize: Does a good program of necessity have a special kind of person who acts as a unifying force, pulling the program together, making it cohesive?

Our next visit was to the Children's Center in Biddeford, Maine. There we found Betty Van Wyck. She fit into the same pattern. People in her program spoke about her in superlatives.

Are there qualities that these people (we came to call them leaders) all possess? The answer to that question was an overwhelming *yes*. These leaders had a dream, a vision of the kind of child care they wanted and they were persevering, willing to fight for it. They never took no as a final answer. We think of Jinny Burke. After long years of futile attempts by others to start a center at the National Institutes of Health, Jinny was able to cut through the red tape, by-pass the negatives, open the right doors, and get a center going. We recall a parent there who said, "NIH had a tiger by the tail, with Jinny!" There was also Ann Doss of Children's World in Colorado Springs, Colorado. Indefatigable, she went in and out of banks until she found one that would do the seemingly impossible — lend her $190,000.00, in a period of economic recession, to build a center. Karen Lieu, of the Chinatown Planning Council's After-School Program, is another example. She was willing to wait, literally in the hall, until the public school that housed her program conceded permanent space in the building for her office. We think, too, of Jerry Ferguson of the Infant-Toddler-Parent Center in Pasadena, California. When she was told that there was no possibility of letting the children in her program use a nearby bathroom, she went in on a Saturday and cut a hole in the wall between her room and the bathroom, to give the children access.

These leaders believed in their programs. They were willing to work long hours. Irma Garay scrubbing the floors at the Children's Pumphouse is a telling example. The leaders were not people who merely sat behind desks, isolated, protected behind masses of paperwork. They didn't feel it was beneath their dignity to do all kinds of jobs, including the so-called dirty work. We remember Ann Doss saying, "There is never a time when I can't drive a bus or cook a meal." But they also knew how to protect themselves from too much work. How to take some time off when necessary; how to say no; how to tackle the most important jobs, leaving the others for later. They conserved their time and energy so that they didn't burn out quickly.

Another quality that these leaders shared was the ability to select a strong group of people with whom they could work well. Peter Buttenwieser, of the Durham School in Philadelphia, was described by a colleague as possessing an "uncanny knack for picking the right people for his school." It was interesting to us that all of the leaders used the same criteria for hiring. They were not overly dazzled by the person's academic credentials. They weren't seduced by a sharp line. Rather, they tried to ascertain what kind of human being the applicant was. They asked themselves how that person felt about children. They tried to determine whether an applicant was open to learning. Marlene Weinstein, of The Learning Center in Philadelphia, noticed whether the candidate got down to the children's level. She found out as much as she could about the way in which this person handled stressful situations. Another basis for hiring was the manner of the candidate in responding to adults, particularly to parents. Here, perhaps, the criteria differ most markedly from the kind of hiring guidelines that are used in the majority of preschools and schools across the country, where it is hard to imagine a teacher's relationships with parents counting for much in hiring.

Another aspect of the techniques used in hiring fascinated us: these leaders did not make snap judgments or quick decisions. Interviews were lengthy, the candidate was observed, and the initial employment contract was provisional. The leaders were going to make sure that they had the right people in their programs. If they made a mistake, they were not averse to firing. "You have to be willing to fire," Betty Van Wyck states. She has found that the wrong people do not leave of their own accord; they stick like glue, programs decline, and the good people begin to leave. Here again, these programs differ from many day care programs and schools, which are notorious for holding on to people long after it has become apparent to everyone that they are not doing a good job.

The leaders saw themselves as taking care of their staffs. Ann Doss says, "Once I was out on the playground and a new child came up to me and asked if I was a teacher. I said no. She asked me what I did. I told her that the teachers took care of her and I was there to take care of the teachers." Ann then asked herself, "I wonder who takes care of me?" Betty Van Wyck feels strongly that the leader of a program must have a supervisor or someone to help them. Ann herself searched until she found the kind of help she needed.

In all of the programs, the leaders and their staffs said

that they felt a family relationship with each other. We reacted to that statement with suspicion. Was that the cliché of the day? The current day care code word? In our time as educators, we have seen that expression used to cover a multitude of misdeeds. We have seen directors or school officials say that they treated their staff like family, which meant lots of free labor and low pay. It also meant, among other things, that the members were close — but competitive. The director would compare one with the other, setting up feelings of stress that were indeed like the sibling rivalry found in some families. Another term we had heard in reference to the director of a program was "father-figure," or "mother-figure." This often meant that the director treated his or her staff like children or dependents. The people on the staff came to lean on the director, awaiting a nod before making a step, nourishing themselves primarily from the director's approval. Now we were hearing "like a family" again, and we were wary. We looked for indications of a family relationship gone sour; we searched, we scoured the dark corners everywhere for dependency on overly competitive relationships. And it must be said, and said emphatically, that nowhere in any of the programs we studied for the book did we find these flaws. We learned that the familylike relationships were grounded in the best attributes of home life, which in no way precluded growing professionalism on the part of all levels of staff.

Each of the leaders in these good programs allowed the staff a large measure of independence. "He lets me be myself," one person said of Peter Buttenwieser. "She gives us real responsibility," another person said in praise of Ann Doss. The leaders gave the people they worked with the opportunity to try things and, more important, to make mistakes without being subjected to censure. In other words, the leaders allowed their staffs to grow and learn. The leaders were like choreographers, modeling the movements. But at the same time these leaders encouraged others to try their own steps. "Because of Betty Van Wyck's confidence in me," reported a staff member at the Children's Center, "I was able to stand up and become the kind of person I wanted to be." "Because of our director's belief in us, we could probably walk across water," another caregiver said.

This is not to say that these leaders were without fault.

Each of them had eccentricities and failings, but these did not include hypocrisy, callousness, or narrowness of view. At their core, they were good, strong, humane people. And they sought and attracted other good, strong, humane people to work *with* them, not for them.

Most of the program leaders made sure the long hours of child care were not too demanding, too draining, or demoralizing for staff members. Teachers or caregivers were usually grouped in pairs. Working together, they could stimulate and encourage each other. We found staff members most involved if they were learning as well as teaching — if, for instance, they were participating in a project together, such as observing the nature of social relationships between one- and two-year-olds or studying the most effective method of grouping the children. We found, too, that it was very important for members of the staff to have some time during the working day for themselves.

Low pay for all those working in child care, caregivers and directors alike, continues to be one of the main problems in the field. Poor salaries weaken the commitment people feel for the work they are doing and the children they are caring for, making it less likely they will stay in their jobs for long periods of time.

Few, if any, of the leaders came to their programs with a refined background in administration. Most of them entered the profession with a good understanding of early-childhood education and a strongly felt sense of urgency about providing high-quality care for young children. Perhaps this was a plus in the beginning, since foreknowledge of the thousands of operational and administrative details might have deterred them. However, each of them learned quite early how dependent his or her center was on a knowledgeable administrator. Betty Van Wyck of the Children's Center says, "I have no doubt that if I hadn't become interested in administration, we either wouldn't be operating or we wouldn't be operating the way we are . . . Running a day care center is running a business first." This in no way is meant to undervalue the importance of program within a center. It is meant to emphasize the importance of good administration, without which the best programs may not survive.

A growing sense of political awareness was characteristic of the program leaders. Even the most apolitical among them found themselves moving into political arenas on the local, state, and federal levels. Everything from licensing procedures to life-blood funding was connected in one way or another to governmental agencies. Because they cared so deeply about their programs, many of them became political activists. Often they were joined by parents, especially when reduced services or withdrawal of funding became an issue that affected their children. These leaders and many parent supporters now fully realize the importance of active participation in helping to shape legislation that is going to affect the quality and amount of child care we have in the future. They are finding ways to make their feelings known and to enlist others in attempting to affect political action.

It was interesting to us to note that not all of these leaders were the directors of programs. In one case, the leader was the staff coordinator; in another, a parent; in still another, a consulting pediatrician. Each of the leaders of the first several places we visited, though, had had a hand in the founding of the program. The possibility that a founding leader was essential to the process of maintaining a good program was discouraging to us — so we were relieved to meet Gardenia White and John Gadson at Penn Center in Frogmore, South Carolina; Lloyd Vicente at the Parent-Child Development Program on the Pueblo of Acoma reservation in New Mexico; and Billie Lockett at the Child Care Resource Center in Minneapolis, Minnesota. Every one of these people came into an already existing concern and was able to take the wheel and move the program into new and promising ground.

The origins of the programs we visited had many similarities. For one thing, they grew out of real need. The people who started them did not do so because money was suddenly available — they were responding to a need. The most obvious need was that of working parents for child care. We think here of the mothers that Irma Garay saw day after day in Harlem, wanting to work, needing the income, but having no place to leave their kids. We think, too, of the employees at the National Institutes of Health, desiring child care so badly that they considered bringing their children to the office of the director of the NIH for a day to see if he would then get the message.

Perhaps at this point one may have a vision of the altruistic founder. This view is only half the truth. The founders of programs had very practical personal reasons for being at that place at that time. Jim and Zoe Nicholie at the Group Family Day Care Project in Minneapolis found that their marriage was better off if they worked together, and they wanted to find a job they could share. Ann Doss in Colorado was a widow with very young children; she had to find some way to support herself. The impetus for starting a program seems a blend, perhaps fortuitous, of personal and social needs.

The programs that we observed were initiated in some cases by parents, in others by professionals. It is significant to us that each sought an alliance with the other before moving very far. The professionals at Pacific Oaks College who began the Infant-Toddler-Parent Center went right to parents to find out what they wanted. The native Americans on the Acoma reservation invited noted academics from all over the country to consult with them, using some things that were said, rejecting others, until they had shaped their own program.

The dichotomy between parents and educational professionals in this country is wide. Professionals usually adopt an attitude of superiority — an attitude of having to fill the gaps and correct the wrongs that the parents have inflicted on the child. "If only that child didn't have that parent," "If only we could have gotten to that child sooner" are typical of statements frequently heard in teachers' conversations. In turn, parents have stood back, sometimes fearfully, awed by what they perceived to be the educator's greater knowledge. It is significant that the child care programs we visited had little of this kind of division. Perhaps this is because both parents and professionals were in on the beginnings of most of the programs. More probably, however, the compatibility and cooperation are related to the respect that both groups had for each other: they valued each other; they knew that they had important things to learn from each other; they knew that they shared jointly the same concerns for children. We saw no child care workers who felt or thought that they could replace the family. They all had the utmost respect for the families they worked with.

We were particularly interested in the values, the goals of each of the programs we studied. We know that goals ultimately determine the shape a program takes. If we had had to guess before we began, we might have predicted that most of these programs would have the same generalized goals (such as promoting the well-being of the child). We would have been wrong. We found that each program had a different emphasis, a different stress. The Children's Center in Biddeford wanted children to learn to do things for themselves, to be independent. The toys and materials were all easily accessible to the children; the dining room had a serving pass to the kitchen so that children could serve and clear for themselves. In fact, every detail of the program, from the placement of the bathrooms to the overall schedule, was planned to encourage independence. Why, we wondered to ourselves, would this particular program have this goal? One answer is obvious: the program serves some children with handicapping conditions. Most of the time people do things for these children: they feed them, dress them, walk them around. There comes a time when children with handicaps need to learn to be on their own. It is the opportunity to do this that the Children's Center offers. It also seemed fitting to us, although we weren't quite sure of its significance, that the Children's Center is in New England, a stronghold of independence. We would be less likely to find such a strong emphasis on teaching independence in New York City, for instance, where, because of the real dangers of city life, children are given constant supervision for a much longer time.

There were, indeed, patterns in the values we found. City programs were often meant to be calm refuges from the overstimulation and overcrowding of the city. Rural programs were set up to help children overcome their shyness and timidity. Programs serving black or immigrant children were more likely aimed at enabling the children to get ahead. Here, education was seen as providing the skills for upward mobility. Programs that enrolled predominantly middle-class children usually stressed socialization, helping children learn to live well together.

We did find geographic differences. It seemed very appropriate that the Children's World program, in the rugged, powerful mountains of Colorado, emphasized physical skills. It seemed equally fitting that the staffs of the programs we visited in the densely populated cities talked about helping people emerge from the separate boxes they had enclosed themselves in and get together.

We came up with one finding that has been borne out in all our observations: the best programs have goals that address themselves to the needs as well as the values of the communities they serve. This is undoubtedly one of our most important findings. It is a powerful argument against mass-produced child care. It is an equally persuasive case against the consolidation of child care centers unless the combined groups are carefully planned to accommodate individual differences and are desired by all the participants. It means that child care at its best should not be prescribed by remote authorities, whether they are the personnel of the Department of Health, Education, and Welfare or the state Department of Social Services or prestigious education departments in colleges and universities. By this we don't mean that the advice of authorities should be ignored; we mean simply that it should be used, adapted, reshaped, and sometimes changed to suit the needs of programs that are truly indigenous.

In the past decades, programs serving minority children have tended to ignore ethnic backgrounds and to concentrate on Americanization — in other words, to homogenize the children and bring them into the general flow of our culture. If the programs we visited indicate a trend, it is the fortunate ending of this era. We saw the start of the new era in Acoma native American children learning about their past, their foods, their music, and their dances. We saw it in Chinese children learning about their Chinese culture. And we saw it in Mexican-American children who were placed in Mexican-American family day care homes, where traditions and cultural background were incorporated into the caregiving. These children were being given insights into both cultures; they were being taught skills to help them survive in the American world as well as pride in their own backgrounds.

There was another quite important pattern we found. Whether programs were home-based or center-based, they all had ties to professionalism in one form or another. The family day care mothers' relationship to WATCH in Pasadena is an example. The Children's Pumphouse maintained a close relationship to Bank Street College, where staff members matriculated for training in early-childhood development. The Learning Center in Philadelphia served as a demonstration school for the Medical College of Pennsylvania and other nearby colleges. Students from universities were accepted for field placement work by the Children's Center in Maine, and by the Preschool Development Program at the National Institutes of Health. In all of the programs the staffs were encouraged to maintain professional contacts, to remain active learners both on the job and through continuing formal education. At the same time these programs showed a willingness to reciprocate by freely sharing their own ideas and methods with observers and student teachers.

A sentence we heard over and over in the programs we visited was "'We want to be an extended family for the parents." This might have seemed trite to us had we not seen so many real, vibrant demonstrations of it. All the programs we visited in institutional settings had a home-like ingredient somewhere in their composition. The Learning Center had a man and a woman at the head of each group, and children clustered in a mixed-age pattern resembling a family. The Family Center at Bank Street College in New York City was set up to look like an apartment. Parents played a large part in the running of that center, as they did in the center at the National Institutes of Health in Bethesda, Maryland. The Children's Center provides one of the best blends of home and institution. It is in the process of establishing a program in which children are taken to family day care homes in the morning, brought to the center for school hours, and returned at the end of the day to their family day care homes.

In fact, all of the adults in these programs helped each other with much more than child care. They brought personal and legal questions to each other for advice; they helped find housing for each other; they helped paint and fix up one another's homes; they helped plant gardens. This aid was not just one-directional — the staff helping parents; it flowed in both directions. They all had occasion to give and to receive help.

Before putting their children in a child care program, most parents felt guilty. "Am I doing the right thing?" they worried. "Will this weaken my relationship with my child?" We found that the younger the child, the more severe the parents' guilt. We asked parents many questions about this guilt: "Have you had your child in other programs? Did you feel guilty then? Do you feel guilty now?" If the guilt had gone away, we asked, "What made that happen?" The parents' answers pointed to one conclusion: their guilt did not subside if they felt they were surrendering their child to a little-known place, if they had a buyer-seller relationship with the program, or if they sensed they had made a wrong decision. Their guilt did dissipate when they understood the program, felt that it was a good one, and knew that they were an integral part of its operation.

There is a tendency in many educational child care programs in this country to have an overriding concern with problems and frailties. The educator all too often sees his or her purpose as saving the child from problems. It was a pleasant surprise to us that in our first visit to most places, we heard almost no derogatory labeling. Children were not described in terms of their deficits ("She's aggressive" or "He's a stutterer" or "She comes from a terrible home"). Frequently, though not always, we noted the same avoidance of depreciation during our subsequent visits. It is a source of great pride to Betty Van Wyck at the Children's Center that visitors can't readily pick out the children who enter her program tagged emotionally disturbed, blind, or cerebral palsied. In most of the programs people were talked about in reference to their strengths: "See that child. She's wonderful with any art material" or "He is the most lovable little boy." This positive attitude toward people did not prevent caregivers from helping children where they needed help, but they did so in an atmosphere charged with optimism.

A positive approach was reflected in these programs' discipline policies. Aberrations of behavior were seen not as the results of children's deficiencies; they were seen as understandable problems demanding resolution. If two children were fighting, the caregiver would not explode in self-righteous indignation against fighting; he or she would get down to the children's level, find out what they were angry about, and then help them find solutions that were alternatives to physical combat.

We also found that the values for curriculum paralleled those for discipline. Most of the caregivers' efforts were geared toward making children feel good about what they could accomplish. Interestingly, it is the curriculum in child care that has stirred up the strongest response when we have discussed our study with friends and colleagues. We have been asked, "How does the curriculum in child care centers compare with that in preschools?" We have been informed that the academic curriculum in child care centers is the weakest link in these programs. We have been reminded that it wasn't long ago that child care programs began to introduce an academic curriculum at all. And, conversely, we have been told that "child care should be a substitution for home and shouldn't emphasize school-type learning at all."

We have visited all kinds of programs — some that take place during school hours and some after school. We have come to agree with Betty Van Wyck's definition of curriculum: "It is what adults and children do as they live together." Children are always learning, whether they are sitting, looking around, painting, playing, or reading books. If we had to rate the curriculum in the programs we visited, we could rate much of it as good. We saw unusually creative learning environments: the modular sky-lighted building in Colorado Springs, with a swimming pool and gymnasium inside, for instance; the series of play yards at the Pacific Oaks Infant-Toddler-Parent Center, designed with psychological and physical development in mind — these were inspired and inspiring spaces. We saw excellent homemade materials. There was the climbing-hiding structure at the Child Care Resource Center in Minneapolis. And there were the fantastic materials at the Parent-Child Development Program on the Pueblo of Acoma: an appealing homemade wheel-toy horse, counting games, the beautifully drawn book *Grab Day at Acoma*, to name just a few. At the Chinatown After-School Program in New York City, many beautiful puzzles, games, and reading books were made by the children themselves.

One way of viewing curriculum is by determining whether it is initiated by the children or the adults. If we use this as a measure — children at one end and adults at the other — we would place the program at Penn Center in Frogmore, South Carolina, near the far end. There, the curriculum was initiated by adults a great deal of the time. The program at the Family Center at Bank Street College and the Infant-Toddler-Parent Program at Pacific Oaks would, perhaps, fall near the other end of the line. There, curriculum activities were often triggered by the children's interests. The other programs fell between — adults organized some teaching times, and children had free-choice times, when they could explore materials, ask questions, and pursue their own interests.

Another way to analyze curriculum is to ascertain how much time the children spend waiting and how much time they spend working or playing. In all but one program there was literally no waiting time. Yet another method evaluating curriculum is based on who talks and when, and what they say. Is it the teachers' voices that predominate, for instance? In all the programs we visited, the air was alive with children's voices. The children were not talking in set or formal ways; their voices were pensive, eager, excited, sad, quiet — always alive.

We did see the children engaged in similar kinds of activities in all the programs: painting, making collages, building with blocks, swinging, and playing in sand piles. And we saw more or less the same daily schedules used all over the country. Furthermore, we did on occasion see some misguided activities: children being asked to discuss a foreign country when they had no idea what a "country" was; children studying desert life and plants when they didn't know what a "desert" was; children coloring pictures of fruit when they would rather have done a hundred other things. We saw children all drawing the same boring pumpkins or making the same prosaic fireman's hats. But we saw no programs so heavily laden with this sort of thing that it was dampening the children's curiosity or squelching their spirit.

When a child's day is lengthened to include day care along with schooling, the arrangement is never quite right. We realized people who understood that the schedule and curriculum for schools and child care programs must be different were grasping an important fact. New curricula are emerging, but there is ample room for more creative work in this area.

Several of these programs had a tangential or direct relationship with another institution. None of these relationships was easy and all had periods of jeopardy. When resources became scarce, whether they were time, money, or space, the child care programs were the first to feel the pinch. We heard tales of trials and tribulations, fundings withdrawn, new restrictive regulations issued from on high.

The tenuous position of many centers seems significant to us. It is a sad comment on the present position of child care within our culture. Child care help is not yet accepted as a social responsibility, except for the neediest members, and is often viewed as an invasion of the parental role. "Perhaps it is because children don't vote," Jim Nicholie of Minneapolis guesses, "or perhaps because child care workers aren't organized." Mary Afcan, in an Alaska child care newsletter called *Enep'ut*, writes, "We demand tax-supported education so our youth may grow to their full greatness; we demand tax-supported jails to protect us from people labeled dangerous; we demand tax-supported animal shelters to protect us from homeless and dangerous dogs; but, perhaps because kids *don't* bite as hard as dogs, we don't demand tax-supported child care."

Where good programs exist, they have been hammered out despite opposition, but they have also been made to come alive by strong support from those who found child care a necessity or were dissatisfied with available programs. They exist because some very committed people believed in them and were willing to act on that belief. "We are what we are because of the individuals who have made it happen," Jerry Ferguson of the Pacific Oaks program says. "We've kept right on going with little or no support from others."

The lack of broad-based support — both in funding and in attitude — is perhaps the most crucial problem in child care, but as with most problems, if you look at it from another vantage point, it can become a source of strength. Because our country has let child care grow untended like a wild field, both weeds and beautiful flowers have grown side by side. This neglect, which in a strange way has allowed for freedom and independence, has produced a much broader spectrum of child care than would have existed if the programs had been carefully supervised by governmental agencies. It has produced programs that belong to the directors, the parents, the teachers, and the children. They have fought for the programs. They are proud of them. And that is as it should be, because child care, which is as broad as society, is at the same time as private as the individual, since it reaches into the very personal realm of parents and children. They are the ones who must decide what this care should be.

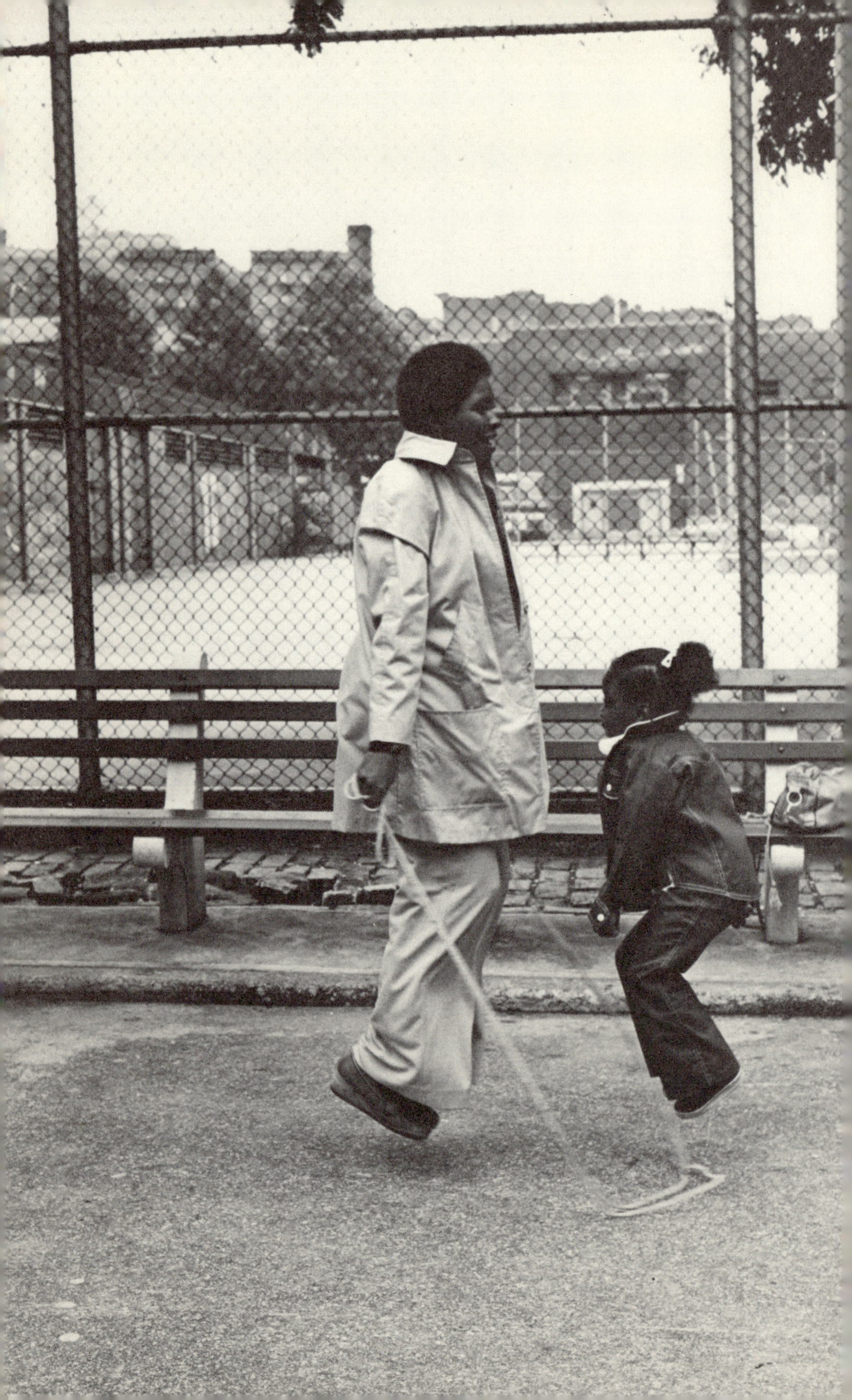

18
The Political Arena

Child care is political. Whether it is for infants or older children, whether it is only custodial and minimal or broadly conceived and comprehensive, it reflects values and beliefs. Legislation and public policy directly and indirectly affect what happens to children in a region that was formerly considered the sole province of the parents: the raising of children. And when parents or professionals feel their rights have been encroached upon by public policy, they usually step into the political arena.

The future of child care has been widely and publicly debated. Sometimes, as we listen to speeches or read statements in newspapers, we have the sense that a new continent has been discovered, provoking a series of skirmishes over who will gain control.

A great deal is known about how organized groups feel about these issues. The National Association of Education for Young Children says child care belongs in the hands of educators trained in early-childhood development. The teachers' unions say child care belongs in schools. The schools support this stand. Some parents disagree. We became interested in looking beyond the public posturing. We suspected that the people who had managed to create good programs would have valuable insights that could be called on for shaping legislation. We asked them, "If you could write child care legislation, what would it be like?"

Our question prompted immediate indictments of present legislation. Wherever we went, we heard the same complaints. For example, Title XX, the major piece of existing federal social-service legislation, is written with a focus on problems. The first two goals of Title XX are directed to parents:

— achieving or maintaining economic self-support to prevent, reduce, or eliminate dependency;

— achieving or maintaining self-sufficiency, including reduction or prevention of dependency.

The remaining goals, although they apply to children, stress problems:

— preventing or remedying neglect, abuse, or exploitation of children and adults unable to protect their own interests, or preserving, rehabilitating, or reuniting families;

— preventing or reducing inappropriate institutional care by providing for community-based care, home-based care, or other forms of less intensive care; or

— securing referral or admission for institutional care whose other forms of care are not appropriate, or providing services to individuals in institutions.

The emphasis in this legislation is on "preventing" and "remedying." It is designed, primarily, to serve parents with problems — parents who, for instance, are economically dependent. It is assumed that, with the availability of child care, these parents might make strides toward becoming economically self-sufficient. The legislation is also intended for children who are neglected, abused, exploited, and for children who are handicapped emotionally or physically and who might otherwise be institutionalized.

On the surface, the emphasis of Title XX may seem supremely fair. After all, parents who are out of work or otherwise in trouble need more help than other parents. It *seems* fair — until one considers that the United States is the only nation to construct its child care programs with such a heavy stress on problems.

The result, according to the people we interviewed, is that child care programs are imbued with strong negative overtones. The emphasis says to parents, in effect, that if they could better themselves, they would rid themselves of the need for child care. It says to the staffs of programs that they are working with a pathological part of the population. It segregates a community by grouping together the poor, the abused, and those with other problems.

Good day care, meeting Title XX specifications, is costly. As a result, in many communities, centers that take Title XX children become too expensive for fee-paying families. These centers end up serving mainly Title XX children, and will continue to do so unless public support shares this cost with a sliding fee scale for families.

Billie Lockett of the Child Care Resource Center in Minneapolis says bitterly that Title XX centers might as well put a sign on their doors stating "Aid for Dependent Children Only." Jinny Burke, of the Preschool Development Program in Bethesda, Maryland, calls these centers "ghettoes" for poor children, saying that, by isolating poverty, they perpetuate poverty. Jim Nicholie, from Minneapolis, feels that segregation by money is a racist policy. "It is segregation by government edict," he points out. "The people aren't segregating themselves."

The money from Title XX is tied in to state welfare systems. In most states, child care comes under the aegis of the state Department of Welfare or the state Department of Social Services. John Gadson, of Penn Center in South Carolina, says, "The Welfare Department is a negative institution and it relates to people in a negative way. The money comes down as negative money, and it gets administered negatively. It takes away from people rather than developing people."

Another criticism of Title XX is that day care centers are funded on a per-child basis. The government purchases services for a certain number of children, or "slots." The drawback to this method is that program staff members come to think of children as numbers instead of as human beings. Billie Lockett says that Title XX day care centers will call her Information and Referral Service and say, "I have three Title Twenty slots. Do you know how I can fill them?" Billie says, "They talk about slots when they should be talking about kids or families. It's getting to the point where slots are more important."

Under the per-child method of funding, centers are allowed a certain amount of money for each full-time child. In addition, the total amount of money given to a program under the slot method is divided into narrow budgetary lines, which become a constraint on innovation and experimentation. This funding method practically predetermines uniformity of programs.

Our interviewees objected strongly to this standardization. They didn't mean that they were against having standards that protect children; they meant that they were against having programs that were carbon copies of one another. They believe that there should be a variety of child care choices in each community, and that child care programs should be responsive to their own populations. Standardization, they feel, sets the stage for rip-offs. It makes it easier for real estate developers to get away with excessively expensive leases. It makes it possible for the misuse of money, or graft. And it makes it probable that programs will become tied to high administrative costs. Billie Lockett deplored the fact that a large proportion of the money intended for child care is "gobbled up at the top," while the people who work directly with children make next to nothing.

Standardized programs are expensive programs. Title XX day care costs for infants range from $75 to $100 per week; $45 to $65 for group care of preschool children. The yearly price tag at the top of this range is $5200 for an infant and $3380 for a preschool child. The cost is extremely high for the government, and completely out of the price range for many families, especially when one considers that some families are at the first stages of their earning capacities or have more than one child who needs care. "Something has to be done about the cost of child care," Jinny Burke says. "It can't go on costing what it does now."

Furthermore, the people we interviewed do not like the amount of control that funding organizations hold over programs. Money is a carrot held in front of them to determine which way they will turn, how fast and how far they will go. "A lot of organizations and foundations and the government sit down and write the definition of what the program should be like," John Gadson says. "They base their funding on that. If you don't let yourself look the way they want you to look, you don't get the funding."

The people we interviewed hated the funding agencies' expectation of instant results, measurable in research statistics. "Everyone thinks you're doing a good job," says Gardenia White of Penn Nursery in Frogmore, South Carolina, "if you tell them something that they can count in numbers. But that isn't what we are trying to do." Her colleague, John Gadson, explains, "When you deal with people and their growth, things can't always one-two-three."

Everyone we talked with agreed that licensing was essential for health and safety. But there was also unanimous agreement that there are serious problems when licensing procedures are used for program content standards. Day care staffs invariably expressed a need for help and consultation, but felt it should come from other sources, not from licensing officials. The following three stories are typical of what we heard in all the places we visited:

- The licensing agency calls up to inform a very chaotic messy center that they will be visiting the following week. Everyone works like crazy, gets the place cleaned up, and it passes the inspection with flying colors. Then the people there go right back to their disorderly ways.
- Licensing personnel visit a center during nap time; all the children are sleeping. They spend five minutes in one room looking through a file; they glance at a bulletin board; then they leave. Their report states that this program has nothing for children to do.
- A well-funded center that passes licensing inspections with no problems turns out to be one that ignores children's needs and parents' values.

We've heard of and even seen (but not in the programs described in this book) dreadful incidents: children being struck, children stashed in wastebaskets, even children sexually assaulted. It is clear that the licensing procedures are not an effective method of ensuring quality. Licensing agencies are too understaffed — the members overworked and often untrained — for the job they are performing. Gardenia White feels that licensing agencies should continue to set standards having to do with fire escape, building, and health codes, but that "they should not be the people who come to help you. They don't know anything about it and they look over your shoulder in a negative way. People get turned off and people get mean. That's what's happened in a lot of the public schools. The principal always tells the teacher what is not good, and the teachers get meaner and meaner and the kids get more frustrated. The best way is to go in and find the ways in which you can be helpful."

Most of the people in the programs we visited were aware of the need for public help but were not in favor of the government's creating a major child care system at the present time. As opposed to what the Washington lobbyists and the press have been saying, these child care people had some concerns about the kinds of programs outlined in recent child care legislation. They feel that with such legislation, the mistakes of the past might be compounded, setting child care on the wrong track. They are worried about plowing huge sums of money into what would probably become standardized day care centers. They feel that such legislation would elevate the cost above what most people could afford. The cry for such standardized centers assumes that the informal child care going on in a community is substandard. Our interviewees didn't share that outlook. Their view was not based simply on the assumption that people, unfettered by systems and bureaucracies, would behave well; they *know* about the quality of child care going on in their neighborhoods. The staff at the Child Care Corner in Minneapolis is in constant communication with neighborhood people. In Portland, Oregon, Alice Collins has spent years studying neighborhood care systems. These people feel that much of the informal child care is potentially good, and should be strengthened rather than eliminated. They don't want to create a child care system that will become another Medicaid — increasingly expensive, impersonal, sometimes riddled with fraud.

We asked, "But what *does* work? How can the quality of good child care be assured? What kinds of legislation are needed? What kinds of funding?"

As with the indictments of current conditions, there was an uncanny degree of agreement among the people we interviewed on the future course of child care. It was as if these people, from all parts of the country, had met previously and mapped out legislative strategies; of course, most of them didn't even know each other. From our conversations with them we have drawn up a list of the principles that we and they would like to see as the basis for any future child care legislation.

1. *"The family is the primary and the most fundamental influence on children; child and family service programs must build upon and strengthen the role of the family . . . "* This is part of the opening statement of S.626, a bill sponsored in the United States Senate by Walter Mondale in 1975. It is the belief of the people we interviewed that this bill makes a critically important point by establishing all programs according to this tenet. Child care programs, they believe, must respect the family and never try

to supplant it. And all of the programs discussed in this book do respect and support the family.

2. *Child care programs should augment and extend the positive things already happening in child care in each community.* The people we interviewed feel that child care programs should not wipe out the child care already occurring in a community, but should use it, improve it, extend it, and, when necessary, create new programs. Perhaps the program at the Pueblo of Acoma is the best example of this approach. It uses the skills of the people who have been doing family day care — the children's grandmothers and aunts, for example. Under the program, these people are entitled to adequate money and to training.

One of the problems with proposed and existing child care legislation is that it is constructed to remedy social deficiencies. And the community must have a deficit — it must be a community without adequate child care. Abt Associates (a private consulting firm in Cambridge, Massachusetts, that has done research into the field of child care) and the Bank Street Day Care Consultation Service have both noted what happens with this mode of public policy. Peter Sauer of Bank Street says, "There are countless communities across the country where a government program has arrived, and the result of it, two years later, is that there are fewer baby sitters and child care options in that community, and the cost of those options has doubled."

3. *Child care programs should take into account all of the families' needs in raising children.* Intellectually, one can categorize children's needs: their physical growth, their language development, their social growth, their health needs, their psychological progress. But people in programs we visited feel that child care programs should not define their territory narrowly, dealing only with certain aspects of the child. They can stress specific goals, but in addition they should be a resource for families in all their needs. If the programs don't provide a particular service, the staff should know where to send parents to find it. We saw this kind of referral being given in the programs we studied. In fact, the CETA program for family day care providers in Pasadena, California, makes a point of inviting people from Pasadena's service agencies to seminars in order for them to meet the family day care providers.

4. *Child care programs should establish positive goals for the healthy child.* This would mean a new direction for all child care, which in the past has been geared to serve mainly the neediest families. We found it interesting that the programs we visited did not accept these restrictions. Many found ways — often very clever ways — to include all strata of American society. In Philadelphia, The Learning Center by-passed the government's restrictions in theory by having its population come from the community, which is poor, and from the Medical College, whose students are only temporarily poor.

5. *Child care should be available to anyone who wants it.* Everyone needs help in raising children.

6. *There should be a wide range of child care within each community.* The choice should be very broad, encompassing, in Marlene Weinstein's words, "as much variety as there are neighborhoods and community needs." Here the issue of who should control child care comes to the fore. Advocates from the teachers' unions and public schools are urging that child care be incorporated within the American public school system. This action would serve their needs very well. The baby boom has ended, and schools, which had expanded to meet the surge in numbers of students, are now faced with empty classrooms. Many communities have been forced to close the doors of elementary schools, and many teachers have lost their jobs. Bringing preschool and child care programs into elementary schools would keep teachers, who would undergo retraining, or would add new teachers to the rosters and fill up some of the empty classrooms.

We found that the people we interviewed were not averse to having child care programs in public schools. They favored a cooperative arrangement with the schools, such as the one at Ayrlawn Elementary School in Bethesda, Maryland. The parents in Bethesda rent space in the school and run their own before- and after-school and holiday programs. The Chinatown Planning Council has a similar arrangement with several public schools in New York City for their after-school and vacation-time programs. While child care people would support a cooperative arrangement with the public schools, they were generally very wary of schools' taking over child care programs. "Public schools don't show concern for parent involvement," Marlene Weinstein states, "and I'm afraid that parents would get lost in the shuffle." Jim Nicholie agrees: "I think that parent control would be very quickly lost in the public schools." He and many others are concerned that teachers trained to work with older children would be transplanted into the preschool, and the result would be a watered-down grade school curriculum for young children. Preschool-age children require teachers who have knowledge in their specific stage of development and who have skills in preschool curriculum development. Jim Nicholie also feels that "the public schools are geared toward the white middle class, despite all efforts to the contrary." He feels this is true for both children and adults. He states that, for the most part, adults can't even enter the public school system without a degree; whereas child care has offered an opportunity "for people to get into it while their kids are young, and work their way up — get some skills and move ahead." Furthermore, Jim feels that "the qualities that one needs to make it in the [public school] system are not the same qualities that you need to do good child care."

We visited several programs where the control resides in the public school system and the programs are responsive, community-centered places. For thirty-three years, Docia Zavitovski has run day care centers in the public schools in Santa Monica, California. These centers are notable for the way they use the resources of the public schools. One, in the John Adams Junior High School, has its child-development and home-economics students working regularly with the young children. In addition, the eighth-grade remedial students help the younger children learn to read and at the same time improve their own reading skills. "You can just see the feeling of accomplishment on the children's faces," Docia says.

The Durham School in Philadelphia offers excellent child care for both infants and preschoolers, but it exists more as a monument to the efforts of Lore Rasmussen and Peter Buttenwieser than to the public school bureaucracy. Peter describes the whole process of creating good child care within the public school system as "very disenchanting." He adds, "What the system wants, in essence, is the product without the process."

It became obvious to us that, given good leaders, good programs can be created within the public education system. We think that child care in the public schools, either under the control of community groups or the schools, is viable if parents have control over the program and staffing, if parents are in constant day-to-day communication with caregivers, and if this is only one part of the spectrum of the child care choices in the community.

7. *Within each community, there should be an organization that disseminates information about local child care options so that parents can make informed choices.* The arguments used most frequently against giving parents a choice in their own child care are: "Parents will make hasty decisions," "Parents aren't knowledgeable enough about education to make choices," and "Parents will do what's most convenient for them, not what's best for the child."

The people who actually work with parents in making choices consider these arguments fallacious, and feel that they reflect an attitude of professional superiority that has very little basis in actuality. The staff at the Child Care Resource Center in Minneapolis feels that parents do "want the best for their children." Regardless of parents' underlying motives, these arguments are nullified when there is a community organization whose purpose is to help parents make educated choices. The staffs of these organizations, such as the Child Care Resource Center in Minneapolis, the Pre-School Association of the West Side in New York City, and the Gathering Place in Ithaca, New York, present parents with several options. They arrange for parents to visit child care settings, and they brief parents on how to judge a child care center or home. After the parent has made a decision, members of the staff follow up with a telephone call to see how things have worked out.

Alice Collins, of Portland, Oregon, has an interesting suggestion for expanding the usefulness of information and referral services: "If I had my way," she says, "I'd have a consultant on the staff of every information and referral service who could spot the people in the neighborhood who are already helping others find baby sitters — the natural helping neighbors — and team up with them." Alice Collins feels that this use of neighbors improves the quality of local child care.

8. *"Child and family service programs . . . must be provided on a voluntary basis only to children whose parents or legal guardians request such services, with a view toward offering families the options they believe are most appropriate for their particular needs."* Again the wording comes from the Mondale bill. And it is a new direction —

away from the current Title XX legislation, whose purpose is ostensibly to reduce the welfare rolls. Obviously, under Title XX there are some instances of parents having been forced to enroll their children in particular centers lest they lose their benefits.

As long as the central purpose of child care is linked to public welfare, it will continue to taint child care. The relationship turns it into something coercive, unpleasant, and unwanted. Child care, according to the people we interviewed, should be strictly voluntary, serving families who want it. And the choice of a particular child care arrangement should never be made for a family. The family should be presented with the possibilities available and then be left to make its own decision.

9. *Parents and community members must have influential decision-making power in their own child care programs.* There have been many attempts to spell out more conclusively what "influential decision-making power" means. Does it mean that 51 percent of the board of directors are parents and community members?

From our experience, we have come to believe that the fulfillment of this requirement should be left to the program planners and initiators themselves, perhaps including some built-in grievance procedures and child advocacy principles. In all the programs we visited, parents were respected, listened to, and influential. But the forms of parent participation varied widely. We saw programs where all the power resided with the parents, and those that were genuinely "open to parents' suggestions" but in which parents had no administrative responsibilities. We think that there should be options in this aspect of child care as in all others.

On the other hand, we think that the creation of local advisory boards is a good idea. The Consortium in Pasadena, California, for instance, seems to work particularly well. Consisting of local leaders in children's services as well as family day care providers, the Consortium is able to agree upon its own goals for child care and then to use clout in bringing those goals to actuality.

10. *It is essential that the funding of such programs be undertaken as a partnership of parents, community, private agencies, and state and local government with appropriate assistance from the federal government.* The main obstacle to basing child care on positive goals for the healthy child and offering it to everyone is the staggering

cost. It is simply too expensive a prospect for the federal government to undertake alone without a reordering of national priorities, an event we consider unlikely. Therefore, the funding of child care has been a problem many people have grappled with, and no one has really solved. We feel that the Mondale bill, from which the above principle is taken, heads in the right direction by insisting that all child care programs have broad-based funding. This is to the advantage of the funding agencies because it lessens the expense that any one segment of society has to pay. It is equally advantageous to those who are funded — it makes them less dependent on one source of revenue and, consequently, less likely to lose their program if a single source of funding withdraws its money.

The best funding plan we heard of was put forward by Stella Alvo of the Women's Action Alliance in New York City, and Susan Angus of the Women's History Project in Denver. They advocate that funding be divided into stages. The first step is for groups to figure out the minimum amount of money they need to operate. This prime level of the program should be self-supporting. "Then, even if the groups get no outside funding," Susan Angus points out, "they can at least operate on that basis. They can have the confidence that they'll exist." The money for this prime level can come from parent fees or from a regular commitment on the part of the parents and staff to fund-raising, or a combination of the two. "The organizations that have done this," Susan says, "have had times when they have had to resort to doing that basic operation with no outside money, living from hand to mouth, hoping for volunteers, and doing bucket drives on the corner every week. But it's meant that they've never had to close down and it's meant that there is some kind of consistency — that they are always there for the community. The important thing is that they are not dependent on outside funding to exist. They are going to exist anyway."

Stella Alvo and Susan Angus think that child care programs should consider budget-planning as one of their most critical jobs — that there should be a person or a committee with the job of overseeing budget-planning and formulating a two- to three-year strategy. Stella Alvo suggests that each child care program look over its local business community and form a "Friends Committee," whose members will be allies and advisers on financial matters. For the second phase of funding, beyond the self-supporting level, they propose that funds should be solicited from as many sources as possible: local businesses, churches, and foundations; national foundations; and county, state, and federal projects. Some portion of the monies that go to child care should be designated for start-up costs: for renovation, or making capital improvements in order to bring a home or center up to licensing standards. Both Alaska and Minnesota have built start-up costs into their state child care programs.

"If funding is broad-based," we asked, "how much should parents pay? Should parents of all income levels pay the same, or should they pay different amounts?" The almost universal response was, "Parents should pay *something*." Gardenia White suggests that if parents don't have any money, they can pay by volunteering their time to help with the children or to make toys and equipment. Most of our respondents feel that parents should pay on a sliding fee scale based on income as determined by regional Bureau of Labor Statistics offices.

Many of the people we interviewed are strongly in favor of having the federal government contribute its share of the cost of child care in the form of vouchers: parents would be given vouchers that could be spent at the child care home or center of their choice. Vouchers would promote diversity of child care arrangements and would put the choice of child care in the hands of parents. Others we spoke to are not in favor of the voucher system, feeling that it would give rise to all kinds of excessive advertising promotions and claims, putting child care on a par with commercial products that are hawked to the American public. Still others feel that vouchers are not a politically feasible alternative. The precedent in our country has been funding of programs, not parents.

"Where would the additional money come from?" we asked. "From existing revenues? From new revenues?" There was general agreement that there is room for new sources of money and that the burden should not fall on the government alone. It was felt that business and industry should take more responsibility in providing child care as a benefit of employment. Here, vouchers seem the ideal solution. The Polaroid Corporation has pioneered in this venture by establishing a child care voucher system for its employees. Polaroid pays a portion of the child care costs, that portion determined by the employee's salary. The payment goes directly from the company to the child care home or center. The Ford Foundation has taken this system a step farther by reimbursing its employees a minimum amount toward child care costs, thus leaving the child care transactions in the hands of the parents rather than having money pass from the corporate pocketbook directly to child care, with the ever-present possibility of corporate control over child care. Industry can also support child care through the donation of space and contributions to maintenance costs.

We asked if there were any provisos that should be placed on child care money. We were told that administrative costs should be curtailed so that, according to Jim Nicholie, no money "is wasted on needless bureaucracy and organizational structures." This is a precept that Alaska has taken well into account. Its recent Day Care Assistance Program requires that 100 percent of the state monies designated for child care must go directly into child care. Any community wishing to partake of the state funds must pay its own administrative costs. When communities pay all administrative costs, there can be immediate and much closer checks and control over the amount of spending.

11. *There should be accountability for every aspect of a child care program.* Traditionally, only the operational aspects of day care centers have been held accountable. The people we interviewed feel that everyone involved — the sponsor and the sponsored — should be held accountable for what he or she does. Children need protection; they need local advocates to help set standards. Sue Aronson of The Learning Center in Philadelphia feels that there can be beneficial monitoring that does not hamper growth. "I am thinking in very concrete terms," she says, "about safety of the environment, about practices that permit parents to have a role in the program and look for concrete evidence of it. I see this very much like hospital or college accreditation — the kind of thing where you have experts who have been in the field to serve as advisers. And then there should be others who carry out those standards. I also think it is important for the standards to be reviewed periodically so that they don't get to be restrictive."

Peer review, which is practiced by the staff and parents of the Preschool Development Program in Bethesda,

Maryland, has proved an effective method of personal accountability.

12. *Every community should have voluntary technical assistance available.* Our interviewees feel strongly that technical assistance should not be linked to guidelines or standards. Technical assistance should be voluntary so that it is readily available to programs. We have seen and heard of some very good examples of technical assistance. The Child Care Corner in Minneapolis is a great source of aid to child care in South Minneapolis — from helping staff write proposals, to building and repairing equipment, to setting up the Toy Lending Library, to providing a van to take children on field trips.

Using CETA monies, the state of Alaska has founded a small cadre of carpenters. All of them have worked in day care before, and know and understand children as well as environments for children. These carpenters maintain a woodworking shop that is a place for child care people to bring equipment for repair or to build things themselves. Mary Afcan, who was instrumental in starting this program, says that these carpenters are also "going out and finding family day care providers who are unlicensed and helping them bring their homes up to licensing standards by building beautiful things for them."

In New York City, where day care seems to go from crisis to crisis, the Bank Street Day Care Consultation Service is often a lifesaver for the child care community. Members of the staff of the Day Care Consultation Service have provided legal and investigatory assistance in helping centers fight closings; they have probed into and uncovered graft and fraud in the original negotiations of day care leases; and they have been successful in helping to prevent the closing of centers. In addition, they have originated joint fund-raising efforts to help save centers that have lost their funding.

13. *The day care program should ultimately help to develop "kith and kin" systems, in which people help each other.* The good child care programs we studied have become extended families to the people they serve. We feel that this principle should be the overarching one in the establishment of child care programs.

With these thirteen principles forming the staves of a legislative program, we began casting about for a way to join them together. Were there any precedents? Were there any bills that resembled a child care bill like the one we envision? Peter Sauer of the Bank Street Day Care Consultation Service had been asking himself the same questions. When we talked with him, he said, "There is the Older Americans Act of nineteen sixty-five. I think something like that for children might be part of the answer."

This bill could be called the "American Family Act." It would provide block grants to citizens' groups to provide services for children and families. The act would include guarantees of citizen participation much like those already written into the Environmental Protection Act. Under these grants, services could not be narrowly defined; that is, a day care center would not be merely a collection of classrooms. Services for children and families would have to have wide scope and several purposes. Furthermore, these grants could enlarge the bounds of child care to include park facilities, health care, or information and referral services. Grants would be made to help communities build on the good child care practices that already exist, and help to establish new programs when needed.

The impact of such legislation would be enormous. It would foster the notion that people can help each other. It would promote creative solutions. It would, in fact, be productive for all involved. In the end, this act would build communities. And, in doing so, it would move away from the fragmentation wrought by an industrialized society of sharply disparate specializations.

Marlene Weinstein has had a dream of what child care could be. With current funding patterns, this dream is almost impossible of realization. Perhaps with an American Family Act, it could be achieved. "I would love to see us operate as a community center in the best sense of the word," she says. "A place where supper is served. We have lots of families who are students, who are on shifts, and it really makes it difficult for one person to come home and make supper. We have a wonderful kitchen here, and all this space, and families could have dinner here together. We have a sewing machine — families could sew here. We could have a library. We could buy one book that could be read by five people, and one newspaper that could be read by ten. This is my personal dream. I don't think it would be ideal for everyone, but it would be for us at The Learning Center."

We are often asked what we think is going to happen in

the field of child care. Will programs continue to tread water, trying not to sink, hoping to stay afloat? Will child care continue to be seen as a do-good society's token for the poor? Will it continue to be linked to welfare? Or will things change?

We do think we have seen a change coming. We have seen it on the parents' faces, heard it in their voices. Many of these parents were raised to believe the maxim that the best parent is one who does everything alone; who gallantly shoulders all responsibility; who is independent. But they found that the maxim isn't true. They have had to toss it aside and seek help. Initially, they feared child care. They worried that their family ties would be loosened. Somewhere they had heard that child care might produce a nation of people whose loyalties were toward groups, a nation of conformists. And they worried about that, too. These parents have found good child care programs; and they have found that *good* child care does not dissolve the family. It fortifies it. And it provides extended families, like the kith and kin groups of past generations. Within this good child care, the children remain individuals, and families remain intact.

We could tell that a change was coming by the very fact that the programs we visited are peopled not just with the most disadvantaged segment of society; their population usually comes from every stratum of society. And if the statistics and predictions are correct, more and more families will be looking into the field of child care. They all won't be looking for the same thing. Some will want drop-in care; some will want center care; some will want after-school care; some will want part-time care. Some will want programs that emphasize school readiness; others will want programs that focus on social development. Some will want to employ neighbors or teen-agers as caregivers; some will want to call on senior citizens. Some will be able to pay the full cost of child care; others won't.

The programs we have looked at all across the country have convinced us that the change that is inevitably coming can be a change for the better. Whether it will is up to all of us.

Selected Readings

Breitbart, Vicki, ed. *The Day Care Book.* New York: Alfred A. Knopf, 1974.
Collins, Alice H. and Watson, Eunice L. *Family Day Care: A Practical Guide for Parents, Caregivers, and Professionals.* Boston: Beacon Press, 1976.
Curtis, Jean. *Working Mothers.* New York: Doubleday and Co., 1976.
Daycare, Child Development Series. Washington, D.C.: Office of Child Development, 1971–1972.
Evans, E. Belle and Saia, George E. *Day Care for Infants.* Boston: Beacon Press, 1972.
Evans, E. Belle; Shub, Beth; and Weinstein, Marlene. *Day Care: How to Plan, Develop, and Operate a Day Care Center.* Boston: Beacon Press, 1971.
Harlow, Nora. *Sharing the Children: Village Child Rearing within the City.* New York: Harper Colophon Books, 1975.
Harris, Robie H. and Levy, Elizabeth. *Before You Were Three.* New York: Delacorte Press, 1977.
Levine, James A. *Who Will Raise the Children? New Options for Fathers (and Mothers).* Philadelphia: J.B. Lippincott, 1976.
McBride, Angela B. *The Growth and Development of Mothers.* New York: Barnes and Noble, 1973.
Poussaint, A.F. *Black Child Care.* New York: Pocket Books, 1976.
Roby, Pamela, ed. *Child Care — Who Cares?* New York: Basic Books, 1973.
Ruopp, Richard; O'Farrell, Brigid; Warner, David; Rowe, Mary; and Freedman, Ruth. *A Day Care Guide for Administrators, Teachers and Parents.* Cambridge, Mass.: The M.I.T. Press, 1973.
Stein, Sara B. *About Handicaps, An Open Family Book for Parents and Children Together.* New York: Walker and Co., 1974.
Steinfels, Margaret O'Brien. *Who's Minding the Children?: The History and Politics of Day Care in America.* New York: Simon and Schuster, 1973.
Stone, L. Joseph and Church, Joseph. *Childhood and Adolescence,* 3rd ed. New York: Random House, 1973.
Willis, Anne and Ricciuti, Henry. *A Good Beginning for Babies.* Washington, D.C.: National Association for the Education of Young Children, 1975.

Index

Abt Associates (Cambridge, Massachusetts), 261
Accountability, need for, in all aspects of child care programs, 268–69
ACD, see Agency for Child Development
Acoma Parent-Child Development Program (San Fidel, New Mexico), 143, 244, 245, 250, 261; Acomita Day Care Center of, 144–45, 151–53; admissions to, 150; beginnings of, 143–48; discipline at, 153–54; food programs at, 155–56; goals of, 149–50; grouping at, 151; health program at, 156; McCartys Day Care Center of, 144–45, 149, 151, 153, 155–56; parent participation at, 154–55; problems and changes at, 158–59; space and daily schedule at, 151–53; staff selection at, 150–51; training at, 156–58
Acomita Day Care Center, see under Acoma Parent-Child Development Program
Admission policies: at Acoma Parent-Child Development Program, 150; at After-School Program (Chinatown), 176–77; at Children's Center, 94–95; at Children's Pumphouse, 78–79; at Children's World, 136; at Infant-Toddler-Parent Center, 68; at The Learning Center, 21–22; at NIH Preschool Development Program, 115–16; at Sakach (Debbie) group family day care home, 195–96, 199
Advisory boards, creation of local, 265
Afcan, Mary, 252, 269
After-School Handbook, 176
After-School Program (P.S. 42, Chinatown, New York City), 240, 250; admissions to, 176–77; beginnings of, 174–76; daily schedule at, 179–81; discipline at, 181–82; food program at, 185; funding of, 185; grouping of, 178; health program at, 185; parent participation at, 182–85; problems and changes at, 186–87; staff selection at, 177–78; training at, 185–86
Agencies, inadequacies in child care, 223–24

Agency for Child Development (ACD, New York City), 79, 85, 86, 87–88; funding of Chinatown After-School Program by, 174, 175, 177, 185
Ainsworth, M.D.S., 16
All-Indian Pueblo Council, 156
Allen, Jennie, 137
Alvo, Stella, 266–67
American Family Act, proposed, 270
Angus, Susan, 266–67
Aragon, Hilda, 145
Aronson, Sue, 13, 268; on beginnings of The Learning Center, 17–18; health plan of, 28; on parent participation, 26–27
Ayrlawn Elementary School (Bethesda, Maryland), 112, 114, 116, 262

Bank Street College of Education (New York City), 86, 247; Day Care Consultation Service of, 211, 261, 269, 270; Family Center at, 35, 36, 47, 48
Bank Street School for Children (New York City), 40, 41, 46–47
Beginnings: of Acoma Parent-Child Development Program, 143–48; of After-School Program (Chinatown), 174–76; of Children's Center, 91–92; of Children's Pumphouse, 76–77; of Children's World, 129–31; of Durham School, 52–53; of Family Center at Bank Street, 36–38; of Gomex (Amparo) family day care home, 204; of Infant-Toddler-Parent Center, 64–65; of The Learning Center, 17–18; of NIH Preschool Development Program, 112–14; of Penn Nursery/Day Care Center, 162–63; of Sakach (Debbie) group family day care home, 194–95
Behavior modification techniques, 138
Belanger, Irene, 96, 100–101, 102
Beller, Kuno, 56
Ben Franklin Institute (Philadelphia), 15–16
Bittle, Calley, 39, 40–41, 47
Bloomfield, Byron C., 130, 133
Board of Education (Philadelphia), 52
Boissonneault, Priscilla, 108
Bowlby Report, 16

273

274   Index

Boyer, Margaret, 227–28, 232, 236
Breitbart, Vicki, ed., *The Day Care Book*, 128
Bronfenbrenner, Uri, 41
Brown, Mrs. Corinne, 162–63, 169
Bureau of Indian Affairs (BIA), 143
Bureau of Labor Statistics, 267
Bureaucracy, unresponsiveness of, to children and families, 224
Burke, Virginia "Jinny" (coordinator, NIH Preschool Development Program): on admissions, 115–16; and beginnings of program, 112–14; on cost of child care, 258; on funding, 123; leadership of, 240; on relationship between NIH and Preschool Development Program, 124–25; on staff selection, 116; on Title XX centers, 257
Buttenwieser, Peter (director, Durham School), 52–53, 240–41, 242, 263
Byrd, Doris, 193

Caldwell, Betty, 17
Caregivers, *see* Staff
Catholic Diocese (Portland, Maine), 92, 104
CETA (Comprehensive Employment Training Act), 193, 261, 269
Chase, Linda, 145, 149, 150, 151
Child Care Corner (Minneapolis), 229, 234, 236–37, 260; four organizations making up, 223, 225–27; technical assistance at, 269. *See also* Child Care Resource Center; Group Family Day Care Project; Southside Child Care Committee; Toy Lending Library
Child Care Resource Center (Minneapolis), 223, 225–27, 236, 244, 250; activities of, 228–33; formation of, 228; funding of, 227–28; help offered to parents at, 264
Children's Center (Biddeford, Maine), 3–4, 239, 248; admissions to, 94–95; beginnings of, 91–92; discipline at, 100–102; food program at, 103; funding of, 104–5; goals of, 93–94, 246; grouping at, 96; health services at, 103–4; parent participation at, 102–3; problems and changes at, 106–9; program at, 92–93; staff selection at, 95–96; training at, 105–6
Children's Pumphouse (New York City), 3, 75–76, 239, 240, 247; admissions to, 78–79; beginnings of, 76–77; discipline at, 80–82; food program at, 84; funding of, 85–86; goals of, 77–78; health services at, 84–85; origin of name, 89; parent participation at, 82–84; problems and changes in, 87–89; space and daily schedule at, 79–80; staff selection at, 79; training of teachers and parents for, 86–87
Children's World Play School Learning Centers (Colorado Springs [Mesa], Colorado), 127–29, 240, 250; admissions and grouping at, 136; beginnings of, 129–31; daily schedule at, 133–35; discipline at, 138; flexible concept of roles at, 137–38; food program at, 135–36; funding of, 140; goals of, 133, 246; health program at, 138; parent participation at, 139; problems and changes at, 140–41; space at, 131–33; staffing procedures at, 136–37; training at, 138–39
Chin, Lois, 178, 181–82, 184, 186
Chinatown Health Clinic (New York City), 185
Chinatown Planning Council (New York City), 173, 182, 240, 262; beginnings of, 174–76; policy of community development of, 185; position of, in union strikes, 187. *See also* After-School Program Chinese Garment Manufacturers Association, 174
Chino, Cyrus, 144
Chisholm, Shirley, 189
Clausen, J. A., 13
Cohen, Allen (director, Chinatown Planning Council): and beginnings of council, 174–76; on parent participation, 182–83, 184–85; on problems with custodians, 186; on staff selection, 177
Coles, Alice, 15, 19, 23
College training, controversy over value of, to day care, 87
Collins, Alice, 264; creation and operation of Day Care Neighbor Service by, 215–21; *Family Day Care* (with Eunice Watson), 212–14; research of, on neighborhood day care, 212, 214–15, 260
Community control, 88
Consortium (Pasadena, California), 191, 265
Cook, Shelia, 102, 106
Cunningham, Edith, 58
Curriculum, academic, in child care centers, 249–51
Curtis, Jean, *Working Mothers*, 111

Daily schedules, 251; at Acoma Parent-Child Development Program, 152–53; at After-School Program (Chinatown), 179–81; at Children's Center, 96–100; at Children's Pumphouse, 79–80; at Children's World, 133–35; at Durham School, 54–57; at Family Center at Bank Street, 39–41; flow of, 9–10; at Gomez (Amparo) family day care home, 206–7; at Infant-Toddler-Parent Center, 68–69; at The Learning Center, 25; at NIH Preschool Development Program, 117–19; at Penn Nursery/Day Care Center, 165–68; at Sakach (Debbie) group family day care home, 197–99

Index   275

Day Care Assistance Program (Alaska), 268
Day Care Neighbor Service (Portland, Oregon): creation of, 215; operation of, 215–21; preliminaries to, 211–15
Department of Agriculture, 123
Department of Health, Education, and Welfare, 247
Department of Public Welfare, 21, 257
Department of Social Services, 247, 257; California, 194, 203; Colorado, 140; Maryland, 123; South Carolina, 164, 165, 168, 170
Directors, see Leaders
Discipline: at Acoma Parent-Child Development Program, 153–54; at After-School Program (Chinatown), 181–82; at Children's Center, 100–102; at Children's Pumphouse, 80–82; at Children's World, 138; at Family Center at Bank Street, 43–45; at Gomez (Amparo) family day care home, 207; at The Learning Center, 25–26; at NIH Preschool Development Program, 119–20; patterns in programs' policies of, 249; at Sakach (Debbie) group family day care home, 199–200
Doss, Ann (founder, Children's World), 132–33, 138, 245; on flexible concept of roles, 137, 138; on food program, 135–36; founding of Children's World by, 129–30; on funding, 140; leadership of, 240, 241, 242; on parent participation, 139; her problems at Children's World, 140–41; on stock-purchase plan, 137; on use of skylight domes, 131
Dudevoir, Duke, 98, 99, 100
Dully, Poppy, 62, 63, 69
Durham School (Philadelphia), Teen-Age Mother Program at, 51–53; goals of, 53–54; health and food at, 57; learning responsibility at, 57–58; problems and changes at, 58–59; space and daily schedule at, 54–57

Eden House (Minneapolis), 232
Education Systems Corporation, 113
Educational Development Corporation, 156
Emlen, Art, 214
Enep'ut, 252
Enrollment, see Admission policies
Environmental Protection Act, 270

Fairbanks, Cheryl, 144, 146, 149–50, 158–59
Family, need for child care programs which respect and support, 260–61
Family Center at Bank Street (New York City), 35–36, 250; absence of director at, 46; beginnings of, 36–38; daily schedule at, 39–41; discipline at, 43–45; funding of, 46–47; goals of, 41–43; groupings at, 38; parent participation at, 45–46, 248; problems and changes at, 47–49; space arrangements at, 39
Family day care (Pasadena, California), 189–93, 239. See also Gomez, Amparo, family day care home of; Sakach, Debbie, group family day care home of
Family Day Care Association (Los Angeles County), 202
Faulkner, Irvina, 168
Featherstone, Joseph, 128
Ferguson, Jerry (founder, Infant-Toddler-Parent Center), 69, 253; child care goals of, 64; on confinement of parenthood, 62; on environment for children, 67–68; founding of center by, 61, 64–65; leadership of, 240; and parent participation, 71; on problems with Pacific Oaks College, 72–73; on relationships among children, 70
Food programs: at Acoma Parent-Child Development Program, 155–56; at After-School Program (Chinatown), 185; at Children's Center, 103; at Children's Pumphouse, 84; at Children's World, 135–36; at Durham School, 57; at Family Center at Bank Street, 40; at Infant-Toddler-Parent Center, 70; at The Learning Center, 28; at NIH Preschool Development Program, 121–22; at Sakach (Debbie) group family day care home, 201–2. See also Lunch and snacks
Ford Foundation, 268
FTE (full-time employment), 136, 140
Funding: of After-School Program (Chinatown), 185; of Child Care Resource Center, 227–28; of Children's Center, 104–5; of Children's Pumphouse, 85–86; of Children's World, 140; divided into stages, 266–67; of Family Center at Bank Street, 46–47; of Gomez (Amparo) family day care home, 208–9; of Infant-Toddler-Parent Center, 71–72; of The Learning Center, 31; need for broad-based, 265–66, 267; of NIH Preschool Development Program, 123; of Penn Nursery/Day Care Center, 164–65; per-child method of, 257–58; of Sakach (Debbie) group family day care home, 202–3; of Southside Child Care Committee, 227–28; voucher system of, 267–68

Gadson, John, 244; on funding, 164–65, 258; on parent participation, 168; on Penn Center, 161, 162, 163; on Welfare Department, 257
Galinsky, Ellen, 36, 38, 41, 45, 48–49
Galinsky, Lara, 35, 38, 41, 43
Garay, Irma (director, Children's Pumphouse), 244; on discipline, 82; on

276　Index

Garay, Irma (*continued*)
ethnic food, 84; formation of Children's Pumphouse by, 76–77; on funding, 85; leadership qualities of, 239, 240; on origin of names "Children's Pumphouse," 89; on parent participation, 83–84; and problem of funding interim center, 87; on training of teachers and parents, 86
Gardening, involving children with, 155–56
Gathering Place (Ithaca, New York), 264
Getze, Linda, 62, 69, 71
Goals: of Acoma Parent-Child Development Program, 143–48; of Children's Center, 93–94, 246; of Children's Pumphouse, 77–78; of Children's World, 133, 246; of Durham School, 53–54; of Family Center at Bank Street, 41–43; of Gomez (Amparo) family day care home, 204–5; of Infant-Toddler-Parent Center, 63–64; of The Learning Center, 18–21; of NIH Preschool Development Program, 114–15; patterns in, among day care programs, 245–47; of Penn Nursery/Day Care Center, 163–64; of Sakach (Debbie) group family day care home, 195
Gomez, Abuelo, 190, 205, 206–7, 208
Gomez, Amparo, family day care home of, 190; beginnings of, 204; discipline at, 207; and formation of WATCH, 192; funding of, 208–9; goals of, 204–5; grouping at, 206; health at, 207; parent participation at, 207–8; problems and changes at, 209; space and daily schedule at, 206–7; training at, 208
Grant, Sandra, 80, 84
Greater Minneapolis Day Care Association, 227, 228
Grose, Deidre, 53–54, 57, 58
Group Family Day Care License (Minnesota), 234
Group Family Day Care Project (Minneapolis), 223, 225–26; activities of, 235–36; formation of, 234–35
Groupings: at Acoma Parent-Child Development Program, 151; at After-School Program (Chinatown), 178; at Children's Center, 96; at Children's World, 136; at Family Center at Bank Street, 38; at Gomez (Amparo) family day care home, 206; at The Learning Center, 23, 248; at NIH Preschool Development Program, 116–17; at Sakach (Debbie) group family day care home, 196–97
Guidelines, for selection of day care program, 7–13
Guilt, parental, 8, 248–49

Handbook for Camping, 180
Handicapped children, *see* Children's Center
Harmon, Darrel Boyd, 130–31
Harriet Tubman Shelter (Minneapolis), 232
Head Start, 52
Health programs: at Acoma Parent-Child Development Program, 156; at After-School Program (Chinatown), 185; at Children's Center, 103–4; at Children's Pumphouse, 84–85; at Children's World, 138; at Durham School, 57; at Gomez (Amparo) family day care home, 208; at The Learning Center, 28–29; at NIH Preschool Development Program, 122–23; at Penn Nursery/Day Care Center, 168; at Sakach (Debbie) group family day care home, 202
Hennepin County (Minnesota) Family Day Care Association, 233
Honig, R., 17
Honoré, Ella, 26
Hooks, William, 36n
Human relationships, 10–11
Humble Oil Company, 89
Hutchenson, Penny, 196

Iba, Barbara, 120
Independence, as goal for day care children, 20, 93, 246
Indian Health Service, 155
Infant-Toddler-Parent Center (Pasadena, California), 61–63, 240, 245; admissions at, 68; beginnings of, 64–65; curriculum at, 250; daily schedule at, 68–69; funding of, 71–72; goals of, 63–64; parent participation at, 69–70, 71, 72; problems and changes at, 72–73; space at, 65–68; staff selection and training at, 70–71
Infants: opposition to out-of-home care for, 16; proponents of day care for, 16–17

John Adams Junior High School (Santa Monica, California), 263
Johnson, Annie Lee, 164
Johnson, Norma, 168, 169
Jones, Coralyn, 112, 113
Jordan, Constance, 195–96

Kelly, Linda, 235–36
"Kentucky Fried Children," 128
King, Martin Luther, Jr., 162
Kingston, Thelma, 141
Kiwanis Club (Willmar, Minnesota), 233
Kleinberg, Judy, 135; *The Day Care Book*, 128
Klopf, Gordon, 37
Kose, Gary, 15, 20

Lake, Alice, *The Day Care Book*, 128
Lambert, Annie, 102
Lauritzen, Phyllis, 191, 193
Leaders, day care: family relationship between staff and, 241–42; low salaries for teachers and, 243; political

Index 277

awareness of, 243–44; qualities of, 239–41, 242–43; reasons for initiation of programs by, 244–45
Learning Center, The (TLC, Philadelphia), 13, 15–17, 241, 247, 262; admission to, 21–22; beginnings of, 17–18; daily schedule at, 25; discipline at, 25–26; funding of, 31; future hopes for, 270; goals of, 18–21; grouping at, 23, 248; health program at, 28–29; parent participation at, 26–28; Policy Advisory Committee (PAC) of, 27; problems and changes at, 31–33; space arrangements at, 23–25; staff selection at, 22–23; training at, 29–31
Lee, David, 184, 187
Lee, Steven, 184
Legislation, child care: indictments of present, 255–58, 260; principles as basis for future, 260–69; and proposed "American Family Act," 270
Levenstein, Phyllis, 146
L'Heureux, Deborah, 102–3
Licensing, 48, 73, 87; procedures, used for program content standards, 258–59
Lieu, Karen (director, Chinatown's After-School Program): on ACD funding, 185; on attitudes of public school teachers, 187; and beginnings of program, 175; on day care versus public school, 187; on discipline, 182; on food program, 185; leadership of, 240; on parent participation, 183; on problems related to Chinese values, 186; qualifications of, 185; on staff selection, 177–78
Lippitt, Ronald, *Socialization and Society*, 13
Lipton, R.C., 16
Lockett, Billie, 236–37; and Child Care Resource Center, 226, 228, 230–33, 244; on misuse of child care funds, 258; on Title XX centers, 257
Lucario, Jack, 155–56
Lucario, Rebecca, 150, 158
Lunch and snacks, 9; at Acoma Parent-Child Development Program, 153; at Children's Center, 99, 101; at Children's Pumphouse, 80, 84; at Children's World, 135; at Family Center at Bank Street, 40; at Infant-Toddler-Parent Center, 70; at NIH Preschool Development Program, 117–19; at Penn Nursery/Day Care Center, 166. *See also* Food programs

McCartys Day Care Center, *see under* Acoma Parent-Child Development Program
Macdonald, Maritza, 45, 49
Macdonald, Pete, 35
Macdonald, Scott, 35, 43, 45
Mai, Andy, 181
Materials, 10, 68, 250

Medicaid, 260
Medical College of Pennsylvania, 17, 21, 28–29, 31, 247, 262
Metropolitan Museum of Art (New York City), 181
Miles, Edith, 116, 119
Mondale, Walter, 260, 264, 266
Montgomery County (Maryland) Community College, 124
Moses, Emma, 85

Nap time, 10; at Children's Center, 101; at Children's Pumphouse, 80; at Family Center at Bank Street, 40–41; at NIH Preschool Development Program, 119
National Association of Education for Young Children, 255
National Institutes of Health (NIH Bethesda, Maryland), Preschool Development Program at, 111–12, 240, 244, 248; admissions to, 115–16; beginnings of, 112–14; discipline at, 119–20; food program at, 121–22; funding of, 123; goals of, 114–15; groupings at, 116–17; health services at, 122–23; parent participation at, 120–21, 248; peer review at, 268–69; problems and changes at, 124–25; space and daily schedule at, 117–19; staff selection at, 116; training at, 123–24
Neighborhood Youth Corps, 228
Nicholie, Benjy, 234
Nicholie, Jim, 236, 252; and Child Care Corner, 226; on child care money, 257, 268; on child care in public schools, 262–63; and Group Family Day Care Project, 234–35; 245; and Toy Lending Library, 234
Nicholie, Zoe, 234–35, 245
NIH, *see* National Institutes of Health
Noxon, Molly (director, Infant-Toddler-Parent Center), 62; course in Infancy taught by, 70; on goals of center, 64; and parent participation, 69, 71

Odione, Olive, 70
Office of Child Development, U.S., 215
Okin-Wertheimer, Judy, 20, 21–22, 31
Older Americans Act (1965), 270
Olson, Kathy, 236

Pacific Oaks College (Pasadena, California), 189; and Infant-Toddler-Parent Center, 61, 64, 71, 72–73, 245; study by, of family day care, 192
Parent-Child Development Program, *see* Acoma Parent-Child Develoment Program
Parent-child programs, *see* Infant-Toddler-Parent Center
Parent-controlled day care, *see* Children's Pumphouse
Parent Handbook, 114

278 Index

Parent participation: at Acoma Parent-Child Development Program, 154–55; at After-School Program (Chinatown), 182–85; at Children's Center, 102–3; at Children's Pumphouse, 82–84; at Children's World, 139; at Family Center at Bank Street, 45–46, 248; at Gomez (Amparo) family day care home, 207–8; at Infant-Toddler-Parent Center, 69–70, 71, 72; at The Learning Center, 26–28; at NIH Preschool Development Program, 120–21, 248; at Penn Nursery/Day Care Center, 168–69; at Sakach (Debbie) group family day care home, 200–201; variation in, among programs, 265
Parent-staff cooperative, see Family Center at Bank Street Parenthood, myth about, 1–2
Parents: guild of, 8, 248–49; initiation of day care programs by, 245; relationship of, to child care program, 11–13
Parents of Preschoolers (POP, Bethesda, Maryland), 114, 116, 120–21, 122
Pasquale, Arlene, 151
Pastor, Jeff, 98, 100
Patterson, Corinne, 54–55
Pederson, Frank A., 16
Penn, William, 162
Penn Community Services, 161
Penn Nursery/Day Care Center (Frogmore, South Carolina), 161–62, 244; beginnings of, 162–63; curriculum at, 250; daily schedule at, 165–68; funding of, 164–65; goals of, 163–64; health program of, 168; parent participation at, 168–69; problems and changes at, 170–71; training at, 169–70
Penn Urban Medical Center, 57
Piaget, Jean, 56
Picasso, Pablo, 181
Planning Council of United Way (Pasadena, California), 191
Polaroid Corporation, 267–68
Politics: of child care, 255; as enemy of day care center, 31–32; need for awareness of, by day care leaders, 243–44; role of parents in, 84. See also Legislation, child care
Port Royal Experiment, 161–62
Portnof, Gabriel, 36
Portnof, Nancy, 36
Pre-School Association of the West Side (New York City), 264
Preschool Development Program, see under National Institutes of Health
Problems and changes: at Acoma Parent-Child Development Program, 143–48; at After-School Program (Chinatown), 186–87; at Children's Center, 106–9; at Children's Pumphouse, 87–89; at Children's World, 140–41; at Durham School, 58–59; at Family Center at Bank Street, 47–49; at Gomez (Amparo) family day care home, 209; at Infant-Toddler-Parent Center, 72–73; at The Learning Center, 31–33; at NIH Preschool Development Program, 124–25; patterns of optimism in dealing with, 249; at Penn Nursery/Day Care Center, 170–71; at Sakach (Debbie) group family day care home, 203–4
Professionalism, ties between day care programs and, 247–48
Profit-making day care centers, see Children's World Play School Learning Centers
Provence, Sally, 16
Public schools, proposed child care in, 262–64

Rasmussen, Lore, 52, 263
Rawley, Gwen, 135, 139
Reisz, Margarete, 127
Roby, Pamela, ed., *Child Care — Who Cares?*, 111, 211
Rudolph, Carol (director, NIH Preschool Development Program): on discipline, 119, 120; on goals, 114; on food, 122; on parent participation, 120, 121; on staff selection, 116; on training, 124
Ruel, Pauline, 91

Saine, Elabio, 205
Saine, Julie, 209
Saint James's Church (Philadelphia), 17–18
St. John-Parsons, Donald, 36
Saint Mary's Episcopal Church (New York City), 76
Sakach, Debbie, group family day care home of, 190–91, 193–94, 204; admissions to, 195–96, 199; beginnings of, 194–95; discipline at, 199–200; food program at, 201–2; funding of, 202–3; goals of, 195; grouping at, 196–97; health services at, 202; parent participation at, 200–201; problems and changes at, 203–4; space and daily schedule at, 197–99; staff selection at, 196; training at, 203
Sale, June, 189, 191, 193, 239
Sanchez, Grandma, 153, 154, 158
Sanshu, Ezilda, 155
Sauber, Doug, 20, 23, 26, 31
Sauer, Peter, 211, 261, 270
Selection and Criteria Committee (NIH Preschool Development Program), 116
Senior citizens, activities of Resource Center for, 232
Shelton, Helen (director, Children's World), 141; on daily schedule, 134–35; on enrollment size, 136; on food program, 135; on goals, 133; multiple tasks performed by, 137; on par-

ent participation, 139; and staff turnover, 137; on training, 138–39
Silverman, Phyllis, 47; and Family Center at Bank Street, 35–36, 39; on food program, 40; on parent participation, 45; on spontaneity, 43
Simons, Sandra, 145–46, 153–54, 156, 158
Smalls, Jean, 169
Smith, Mrs., 213–14
Southern Christian Leadership Conference, 162
Southside Child Care Committee (Minneapolis), 223, 225–27, 236; funding of, 227–28; Needs Assessment Committee of, 227; operation of, 227–28; Outreach Committee of, 227; Proposal Review Committee of, 228; and Resource Center, 228, 229
Space arrangements, 10; at Acoma Parent-Child Development Program, 151–52; at Children's Center, 96–100; at Children's Pumphouse, 79; at Children's World, 131–33; at Durham School, 54; at Family Center at Bank Street, 39; at Gomez (Amparo) family day care home, 206–7; at Infant-Toddler-Parent Center, 65–68; at The Learning Center, 23–25; at NIH Preschool Development Program, 117–19; at Sakach (Debbie) group family day care home, 197
Special Food Services Act (Maine), 104
Spitz, René, 16
Staff, selection of: at Acoma Parent-Child Development Program, 150–51; at After-School Program (Chinatown), 177–78; at Children's Center, 95–96; at Children's Pumphouse, 79; at Children's World, 136–37; at Infant-Toddler-Parent Center, 70; at The Learning Center, 22–23, 241; at NIH Preschool Development Program, 116; patterns in, 240–41; at Sakach (Debbie) group family day care home, 196
Stein, Susan, *Child Care — Who Cares?*, 111
Steinfels, Margaret O'Brien, *Who's Minding the Children?*, 211–12
Suburban Hospital (Bethesda, Maryland), 123
Support, lack of broad-based, for child care, 251–53
Swimming, importance of, at Children's World, 134–35

Tannenbaum, J., 17
Teachers, *see* Staff
Technical assistance, need for voluntary, 269
Teen-age mothers, *see under* Durham School
Title XX (Social Security Act), 31, 104; criticisms of, 256–58; focus of, on problems, 255–56; purpose of, 265

Torres, Yolanda, 193
Towne, Laura, 162
Toy Lending Library (Minneapolis), 223, 225–26, 235, 269; operation of, 233–34
Training: at Acoma Parent-Child Development Program, 156–58; at After-School Program (Chinatown), 185–86; at Children's Center, 105–6; at Children's Pumphouse, 86–87; at Children's World, 138–39; at Gomez (Amparo) family day care home, 208; at Infant-Toddler-Parent Center, 70; at The Learning Center, 29–31; at NIH Preschool Development Program, 123–24; at Penn Nursery/Day Care Center, 169–70; at Sakach (Debbie) group family day care home, 203
Trimbur, John, 27, 29

United Federation of Teachers (UFT), 187
United Fund, 220
University of Maryland, 123, 124
University of New Mexico, 156

Van Wyck, Betty (director, Children's Center), 4, 91; admiration for, 239; on admissions, 94–95; atmosphere of optimism in her program, 249; and beginnings of Children's Center, 92–93; her definition of curriculum, 250; on discipline, 100, 101; on firing, 241; and funding, 104–5 goals of, for handicapped children, 93–94; on grouping, 96; on interaction between children and adults, 99–100; on knowledge of administration, 243; leadership qualities of, 242; on parent participation, 102; on problems and changes at Children's Center, 106–9; on selection of child care programs, 8; on staff selection, 95–96; and training, 105, 106
Verbal Interaction Project, 146–47
Vicente, Lloyd (director, Acoma Parent-Child Development Program), 145, 146, 244; on discipline, 154; on goal of positive self-image, 149; on health services, 156; on staff selection, 150
VISTA, 227

Waconda, Lois, 154, 155, 156
Waldman, Joanna, 55–56
Walker, Steve, 26
WATCH (Women Attentive to Children's Happiness; Pasadena, California), 192–93, 202, 203–4, 208, 247
Watson, Eunice: creation and operation of Day Care Neighbor Service by, 215–20; *Family Day Care* (with Alice Collins), 212–14; research of, on neighborhood day care, 212, 214–15
Weinberger, Cyrus, 41, 45
Weinberger, Paula, 36, 45–46, 49

280 Index

Weinstein, Marlene (director, The Learning Center), 262, 270; becomes director, 18; on day care problems, 32–33; on discipline, 25–26; on funding by Medical College of Pennsylvania, 31; on goals, 19, 20; on parent participation, 27; and playground equipment, 24–25; on staff selection, 22–23, 241

Which Way Guide to Child Care in South Minneapolis, 231

White, Gardenia (director, Penn Center), 171, 244; becomes director, 163; on funding, 164–65, 258; on licensing agencies, 259; on parents unable to pay for child care, 267; on training, 169–70

Whiting, Beatrice, 40

Wilson, Liz and Herb, 190
Winnaki House (Minneapolis), 232
Woman's Action Alliance (New York City), 266
Women's History Project (Denver), 266
Wong, Lucy, 181, 186
Wright, C., 17
Wynder, Ralph, 20

Yannapoulis, Ion, 38, 39, 41, 43
Yannapoulis, Rena, 38, 41
Yarrow, Leon J., 16
Yee So Leong, 176, 184
Yu, Albert, 117
Yu, Leepo, 117
Yuen, Gilna, 177

Zavitovski, Docia, 263